**DOCTRINA NOVAE
HIEROSOLYMAE DE FIDE /
TEACHING OF THE NEW JERUSALEM
CONCERNING FAITH**

DOCTRINA
NOVAE HIEROSOLYMAE
DE FIDE

AB

EMANUEL SWEDENBORG

EDITED BY JOHN ELLIOTT

LONDON
THE SWEDENBORG SOCIETY
2019

TEACHING OF THE NEW JERUSALEM CONCERNING FAITH

BY

EMANUEL SWEDENBORG

TRANSLATED BY JOHN ELLIOTT

LONDON
THE SWEDENBORG SOCIETY
2019

Published by the Swedenborg Society
Swedenborg House, 20-21 Bloomsbury Way, London WC1A 2TH

© Swedenborg Society 2019

Cover artwork: Stephen McNeilly
Typeset in Palatino at Swedenborg House
Printed and bound in Great Britain
at TJ International, Padstow

ISBN 978-0-85448-212-2

British Library Cataloguing-in-Publication Data
A catalogue record for this book
is available from the British Library

CONTENTS

Editor and Translator's Introduction	page vii
Abbreviations	ix
Doctrina Novae Hierosolymae de Fide	2
Teaching of the New Jerusalem concerning Faith	3
Table of Parallel Passages	75

EDITOR AND TRANSLATOR'S INTRODUCTION

Being the fourth of the seven works which Emanuel Swedenborg published in Amsterdam in 1763-4, **Doctrina Novae Hierosolymae de Fide** (**FI**) needs no more than a short introduction; for most of what could be stated here appears already in the Editor and Translator's Introduction to **Doctrina Novae Hierosolymae de Domino** (**DD**), the first of the seven.

Relation to Apocalypsis Explicata

In that introduction to **DD** I discussed at some length the connections that all seven works published in 1763-4 have with **Apocalypsis Explicata** (**AE**), the long but never-completed work that Swedenborg began in or before 1759. In addition to its continuous verse-by-verse explanation of the Book of Revelation, this long work contains separate sections dealing with particular subjects; and some of these subjects may be regarded as forerunners to what appears in 'the Amsterdam Seven'. Not only the introduction to **DD** but also the introductions to the second and third of the seven – namely **Doctrina Novae Hierosolymae de Scriptura Sacra** (**SS**) and **Doctrina Vitae pro Nova Hierosolyma ex Praeceptis Decalogi** (**VI**) – point out the actual sections containing the subjects in **AE** that are the predecessors to those three works. But in **AE** no such section exists containing subject matter that may be called a predecessor to **FI**. However, since *fides separata a charitate*, which I have rendered *faith separate from the love of others*, is the subject in the second half of **FI**, a subject that occurs again and again in the main part of **AE** – especially in chapters 12 and 13 explaining the vision of the Woman and the Dragon, and then the vision of the Dragon's Beasts – it seems right to say that **FI** has a definite connection with **AE**.

Relation to Schmidt's Latin Version of the Bible

When quoting from the Bible Swedenborg generally follows the same system of versification as that used by Sebastian Schmidt in his

Latin version first published in 1696, a system that varies sometimes from that found in English versions. In the latter, for example, the book of the prophet Joel consists of three chapters, but in Schmidt's Latin version there are four. Or, to give another example, chapter 22 of Matthew's Gospel is divided into 46 verses in English versions, but only 44 in Schmidt's. So it is because he is following Schmidt that some verses quoted from Matthew 22 by Swedenborg in his religious works are numbered differently from what they are in English copies of the Scriptures. Yet very occasionally Swedenborg's enumeration of a verse of Scripture is different from Schmidt's and in keeping with English versification. One such verse in Isaiah is 15:2 in Schmidt but 14:29 in Swedenborg's quotations of it, as below in §53 and elsewhere in his works. But in this instance Swedenborg may have been relying on Schmidt's two language Hebrew-Latin edition of the Old Testament published in 1740, in which the verse in Isaiah is numbered 14:29, as it is in other presentations of the Hebrew text.

Acknowledgements

Once again I must express my thanks to Revd Robert Gill, my consultant, for his diligence in ensuring that the Latin text has been edited correctly and translated satisfactorily. As before, his thorough attention to detail has been excellent. Thanks are again due to Revd Norman Ryder, Stephen McNeilly, James Wilson, and Judy my wife, for all the reasons mentioned in the introductions to the three works referred to above. And thanks be to Him who is the bedrock of true faith.

London 2017   *John Elliott*

ABBREVIATIONS

Works cited in Editor and Translator's Introduction and footnotes

AC	**Arcana Coelestia**	
	All editions	
AE	**Apocalypsis Explicata**	
	Unfinished work, published after Swedenborg's death	
AR	**Apocalypsis Revelata**	
	All editions	
DD	**Doctrina Novae Hierosolymae de Domino**	
	All editions	
FI	**Doctrina Novae Hierosolymae de Fide**	
	All editions	
FI¹	**Doctrina Novae Hierosolymae de Fide**	
	First edition 1763	
FI²	**Doctrina Novae Hierosolymae de Fide**	
	Second edition 1835, editors L Hofaker and G Werner	
FI³	**Doctrina Novae Hierosolymae de Fide**	
	Third edition 1889, editor Samuel H Worcester	
SE	**Summaria Expositio Doctrinae Novae Ecclesiae**	
	All editions	
VI	**Doctrina Vitae pro Nova Hierosolymae ex Praeceptis Decalogi**	
	All editions	
VR	**Vera Christiana Religio**	
	All editions	

DOCTRINA NOVAE
HIEROSOLYMAE DE FIDE /
TEACHING OF THE NEW JERUSALEM
CONCERNING FAITH

Doctrina Novae Hierosolymae de Fide

Quod fides sit agnitio interna veri

1. Per fidem hodie non aliud intelligitur quam cogitatio quod ita sit quia ecclesia docet, et quia non patet coram intellectu; dicitur enim, Crede et non dubita. Si respondetur, Hoc non comprehendo, dicitur quod ideo credendum sit. Quare hodierna fides est fides ignoti, et vocari potest fides caeca; et quia est dictamen alterius in altero, est fides historica. Quod haec non fides spiritualis sit, videbitur in sequentibus.

2. Ipsa fides non aliud est quam agnitio quod ita sit quia est verum, ita enim cogitat et loquitur qui in ipsa fide est, Hoc verum est, ideo credo. Fides enim est veri et verum est fidei. Is etiam, si non comprehendit quod verum sit, dicit, Non scio num verum sit, ideo nondum credo; quomodo credam quod non comprehendo? Forte potest falsum esse.

3. Sed communis sermo est quod non aliquis possit comprehendere spiritualia seu theologica, quia sunt supernaturalia. Sed vera spiritualia aeque comprehendi possunt quemadmodum vera naturalia; et si non clare, usque, dum audiuntur, cadunt in perceptionem num vera sint vel non, hoc maxime apud illos qui afficiuntur veris. Hoc datum est mihi scire ex multa experientia. Datum est loqui cum ignaris, cum obscuris, cum stupidis, et quoque cum illis qui in falsis fuerunt, et qui in malis, qui intra ecclesiam nati sunt, et audiverunt aliquid de Domino, de fide et charitate. Et loqui datum est cum illis arcana sapientiae; et illi comprehenderunt omnia, et agnoverunt. Sed erant tunc in luce intellectus quae est cuivis homini, et simul in gloria quod

Teaching of the New Jerusalem concerning Faith

Faith is an inward acceptance of truth

1   At the present day faith is taken to mean nothing else than people's believing something is so because that is what the church teaches them and because it does not lie open to human understanding; for they are told, Believe and do not doubt. If anyone replies, This I do not at all understand, they are then told, That is why it is necessary to believe it. So faith at the present day consists in people believing what they do not know and may be termed blind faith; and because it is one person's say-so present in another it is historical faith. And this is not spiritual faith, as will be seen in what follows.

2   Real faith is nothing other than an acceptance that something is so because it is true, for the thought and utterance of people who possess real faith is, This is true, therefore I believe it. For faith is a belief in what is true, and what is true is the substance of faith. Also, if these people do not understand some truth they say, I do not know whether it is true, therefore I cannot as yet believe it. How am I to believe what I do not understand? It may even be a falsity.

3   It is common for it to be said however that no one can grasp spiritual, that is, theological ideas because these belong on a level above those that are natural. But spiritual truths are able to be grasped just as much as natural ones are. There may not be any clear understanding of them, yet when they are heard people detect whether they are truths or not, most of all those who are filled with a love of truths. Many experiences have allowed me to know of all this. I have been allowed to talk to people who are illiterate, those of humble birth, and those with little intelligence, also those with false ideas and those whose ways are evil, who were born within the church and have heard something about the Lord, and about faith and the love of others. I have been allowed to speak of profound matters of wisdom to them, every one of which they grasped and accepted. But whenever I was speaking of those matters these people were seeing things with that light of understanding that every human being possesses, and at the same time in the glory of their

essent intelligentes. Sed haec in commercio cum spiritibus. Ex his convicti sunt plures mecum quod spiritualia aeque ac naturalia possint comprehendi, sed tunc quando audiuntur aut leguntur; sed aegre ab ipso homine cum ex se cogitat. Causa quod spiritualia comprehendantur, est quia homo quoad intellectum potest elevari in lucem caeli, in qua luce non alia apparent quam spiritualia, quae sunt vera fidei. Lux enim caeli est lux spiritualis.

4   Inde nunc est quod agnitio interna veri sit illis qui in spirituali affectione veri sunt. Quia angeli in illa affectione sunt, prorsus respuunt illud dogma quod intellectus erit sub obedientia fidei; dicunt enim, Quid est credere et non videre num verum sit? Et si aliquis dicit quod usque credendum sit, respondent, Num putas te Deum esse, cui credam? aut me insanum, quod credam dicto in quo non video verum? fac itaque ut videam. Ita dogmaticus ille recedit. Sapientia angelica in eo unice consistit, ut videant et comprehendant quae cogitant.

5   Est idea spiritualis, de qua pauci aliquid norunt, quae influit apud illos qui in affectione veri sunt, et interius dictat quod hoc, quod auditur aut legitur, verum sit vel non. In hac idea sunt illi qui in illustratione a Domino legunt Verbum. In illustratione esse non aliud est quam in perceptione esse, et inde in agnitione interna, quod hoc et illud verum sit. Hi sunt qui vocantur docti a Jehovah, Esai.54:13; Joh.6:45; et de quibus dicitur apud Jeremiam,

Ecce dies venientes, quibus pangam novum faedus. Faedus hoc erit: Dabo legem Meam in medio eorum, et super cor eorum scribam illam. Et non docebunt vir amplius socium suum, aut vir fratrem suum, dicendo, Cognoscite Jehovam; omnes enim cognoscent Me. 31:31,33,34.

6   Ex his patet quod fides et veritas unum sint. Quare etiam antiqui, qui ex affectione in cogitatione de veris prae nostratibus fuerunt, loco fidei dixerunt veritatem. Inde quoque

being intelligent. But these experiences occurred when I was in contact with spirits. Many people present with me have been convinced by these experiences that spiritual ideas can be grasped just as much as natural ones, that is, when they are heard or read, yet hardly at all by someone thinking from self. The reason why spiritual ideas are grasped is that the understanding of the human being is able to be raised into the light of heaven, and in that light nothing other than spiritual ideas, that is, the truths of faith, are seen. For the light of heaven is spiritual light.

4   So it is, then, that an inward acceptance of truth exists with those who possess a spiritual desire for truth. Because angels possess that desire they utterly reject the dogma that the understanding must be kept subservient to faith; for they say, How can we believe something without seeing whether it is true? And if someone says it is still necessary for you to believe it, the angels reply, Do you imagine yourself to be God whom I need to believe? Or do you imagine I'm mad enough to believe something I'm told without my seeing any truth in it? Help me therefore to see this in it. At this the one upholding the dogma departs. Angels' wisdom lies solely in their seeing and having a proper grasp of what they think.

5   There is a spiritual way of thinking, which few know anything about, that enters the mind of those who possess the desire for truth and tells it whether or not something they hear or read is true. This way of thinking exists with those who are enlightened by the Lord when they read the Word. Such enlightenment is nothing other than a perception and consequent inward acceptance that this or that is true. These are they who – in Isa.54:13, John 6:45 – are spoken of as ones taught by Jehovah, and of whom in Jeremiah it says,

Behold, the days are coming in which I will make a new covenant. This will be the covenant: I will put My law in the midst of them, and will write it on their heart. No more will every man teach his companion or every man his brother, saying, Know Jehovah. For they will all know Me. 31:31,33,34.

6   From all this it is evident that faith and truth are one and the same as each other. This also explains why the ancients, who because of their desire for truths gave more thought to them than people in our own times do, spoke of truth instead of faith. And

est quod in Hebraea lingua veritas et fides una vox sint, quae vocatur Amuna seu Amen.

7 Quod fides dicatur a Domino apud Evangelistas et in Apocalypsi, erat quia Judaei non crediderunt verum esse quod Dominus esset Messias a prophetis praedictus; et ubi veritas non creditur, ibi fides dicitur. At usque aliud est fidem habere et credere in Dominum, et aliud fidem habere et credere alicui. De differentia dicetur infra.

8 Fides separata a veritate intravit et invasit ecclesiam cum dominio papali, quoniam praecipuum tutamen religionis istius fuit ignorantia veri; quare lectio Verbi etiam vetabatur. Alioquin non potuissent coli ut numina, ac sancti eorum invocari, ac in tantum introduci idololatriae ut cadavera, ossa, et sepulchra illorum sancta crederentur, et inde lucrarentur. Ex quo patet quam enormes falsitates fides caeca potest producere.

9 Fides caeca etiam permansit postea apud plures Reformatos, ex causa quia separaverunt fidem a charitate; et qui separant illas non possunt non in ignorantia veri esse, et cogitationem quod ita sit separatam ab agnitione interna quod ita sit, nominare fidem, Apud hos ignorantia est tutamen dogmatum, nam quamdiu ignorantia regnat, et persuasio quod theologica transcendant, possunt loqui et non contradici, et credi quod vera sint, et quod ii intelligant illa.

10 Dixit Dominus ad Thomam,

Quia vidisti Me, Thoma, credidisti; beati qui non vident, et credunt. Joh.20:29.

Per quod non intelligitur fides ab interna agnitione veri separata, sed quod beati sint qui non oculis vident Dominum,

this furthermore is why the word Amuna or Amen[1] in the Hebrew language means truth or faith.

7   The reason why in the Gospels and the Book of Revelation the Lord speaks of faith is that the Jews did not believe it to be true that the Lord was the Messiah foretold by prophets; and where there is no belief in the truth faith is spoken of instead. However, it is one thing to have faith and believe in the Lord, and another to have faith and believe in someone other. The difference will be spoken of below.

8   Together with the supremacy of the Pope faith separated from the truth entered in and pervaded the church, for the chief form of defence of that religious system lay in keeping people ignorant of the truth, which is why reading the Word was forbidden too. If none of this had come about it would have been impossible for popes to be worshipped as gods, for their saints to be ones who were prayed to, and for idolatry to enter in, so great that even their dead bodies, bones, and tombs were believed to be holy, and consequently became a source of monetary gain. From this it is evident that blind faith can produce hideous falsities.

9   Blind faith continued to exist subsequently among very many in the Reformed Churches as well, for the reason that those people separated faith from the love of others; and anyone who separates these two is inevitably ignorant of what is true and uses the word faith to describe a thinking that something is so, quite apart from any inward acceptance of it. In the case of these people such ignorance serves to protect dogmatic assertions; for as long as ignorance reigns, and a firm belief exists that theological matters rise above human understanding, those people are able to make declarations without being contradicted, and to be believed when they assert that their declarations are true and that they themselves have an understanding of them.

10   The Lord said to Thomas,

Because you have seen Me, Thomas, you have believed. Blessed are those who do not see, yet believe. John 20:29.

By these words is not meant faith separate from an inward acceptance of truth; their meaning is, rather, that they are blessed who do

---

1   Generally this Hebrew word is an adverb, meaning *truly, verily,* but it can also be a noun, as at Isa.65:16, where *Elohim Amen* occurs twice. This is rendered variously in English – *God whose name is Amen, God of truth,* etc.

sicut Thomas, et usque credunt quod Ipse sit; hoc enim in luce veritatis est ex Verbo.

11 Quia agnitio interna veri est fides, et quia fides et veritas unum sunt, ut supra, n.2,4-6, dictum est, sequitur quod agnitio externa absque interna non sit fides, nec quod persuasio falsi sit fides. Agnitio externa absque interna est fides ignoti; et fides ignoti est solum scientia, quae memoriae est, quae si confirmatur fit persuasio. Et qui in illis sunt cogitant quod verum sit quia alius ita dixit, vel cogitant quod verum sit ex confirmato; et tamen falsum aeque confirmari potest quam verum, et quandoque fortius. Per cogitare quod verum sit ex confirmato, intelligitur cogitare illud verum esse quod ab alio dicitur, et illud non prius explorare sed modo confirmare.

12 Si quis cogitat secum aut dicit alteri, Quis potest habere agnitionem internam veri quae fides, ego non possum? Sed illi dicam, quomodo possit: Fuge mala ut peccata et adi Dominum, et habebis quantum desideras. Quod ille qui fugit mala ut peccata in Domino sit, videatur in **Doctrina Vitae pro Nova Hierosolyma**, n.18-31; quod ille amet verum, et videat illud, n.32-41 ibi; et quod ille fidem habeat, n.42-52 ibi.

not see the Lord with their eyes as Thomas did, and yet they believe that He exists, for they see this to be so in the light of truth that flows from the Word.

11   Because an inward acceptance of truth constitutes faith, and because, as was stated above, §§2,4-6, faith and truth are a single entity, it follows that an outward without inward acceptance is not faith, and that a strong belief in what is false is not faith, either. Outward acceptance without inward amounts to faith in what is unknown, and such faith consists solely in factual knowledge residing in the memory, which if substantiated becomes a firm conviction. People who possess this faith and strong conviction think that something is true because another has said it is so, or they think it is true as a result of substantiating it. But what is false just as much as that which is true can be substantiated, sometimes more strongly. By thinking something to be true as a result of substantiating it is meant thinking that to be true which is said by another and not first of all examining it, only substantiating it.

12   Some people may think to themselves or say to another, Is there anyone who is able to possess an inward acceptance of truth which is faith, I cannot? If they do think or say this, let me tell them how it is possible to do so, namely, Shun evil ways as sins, go to the Lord, and you will possess as much as you desire. Those who shun evil ways as sins abide in the Lord, see **Teaching for the New Jerusalem concerning Life**, §§18-31; they love truth and see it, §§32-41; and they possess faith, §§42-52.

Quod agnitio interna veri, quae fides, non detur apud alios quam qui in charitate sunt

13   Supra dictum est quid fides, hic dicetur quid charitas. Charitas in sua prima origine est affectio boni; et quia bonum amat verum, producit illa affectionem veri, per hanc agnitionem veri, quae est fides; per has in sua serie affectio boni existit et fit charitas. Haec est progressio charitatis a sua origine, quae est affectio boni, per fidem quae est agnitio veri, ad finem suum qui est charitas; finis est actus. Ex his patet quomodo amor, qui est affectio boni, producit fidem, quae est idem cum agnitione veri, et per hanc producit charitatem, quae est idem cum actu amoris per fidem.

14   Sed clarius. Bonum non aliud est quam usus, quare charitas in sua prima origine est affectio usus. Et quia usus amat media, producit illa affectionem mediorum, ex qua cognitio illorum; et per has in sua serie affectio usus existit et fit charitas.

15   Progressio illorum est, quemadmodum est progressio omnium voluntatis per intellectum in actus in corpore. Voluntas nihil producit ex se absque intellectu, nec intellectus aliquid ex se absque voluntate; agent in conjunctione ut aliquid existat. Seu quod idem, affectio quae est voluntatis, nihil producit ex se nisi per cogitationem quae est intellectus, nec vicissim; agent in conjunctione ut aliquid existat. Expende, si a cogitatione removeas affectionem, quae est alicujus

---

7   boni: veri *FI*

An inward acceptance of truth, which is faith, does not exist with any but those who possess charity or the love of others

13   Above it is stated what faith is, here it will be what charity or the love of others is. To begin with, the love of others exists as a desire for that which is good; and since good is in love with truth that desire produces a desire for truth; and through the desire for truth comes an acceptance of truth, which is faith. By means of this desire and acceptance, in that order, the desire for that which is good manifests itself and becomes the love of others. This is the way in which the love of others progresses from its beginning, which is the desire for what is good, through faith, which is an acceptance of truth, to its end in view, which is the love of others, an end that is realized in actions. From all this it is evident how love, which is the desire for that which is good, produces faith, which is the same as an acceptance of truth, and through that acceptance produces the love of others, which is the same as actions performed by love through faith.

14   But to make this clearer. Goodness consists in nothing other than usefulness; therefore the love of others is, to begin with, the desire for usefulness. And because usefulness loves the means to make itself a reality, that desire engenders a desire for those means, and this desire leads on to a recognition of what they are. By means of these stages, in that order, the desire for usefulness manifests itself and becomes the love of others.

15   The way in which these stages progress from one into another is the same as that by which all desires belonging to the will pass by means of the understanding into actions within the body. The will engenders nothing by itself, without the understanding, and the understanding does not engender anything by itself without the will, either; they must act jointly for anything to become a reality. Or what amounts to the same thing, desire belonging to the will achieves nothing by itself except by means of thought belonging to the understanding, and vice versa; they must act jointly for anything to become a reality. Look at it this way: if you take away from thought the desire belonging to whatever kind of love, are you able

amoris, num potes cogitare? Aut si ab affectione removeas cogitationem, num potes affici aliqua re? Aut, quod simile, si a cogitatione removeas affectionem, num poteris loqui? Vel si ab affectione removeas cogitationem seu intellectum, num poteris agere aliquid? Simile est cum charitate et fide.

16 Illustrari haec possunt per comparationem cum arbore. Arbor in sua prima origine est semen, in quo est conatus producendi fructum. Hic conatus excitatus a calore, primum producit radicem, et ex illa virgam seu caulem cum ramis et foliis, et demum fructus; et sic conatus fructificandi existit. Ex quibus patet quod conatus producendi fructus sit perpetuus in omni progressione, usque dum existit, nam si ille desineret, facultas vegetandi illico moreretur. Applicatio haec est: Arbor est homo; conatus producendi media est apud hominem a voluntate in intellectu; virga seu caulis cum ramis et foliis sunt apud hominem media per quae, et vocantur vera fidei; fructus qui sunt ultimi effectus conatus fructificandi in arbore, sunt apud hominem usus; in his voluntas existit. Ex his potest videri quod voluntas producendi usus medio intellectu sit perpetua in omni progressione, usque dum existit. De voluntate et de intellectu, et de conjunctione illorum, videatur in **Doctrina Vitae pro Nova Hierosolyma**, n.43.

17 Ex nunc dictis patet quod charitas, quatenus est affectio boni seu usus, producat fidem, ut medium per quam existat; consequenter, quod charitas et fides, in operando usus, conjunctim agant. Tum quod fides non producat bonum seu usum ex se sed ex charitate, fides enim est charitas media. Fallacia itaque est, quod fides producat bonum sicut arbor fructum; arbor non est fides, sed arbor est homo.

18 Sciendum est quod charitas et fides faciant unum sicut voluntas et intellectus, quoniam charitas est voluntatis et fides est intellectus. Similiter, quod charitas et fides faciant unum sicut affectio et cogitatio, quoniam affectio est voluntatis et cogitatio est intellectus. Similiter, quod charitas et fides faciant

to think? Or if you take thought away from desire, are you able to feel a desire for anything? Or, similar to this, if you take desire away from thought, will you be able to speak? Or if you take thought – or understanding, that is – away from desire, will you be able to do anything? Love of others and faith are in a similar way inseparable.

16   Comparison with a tree may help to clarify all this. To begin with the tree is a seed containing an endeavour to produce fruit. Stimulated by warmth, this endeavour first produces a root, and from out of the root produces a trunk or stem, together with branches and leaves, and finally the fruit; and in this way the endeavour to produce fruit manifests itself. From this it is evident that the endeavour to produce fruit is constantly present within that whole process, right through to the manifestation of itself; for if it ceased to be present the ability of the tree to grow would instantly perish. The application of the comparison is this: The tree stands for a person; its endeavour to produce means for itself stands for that in the person which springs from the will and resides in the understanding; the trunk or stem, together with branches and leaves, stand for these means established in the person through which the endeavour operates and which are called the truths of faith; the fruit which are the final result of the endeavour in the tree to be fruitful stand for forms of usefulness the person performs, in which the will manifests itself. From all this it may be seen that the will desiring to engender forms of usefulness by means of the understanding is constantly present within the whole process, right through to that manifestation of itself. Regarding will and understanding and their being linked together, see **Teaching for the New Jerusalem concerning Life**, §43.

17   From what has now been stated it is evident that, to the extent the desire for a form of good or usefulness exists, the love of others produces faith as the means through which it manifests itself; consequently the love of others and faith act jointly in the performance of usefulness. Faith does not as a result of its own existence produce that which is good or useful, but as a result of the existence of the love of others; for faith is the means through which the love of others acts. It is wrong therefore to say that faith produces that which is good as the tree produces fruit; faith is not the tree, the person is.

18   It should be realized that love of others and faith make one, just as will and understanding do, because the love of others belongs to the will and faith to the understanding. In like manner love of others and faith make one just as desire and thought do, because desire belongs to the will and thought to the understanding. In like manner love of others and faith make one just as goodness and truth

unum sicut bonum et verum, quia bonum est affectionis quae voluntatis et verum est cogitationis quae intellectus.

Verbo, charitas et fides faciunt unum sicut essentia et forma, quoniam essentia fidei est charitas et forma charitatis est fides. Ex quibus patet quod fides absque charitate sit sicut forma absque essentia, quae non est aliquid; et quod charitas absque fide sit sicut essentia absque forma, quae nec est aliquid.

19   Charitas et fides apud hominem prorsus se habent sicut motus cordis, qui vocatur systole et diastole, et motus pulmonis, qui vocatur respiratio. Est quoque illorum plenaria correspondentia cum voluntate et intellectu hominis, ita cum charitate et fide. Quare etiam voluntas et ejus affectio intelligitur per cor in Verbo, ac intellectus et ejus cogitatio per animam in Verbo, et quoque per spiritum; ideo emittere animam est non amplius animare, et emittere spiritum est non amplius respirare. Ex quibus sequitur quod non dari queat fides absque charitate, nec charitas absque fide, et quod fides absque charitate sit sicut respiratio pulmonaris absque corde, quae non dari potest in aliquo vivo sed solum in automato, et quod charitas absque fide sit sicut cor absque pulmone, ex quo non aliquod vivum sentitur; consequenter, quod charitas per fidem operetur usus, sicut cor per pulmonem actus. Tanta similitudo intercedit inter cor et charitatem, ac inter pulmonem et fidem, ut in mundo spirituali quisque noscatur ex sola respiratione, qualis ei fides est, et ex pulsu cordis, qualis ei charitas est. Angeli enim et spiritus aeque ac homines vivunt corde et respiratione; inde est quod illi similiter ac homines in mundo sentiant, cogitent, agant, et loquantur.

20   Quia charitas est amor erga proximum, dicetur etiam quid proximus. Proximus in naturali sensu est homo in composito et in individuo. Homo in composito est ecclesia, patria, et societas; et homo in individuo est concivis, qui in Verbo vocatur frater et socius. At proximus in spirituali sensu est bonum, et quia usus est bonum, est proximus in spirituali sensu usus. Quod usus sit spiritualis proximus, quisque agnoscet; quis enim amat hominem solum ut personam? Sed

do, for goodness is the object of desire belonging to the will and truth is the object of thought belonging to the understanding.

In short, love of others and faith make one just as inward essence and outward form do, because the inward essence of faith is the love of others and the outward form of the love of others is faith. From these considerations it is evident that faith without the love of others is like outward form without inward essence, which is not anything, and that love of others without faith is like inward essence without outward form, which is not anything, either.

19   The love of others and faith in a person are exactly like the motion of the heart, termed systole and diastole, and that of the lungs, termed respiration. There is also a complete correspondence of the two with a person's will and understanding, and so with love of others and faith. Also, therefore, the will and its desire is meant in the Word by heart, and the understanding and its thought is meant in the Word by breath or life, and by spirit too. Thus letting go one's breath stands for ceasing to be alive any more, and letting go one's spirit for ceasing to draw breath any more. From all this it follows that faith cannot exist without love of others, nor can love of others without faith; and that faith without love of others is like respiration, the function of the lungs, without a heart, which can never be so in any living being, only in an automaton, and that love of others without faith is like heart without lungs, as a result of which there is no consciousness. So, love of others accomplishes forms of usefulness by means of faith, just as the heart performs its actions by means of the lungs. So great is the similarity between heart and love of others, and between lungs and faith, that in the spiritual world what people's faith is like is recognized solely from the way they draw breath, and what their love of others is like from the way their heart beats. For angels and spirits, just as much as people, live in possession of heart and respiration, and this is why, like people in the world, they have sensory feelings, think, act, and speak.

20   Since charity denotes love towards the neighbour, what is meant by neighbour must also be mentioned. In the natural sense neighbour means people corporately and singly. People corporately are one's church, country, and community, singly they are one's fellow citizen, who in the Word is called brother and companion. But in the spiritual sense neighbour means a form of good, and because usefulness constitutes the form of good, neighbour in the spiritual sense means usefulness. All will accept that this is what is meant by the spiritual neighbour, for is anyone's love of others limited to their outward demeanour? Rather, anyone loves others because of

amat illum ex eo quod in illo est, ex quo est talis, ita ex quali ejus, hoc namque est homo. Hoc quale, quod amatur, est usus, et vocatur bonum; inde est hoc proximus. Quia Verbum in sinu suo est spirituale, ideo illud est amare proximum in spirituali ejus sensu.

21   Sed aliud est amare proximum ex bono aut usu in illo erga se, et aliud est amare proximum ex bono aut usu in se erga illum. Amare proximum ex bono aut usu in illo erga se, potest etiam malus, sed amare proximum ex bono aut usu in se erga illum non potest nisi bonus, nam hic ex bono amat bonum, seu ex affectione usus amat usum. Horum et illorum discrimen describitur a Domino apud Matt.5:42-47; Luc.6:32,33,seq. A multis dicitur, Amo illum quia me amat et bonum mihi facit. Sed usque amare illum propter ea solum, non est interius amare illum, nisi ipse in bono sit, et ex illo amet bonum ejus. Hic in charitate est, ille autem in amicitia est, quae non est charitas. Is qui ex charitate amat proximum conjungit se cum bono ejus, et non cum persona nisi quantum et quamdiu in bono est; hic spiritualis est et spiritualiter amat proximum. At qui ex sola amicitia amat alterum, is conjungit se cum persona, et simul tunc cum ejus malo. Hic post mortem a persona, quae in malo est, aegre separari potest, alter autem potest. Charitas hoc facit per fidem, quae fides est veritas; et homo qui in charitate est, per veritatem scrutatur et videt quid amandum est, et spectat quale usus in amando et benefaciendo.

22   Amor in Dominum est proprie amor, et amor erga proximum est charitas. Non datur apud hominem amor in Dominum nisi in charitate; in hac Dominus Se conjungit cum homine. Quia fides in sua essentia est charitas, sequitur quod nemo possit habere fidem in Dominum nisi in charitate sit; ex hac per fidem est conjunctio, per charitatem conjunctio

---

12-13   Matt.5:42-47; Luc.6:32,33,seq: Matt.5:32,33,seq Fl^1; Matt.5:43,44,seq Fl^2; Matt.5:42-47,seq Fl^3

whatever it is within them that makes them the kind of people they are, that is, they are loved because of their inward character, for this is what constitutes a human being. This character loved by others conditions their kind of usefulness and is called their form of good; and this consequently is what is meant by neighbour. Since the Word inwardly is spiritual that love of what is good is therefore meant in its spiritual sense by loving the neighbour.

21 It is one thing however to love a neighbour because of the good or usefulness in that person which is rendered to oneself, and another to love a neighbour because of the good or usefulness in oneself rendered to that person. Even those who are evil are able to love a neighbour because of the good or usefulness in that person rendered to themselves, but only those who are good are able to love a neighbour because of the good or usefulness in themselves rendered to that person. For these out of what is good love what is good, or out of desire for usefulness love usefulness. The difference between the latter kind of people and the former is described by the Lord in Matt.5:42-47; Luke 6:32,33, and following verses. Many say, I love that person because he or she loves me and does for me that which is good. But loving that person for these reasons alone is not an inward loving of him or her, if what is good does not reign within self and cause the good in the other to be loved. With the latter, in whom that goodness reigns, the love of others exists; but with the former, it is friendliness, which is not the same as the love of others. Those who love a neighbour out of a love of others link themselves to that neighbour's goodness, and not to the person except insofar as, and as long as, the person is governed by what is good. These people are spiritual and love their neighbour in a spiritual manner. But those who love another solely out of friendliness link themselves to the person, and at the same time to that person's evil. After death these are hardly able to be separated from the person immersed in evil, but the former can be. The love of others achieves this by means of faith, faith that consists in truth; and through truth those governed by the love of others look for and recognize what ought to be loved, and perceive the nature of the usefulness that resides in loving and doing what is good.

22 Love to the Lord is, strictly speaking, love, while love towards the neighbour is charity or the love of others. No love to the Lord resides with a person except within the love of others; and within this love of others the Lord links Himself to the person. Because faith in respect of its inward essence is the love of others it follows that none can possess faith in the Lord unless the love of others exists with them. From that love of others given form by faith

Domini cum homine, et per fidem conjunctio hominis cum Domino. Quod conjunctio reciproca sit, videatur in **Doctrina Vitae pro Nova Hierosolyma**, n.102-107.

23   In summa, quantum quis fugit mala ut peccata et spectat ad Dominum, tantum in charitate est, proinde tantum in fide est. Quod quantum quis fugit mala ut peccata et spectat ad Dominum, tantum in charitate sit, videatur in **Doctrina Vitae pro Nova Hierosolyma**, n.67-73, tum n.74-91; et quod tantum fidem habeat, n.42-52; quid charitas in proprio sensu, n.114 ibi.

24   Ex omnibus quae hactenus dicta sunt, constare potest quod fides salutifera, quae est agnitio interna veri, non dari queat apud alios quam qui in charitate sunt.

is the linking together brought about – through love of others the Lord is linked to the person, and through faith the person is linked to the Lord. Regarding the reciprocal nature of this linking together, see **Teaching for the New Jerusalem concerning Life**, §§102-107.

23   In short, to the extent that people shun evil deeds as sins and look to the Lord, the love of others exists with them, and faith consequently does so too. Regarding the existence in people of the love of others to the extent that they shun evil deeds as sins and look to the Lord, see **Teaching for the New Jerusalem concerning Life**, §§67-73, also §§74-91; and that faith does so too, §§42-52. For what is meant, strictly speaking, by the love of others, see §114 in that small work.

24   From all that has been stated so far it is clear that a wholesome faith, that is, an inward acceptance of truth, cannot exist with any but those who have a love of others.

Quod cognitiones veri et boni non sint fidei antequam homo in charitate est, sed quod sint promptuarium ex quo fides charitatis formari potest

25. Est homini affectio sciendi ex prima pueritia; per hanc discit plura quae illi usui erunt, et plura quae non usui. Cum adolescit, ex applicatione ad quoddam negotium, haurit illa quae rei negotii sunt; hoc fit ei tunc usus, quo afficitur. Sic inchoat affectio usus, quae producit affectionem mediorum per quae venit ad negotium suum, quod ejus usus est. Haec progressio est apud unumquemvis in mundo, quia unicuique est aliquod negotium – ad quod ab usu qui est finis per media ad ipsum usum qui est effectus – procedit. Verum quia hic usus cum mediis ejus est pro vita in mundo, est ejus affectio naturalis.

26. Sed quia omnis homo non modo spectat usus pro vita in mundo sed etiam spectabit usus pro vita in caelo – in hanc enim post vitam in mundo veniet, et in hac post illam vivet in aeternum – ideo quisque a pueritia comparat sibi cognitiones veri et boni ex Verbo, aut ex doctrina ecclesiae, aut ex praedicatione, quae pro illa vita erunt, et reponit illas in memoria naturali, in majore aut minore copia secundum affectionem sciendi connatam, et per varia excitamenta auctam.

27. Sed omnes hae cognitiones, quotcunque et qualescunque sunt, modo sunt promptuarium ex quo fides charitatis formari potest; et haec fides non formatur nisi quantum fugit mala ut peccata. Si fugit mala ut peccata, tunc cognitiones illae fiunt fidei, cui vita spiritualis inest. Si autem non fugit mala ut

Items of knowledge of truth and goodness are not constituents of faith before the love of others exists in a person, but they serve as the store from which faith that goes with the love of others can be formed

25   From earliest childhood people have a desire to know things, a desire that leads them to learn many which will be of use to them and many that will not. When they grow up, by their application of those things to some kind of worldly occupation or other, they take in what is of importance in that occupation. At this point the occupation becomes their form of usefulness in life, and this usefulness governs their desire. This is the way in which the desire to be useful begins, and that desire gives rise to a further desire for the means by which they enter their occupation, that is, their form of usefulness. Everyone's life in this world develops in this way, because everyone has some kind of occupation; for they come to it from an aim to perform some form of usefulness, through the means that bring them to the actual performance of the usefulness. However, since this usefulness exists, together with those means, for the sake of life in the world, the desire for it is a natural one.

26   But because every person gives consideration not only to forms of usefulness that exist for the sake of life in the world, but must also give consideration to those that exist for the sake of life in heaven – for they will enter this and live for ever there after life in the world – each person from childhood therefore gathers from the Word items of knowledge about what is true and good, or else from the teaching of the church, or else from sermons. People acquiring these items of knowledge for the sake of the life in heaven store them away in their natural memory, in greater or smaller measure determined by the desire to know things that is innate within them and increases through the various incentives to do so.

27   But all these items of knowledge, however many and of whatever kind they may be, are simply a store of them from which the faith that goes with the love of others can be formed, and this faith is not formed except insofar as people shun evil ways as sins. If they do shun evil ways as sins those items of knowledge then become constituents of a faith that has spiritual life within it. But if

peccata, cognitiones illae non sunt nisi quam cognitiones, et non fiunt fidei cui aliqua vita spiritualis inest.

28 Hoc promptuarium maxime necessarium est, quoniam absque illo non formari potest fides, cognitiones enim veri et boni fidem intrant et faciunt illam. Si nullae sint, fides non existit; fides prorsus vacua et inanis non datur. Si paucae sint, fides fit pusilla et egena. Si multa sint, fides fit locuples et plena secundum copiam.

29 At sciendum est quod cognitiones genuini veri et boni faciant fidem, et prorsus non cognitiones falsi; fides enim est veritas, ut supra, n.5-11, dictum est, ac falsitas, quia est opposita veritati, destruit fidem. Nec potest charitas existere ubi merae falsitates sunt, nam – ut supra, n.18, dictum est – charitas et fides unum faciunt sicut bonum et verum faciunt unum, Ex his quoque sequitur quod nullae cognitiones genuini veri et boni nullam fidem faciant, quod paucae aliquam fidem, et quod multae fidem illustrem secundum plenitudinem. Qualis est homini fides ex charitate, talis est ei intelligentia.

30 Dantur etiam multi qui non agnitionem internam veri habent, et tamen fidem charitatis; qui sunt qui in vita spectaverunt ad Dominum, et ex religione evitaverunt mala, sed a curis in mundo et negotiis detenti a cogitando de veris, et quoque a defectu veri apud docentes. Sed illi usque interius seu in suo spiritu in agnitione veri, quia in affectione ejus, sunt; quare illi post mortem, dum fiunt spiritus et instruuntur per angelos, agnoscunt vera et cum gaudio recipiunt illa. Aliter vero illi qui in vita non spectaverunt ad Dominum et non ex religione evitaverunt mala. Hi non interius seu in suo spiritu in aliqua affectione veri et inde nec in aliqua agnitione ejus sunt; quare ii post mortem, cum fiunt spiritus et instruuntur per angelos, non volunt agnoscere vera, et inde non recipiunt illa. Malum vitae enim interius odit vera, at bonum vitae interius amat vera.

they do not shun evil ways as sins those items of knowledge are no more than items of knowledge and do not become constituents of a faith that has any spiritual life within it.

28 This store of knowledge is absolutely vital, because without it faith cannot begin to take shape; for the items of the knowledge of what is true and good enter into and compose faith. If there are none, no faith comes forth; faith completely empty and devoid of them has no existence. If there are only a few, faith is rendered poor and needy; if there are many, it is made rich and well provided according to the abundance of them.

29 But it should be recognized that items of knowledge of what really is true and good constitute faith, and none at all of anything false. For faith is one and the same as truth, as mentioned above at §§5-11, and falsity, being the opposite of truth, is destructive of faith. Nor can the love of others manifest itself where sheer falsities are, for – as mentioned above at §18 – love of others and faith make one just as goodness and truth make one. From this it follows also that an absence of any items of knowledge of what is really true and good amounts to an absence of any faith, the presence of a few amounts to the presence of some faith, and the presence of many amounts to faith enlightened according to the plentifulness of them. The quality of a person's faith grounded in the love of others determines the quality of the person's ability to understand.

30 There are many people who do not possess an inward acceptance of truth, yet they do possess faith that goes with the love of others. They are those who have in life looked to the Lord and have from a religious motive avoided evil ways. But they have been held back from giving thought to matters of truth by anxious cares and pursuit of their occupations in the world, and also by an ignorance of what is true on the part of those teaching them. Even so, an acceptance of truth resides inwardly, that is, within their spirit, because they have a desire for what is true. Consequently when after death these people become spirits and receive instruction through angels they accept truths and embrace them joyfully. But it is different in the case of those who have not in life looked to the Lord and have not from a religious motive avoided evil ways. No desire for what is true resides inwardly, that is, within their spirit, and therefore no acceptance of it, either. Consequently when after death these people become spirits and receive instruction through angels they have no wish to accept truths and do not therefore embrace them. For inwardly an evil way of life detests truths, but a good way of life loves them.

31 Cognitiones veri et boni, quae praecedunt fidem, apparent quibusdam quod fidei sint, sed usque non sunt. Quod opinentur et dicant se credere, non ideo credunt, et nec illae sunt fidei, sunt enim solius cogitationis quod ita sit, sed non sunt agnitionis internae quod veritates sint; ac fides quod veritates sint, dum nescitur quod sint, est species persuasionis remotae ab agnitione interna. Ut primum autem charitas implantatur, tunc cognitiones illae fiunt fidei, sed non plus quam charitas in illa est. In primo statu, antequam charitas percipitur, apparet illis fides sicut primo loco sit et charitas secundo; sed in altero statu, cum charitas percipitur, fit fides secundo loco et charitas primo. Primus status vocatur reformatio, alter status vocatur regeneratio. Cum homo in hoc statu est, tunc apud illum indies crescit sapientia, ac indies bonum multiplicat vera et fructificat illa. Est homo tunc sicut arbor quae fructum fert, et in fructu ponit semina, ex quibus novae arbores, et tandem hortus. Fit tunc vere homo, et post mortem angelus, cujus vitam facit charitas, et fides formam, pulchram secundum quale ejus; at fides tunc non amplius vocatur fides sed intelligentia. Ex his constare potest quod omne fidei sit ex charitate, et nihil ejus ex se; tum etiam quod charitas producat fidem et non fides charitatem. Sunt cognitiones veri quae praecedunt, prorsus sicut penuarium in horreo, quod non nutrit hominem, nisi appetens victum inde frumentum desumit.

32 Dicetur etiam quomodo formatur fides ex charitate. Cuivis homini est mens naturalis et mens spiritualis – mens naturalis pro mundo et mens spiritualis pro caelo. Homo quoad intellectum est in utroque, non autem quoad voluntatem, priusquam fugit et aversatur mala ut peccata. Cum hoc facit, tunc aperitur mens spiritualis etiam pro voluntate; qua aperta, influit inde in mentem naturalem calor spiritualis e caelo, qui calor in sua essentia est charitas, ac vivificat cognitiones veri et boni quae ibi sunt, et ex illis format fidem. Fit etiam hoc sicut cum arbore, quae non vitam

31 The items of knowledge of what is true and good which come in advance of faith seem to some people to constitute faith; nevertheless they do not. Therefore the fact that they think and say they believe is no guarantee that they actually believe, or that those items of knowledge are the constituents of faith since they go with no more than the thought that this or that is so and not with any inward acceptance of them as embodiments of truth. And believing them to be embodiments of truth without the knowledge that they are such is a kind of conviction far removed from any inward acceptance. However, as soon as a love of others is implanted they do become the constituents of faith, yet only insofar as the love of others resides within it. Initially, before there is a perception of the love of others, faith seems to such people to be primary and the love of others secondary; but subsequently, when they have a perception of the love of others, faith becomes secondary and the love of others primary. The first stage is termed reformation, the second regeneration. Once people reach this second stage they grow in wisdom day by day, and day by day goodness causes truths to multiply and to make them fruitful. At this time people are like a tree that brings forth fruit, and within the fruit lays seeds from which new trees grow and at length a garden is established. Those people then become truly human, and angels after death, with the love of others composing their life, and faith the outward form this takes – a form, the beauty of which is determined by the quality of their love of others. Then, however, faith is no longer termed faith but discernment. From these considerations it becomes clear that the whole of faith exists by virtue of the love of others and not at all by virtue of itself; also that the love of others engenders faith and not faith the love of others. The items of knowledge of what is true that come in advance of faith are exactly like a store of grain in a barn, which does not serve to nourish people unless they have a desire for food and take the grain out of there.

32 The way in which faith is shaped by the love of others must also be mentioned. Every person has a natural level of mind and a spiritual level – a natural level for the world and a spiritual level for heaven. In respect of their understanding, people function on both levels, but not in respect of their will before they shun and detest evil ways as sins. When they do so the spiritual level of mind is opened for the will also, and once this has been opened spiritual warmth from heaven flows from it into the natural level. In essence that warmth is the love of others and gives life to the items of knowledge of what is good and true present on the natural level, and forms faith out of them. This too is like that which happens with

vegetativam accipit prius quam calor e sole influit et conjungit se cum luce, ut fit tempore veris. Plenus etiam paralelismus est inter vivificationem hominis et vegetationem arboris, in eo quod hanc faciat calor mundi et illam calor caeli. Quare etiam homo toties assimilatur arbori a Domino.

33   Ex his paucis constare potest quod cognitiones veri et boni non sint fidei antequam homo in charitate est, sed quod sint promptuarium ex quo fides charitatis formari possit. Cognitiones veri fiunt vera apud regeneratum; etiam cognitiones boni, nam cognitio boni est in intellectu, at affectio boni in voluntate, ac verum vocatur id quod in intellectu est et bonum id quod in voluntate.

a tree. The tree does not receive the life enabling it to develop before warmth from the sun flows in and links itself to the light, as happens in springtime. A perfect parallel also exists between the invigoration of life in a human being and the stimulation of growth in a tree, in that warmth in the world brings about the latter and the warmth of heaven the former. That is also why a person is often likened by the Lord to a tree.

33   From these few observations it becomes clear that the items of knowledge of what is true and good do not constitute faith before the love of others has a place in a person, but are a store from which faith that goes with the love of others can be formed. Items of knowledge of that which is true become forms of truth with one who is regenerate; and so do items of knowledge of what is good, for knowledge of what is good resides in the understanding, whereas desire for it resides in the will, and what resides in the understanding is called truth, and that in the will is called good.

Fides Christiana in universali idea

34   Fides Christiana in universali idea, haec est –

Quod Dominus ab aeterno, qui est Jehovah, in mundum venerit ut subjugaret inferna et glorificaret Humanum Suum, et quod absque eo nemo mortalium salvari potuerit, et quod salventur qui credunt in Ipsum

35   Dicitur in universali idea, quia hoc est universale fidei, ac universale fidei est quod in omnibus et singulis erit. Universale fidei est quod Deus sit unus persona et essentia, in quo Trinitas, et quod Dominus sit ille Deus. Universale fidei est quod nullus mortalium salvari potuerit nisi Dominus in mundum venerit. Universale fidei est quod in mundum venerit ut removeret infernum ab homine, et quod removerit illud per pugnas contra illud et per victorias super illud; ita subjugavit illud, et redegit illud in ordinem et sub Suam obedientiam. Universale fidei etiam est quod in mundum venerit ut Humanum quod in mundo suscepit glorificaret, hoc est, uniret Divino a quo; sic infernum ab Ipso subjugatum in ordine et sub obedientia Sua in aeternum tenet. Quoniam utrumque hoc non fieri potuit nisi quam per tentationes usque ad ultimum illarum, ac ultimum illarum fuit passio crucis, ideo illam subivit. Haec sunt universalia fidei Christianae de Domino.

36   Universale fidei Christianae a parte hominis est, ut credat in Dominum, nam per credere in Ipsum fit conjunctio cum Ipso, per quam salvatio. Credere in Ipsum est fiduciam habere quod Ipse salvet; et quia fiduciam habere non potest

---

2   idea *AR, FI*: forma *SE, VR*
7   ditto
9-10   persona et essentia *AR, FI*: essentia et persona *SE, VR*
14   quod removerit *VR*: removit *AR, FI, SE*

The general pattern of the Christian faith

34   The general pattern of the Christian faith is this –

The Lord existing from eternity, that is, Jehovah, came into the world to subdue the hells and to glorify His Human; without His doing so none who are mortal could have been saved; and those are saved who believe in Him.

35   This is being called a general pattern because it is the general feature of the faith, and this general feature must exist in every single detail. It is a general feature of the faith that God is one in person and essence, in whom there is the Trinity, and the Lord is that God. It is a general feature of the faith that no mortal could have been saved unless the Lord came into the world. It is a general feature of the faith that He came into the world to move hell away from people, and that He moved it away by means of conflicts with it and victories over it, and in so doing subdued it and reduced it to order, making it subject to His command. It is also a general feature of the faith that He came into the world to glorify the Human He assumed in the world, that is, to unite it to the Divine it sprang from; thus He keeps hell which has been subdued by Him in order, subject for ever to His command. Since neither of these reasons for His coming could have been accomplished except by mean of temptations right through to the last of them, the passion on the cross, He therefore suffered this too. These are general features of the Christian faith concerning the Lord.

36   It is a general feature of the Christian faith that people, on their part, are to believe in the Lord, for by believing in Him they become linked to Him and thereby saved. Believing in Him is having trust in Him to save; and since people are not able to have such

nisi qui bene vivit, ideo etiam hoc per credere in Ipsum intelligitur.

37   De binis his fidei Christianae universalibus actum est in specie – de primo, quod Dominum spectat, in **Doctrina Novae Hierosolymae de Domino**, et de altero, quod hominem spectat, in **Doctrina Vitae pro Nova Hierosolyma**. Quare illa hic amplius diducere non opus est.

trust unless they are leading a good life, this too is meant by believing in Him.

37   These two general features of the Christian faith have already been dealt with in detail – the first, regarding the Lord, in **Teaching of the New Jerusalem concerning the Lord**, and the second, regarding people, in **Teaching for the New Jerusalem concerning Life**. There is no need therefore for any discussion of them here.

Fides hodierna in universali idea

38   Fides hodierna in universali idea, est haec –

Quod Deus Pater miserit Filium Suum, ut satisfaceret pro humano genere, et quod propter id Filii meritum misereatur, et salvet illos qui id credunt. (Alii, Qui id credunt, et simul bona faciunt.)

39   Sed ut videatur clarius qualis illa Fides est, velim adducere in ordine varia quae ponit. Hodierna Fides

i   Ponit Deum Patrem et Deum Filium ut duos, utrumque ab aeterno

ii   Ponit Deum Filium in mundum venisse ex voluntate Patris, ut satisfaceret pro humano genere, quod alioquin ex Divina Justitia, quam etiam vindicativam vocant, morte aeterna periisset

iii   Ponit satisfactionem a Filio per impletionem Legis et per passionem crucis

iv   Ponit misericordiam Patris propter illa Filii

v   Ponit imputationem meriti Filii erga illos qui id credunt

vi   Ponit hoc momentaneum, et ideo, si non prius, etiam circa ultimam mortis horam

vii   Ponit aliquid tentationis, et tunc liberationem per fidem istam

viii   Ponit apud hos imprimis fiduciam et confidentiam

The general pattern of the present-day faith

38   The general pattern of the present-day faith is this –

God the Father sent His Son to make satisfaction on behalf of the human race, and on account of this – the Son's merit – takes pity and saves those who believe this. (Others say, Those who believe this and at the same time perform good works.)

39   But so that people may see more clearly the nature of this Faith I would like to set out in order various assertions made by the present-day Faith –

i   It asserts that God the Father and God the Son are two, both existing from eternity
ii   It asserts that God the Son came into the world, because it was the Father's will, to make satisfaction on behalf of the human race; had He not done so it would have perished in eternal death because of what Divine justice demanded, which is also spoken of as retributive justice
iii   It asserts that the satisfaction was made by the Son through His fulfilment of the Law and His passion on the cross
iv   It asserts that the Father takes pity because of those deeds of the Son
v   It asserts that the Son's merit is imputed to those who believe this
vi   It asserts that this is performed instantaneously, even therefore at the final hour of death, if not before
vii   It asserts that if people undergo any kind of temptation they are then delivered from it by means of such faith
viii It asserts that trust and confidence exist in particular with these people

ix   Ponit apud hos imprimis justificationem, et plenariam gratiam Patris propter Filium, et remissionem omnium peccatorum et sic salvationem

x   Doctiores ponunt apud hos conatum ad bonum, qui occulte operatur, et non manifeste movet voluntatem. Alii ponunt operationem manifestam. Uterque per Spiritum Sanctum

xi   Plerique, qui se confirmant in eo quod nemo possit facere bonum a se quod bonum est, et nisi sit meritorium, et quod non sint sub jugo Legis, illi omittunt, et non cogitant de malo et de bono vitae, dicunt enim in se quod non bonum opus salvet, nec malum damnet, quia sola fides facit omnia

xii   In genere ponunt intellectum sub obedientia hujus fidei, vocantes id fidei quod non intelligitur

40   Sed haec singillatim lustrare et expendere num veritates sint supersedetur. Patent manifeste ex illis quae hic supra dicta sunt, imprimis ex illis quae in **Doctrina Novae Hierosolymae de Domino**, et in **Doctrina Vitae pro Nova Hierosolyma**, ex Verbo demonstrata sunt et simul rationaliter confirmata.

41   At usque ut videatur qualis fides separata a charitate est et qualis fides non separata ab illa est, velim communicare quae ab angelo caeli audivi. Dixit ille quod loquutus sit cum multis Reformatis, et audiverit qualis fides illorum est; et retulit quid cum uno qui in fide separata a charitate fuit, et quid cum altero qui in fide non separata, loquutus est, et ab illis audivit. Dixit quod interrogaverit illos, et quod illi responderint. Quae quia illustrare possunt, velim colloquutiones illorum hic afferre.

42   Angelus dixit quod cum illo qui in fide separata a charitate ita loquutus sit –

ix   It asserts that these in particular are made righteous, that the fullness of the Father's grace on account of the Son abides with them, and that all their sins have been forgiven, as a consequence of which they have been saved

x   The teachers among them assert that those people possess the endeavour to do what is good. It works secretly within them and is not manifestly motivating their will. Other teachers assert that this activity is manifest. Both kinds of teachers say this is through the Holy Spirit

xi   The majority of those who are firmly convinced that none can from self perform any good deed that is good, apart from one that is merit-seeking, and that they are not subject to the Law, set aside and give no consideration to the performance in life of what is evil or good. For they say to themselves that a good work does not save and an evil one does not condemn either, because faith alone accomplishes all things

xii   In general they assert that the understanding must be kept subject to this faith; and that which is not intelligible they call a matter of faith.

40   But there is no need to examine these assertions one by one and weigh up whether there is any truth in them. This is plainly evident from what has been stated above in this small work, and especially from what has been presented from the Word and at the same time substantiated rationally in **Teaching of the New Jerusalem concerning the Lord**, and **Teaching for the New Jerusalem concerning Life**.

41   Nevertheless, so that it can be seen what faith separate from the love of others is like and what faith not separate from it is like, may I share what I've learned from an angel of heaven. He said he had conversed with many members of the Reformed Church and learned what their faith was like. He repeated what he had said to and learned from one of those who adhered to faith separate from the love of others and from another who adhered to faith not separate. He said that he asked them questions, and they replied to them. And because these questions and replies are illuminating I would like to set out here the conversations he had with these two.

42   The angel said that the conversation he had with the one who adhered to faith separate from the love of others went like this –

Amice, quis es? Respondit ille, Sum Reformatus Christianus.
Quae tua doctrina, et inde religio? Respondit quod sit fides.

Dixit,

Quae tua fides? Respondit, Fides mea est *Quod Deus Pater miserit*
Filium, ut satisfaceret pro humano genere, et quod salventur qui id credunt.

Interrogavit tunc dicendo,

Quid scis plus de salvatione? Respondit quod salvatio sit per solam illam fidem.

Porro dixit,

Quid scis de redemptione? Respondit quod facta sit per passionem crucis, et quod meritum Filii imputetur per illam fidem.

Porro,

Quid scis de regeneratione? Respondit quod fiat per illam fidem.
Quid scis de paenitentia et remissione peccatorum? Respondit quod per illam fidem.
Dic, quid scis de amore et charitate? Respondit quod sint illa fides.
Dic, quid scis de bonis operibus. Respondit quod sint illa fides.
Dic, quid cogitas de omnibus praeceptis in Verbo. Respondit quod sint in illa fide.

Tunc dixit,

Ergo nihil facies. Respondit, Quid faciam? non possum facere bonum, quod bonum est, a me.

Dixit,

Num fidem potes habere a te? Respondit, Non possum.

Dixit,

Quomodo tunc potes fidem habere? Respondit, In hoc non inquiro; habebo fidem.

Friend, who are you? He replied, I am a Reformed Christian.

What constitutes your teaching and the religion based on it? He replied that it is faith.

What, the angel said, constitutes your faith? He replied, My faith is this: *God the Father sent the Son to make satisfaction on behalf of the human race, and that they are saved who believe this.*

What more do you know, the angel at this point asked, about salvation? He replied that salvation comes through that faith, alone.

What do you know, the angel added, about redemption? He replied that it was accomplished through the passion on the cross, and that the Son's merit is imputed through that faith.

What do you know, he added, about regeneration? He replied that it is effected through that faith.

What do you know about repentance and forgiveness of sins? He replied that they are accomplished through that faith.

Tell me, what do you know about love and charity? He replied that they are that faith.

Tell me, what do you know about good works? He replied that they are that faith.

Tell me, what do you think of all the commands contained in the Word? He replied that they are included within that faith.

So, the angel at this point said, you do not have to do anything. He replied, What am I to do? I cannot from self do anything good that is good.

Can you from self, said the angel, possess faith? He replied, I cannot.

How then, the angel said, are you able to possess faith? He replied, That is a question I do not ask; I must possess faith.

Tandem dixit,

Omnino scis aliquid praeterea de salute. Respondit, Quid praeterea, cum per solam illam fidem salvatio?

Sed tunc dixit angelus,

Respondes sicut qui canit uno tono tibiae; non audio nisi fidem. Si illam scis, et non praeterea, nihil scis. Abi et vide socios.

Et abivit et offendit illos in deserto ubi non gramen. Quaesivit cur ita; dixerunt, Quia illis nihil ecclesiae.
43 Angelus cum illo qui in fide non separata a charitate, ita loquutus est –

Amice, quis es? Respondit, Sum Christianus Reformatus. Quae tua doctrina, et inde religio? Respondit, Fides et charitas.

Dixit,

Haec sunt duo. Respondit, Non separari possunt.

Dixit,

Quid fides? Respondit, Credere quod Verbum docet.

Dixit,

Quid charitas? Respondit, Facere quod Verbum docet.

Dixit,

Num solum credideris illa, vel num etiam feceris? Respondit, Etiam feci.

Angelus caeli tunc aspexit illum et dixit, Mi amice, veni mecum et habita nobiscum.

You surely know something more than that about salvation, said the angel at length. He replied, What more do I need to know when salvation is accomplished through that faith, alone?

But at this point the angel said,

You reply like a person playing a single note on a flute; I'm hearing of nothing but faith. If faith is all you know and nothing else, you know nothing. Go off and see your comrades.

So he went off and met up with them in a wilderness where there was no grass. When he asked why there was not any he was told, Because they have nothing of the church in them.

43   The angel's conversation with the one who adhered to faith not separate from the love of others went like this –

Friend, who are you? He replied, I am a Reformed Christian.
What constitutes your teaching and the religion based on it? He replied, Faith and the love of others.
These, the angel said, are two things. He replied, They are inseparable.
What, said the angel, is faith? He replied, Believing what the Word teaches.
What, the angel said, is the love of others? He replied, Doing what the Word teaches.
Have you merely believed these things, said the angel, or have you also put them into practice? He replied, I have also put them into practice.

The angel of heaven at that point looked at him and said, My friend, come with me and dwell among us.

Qualis fides separata a charitate est

44   Ut fides separata a charitate videatur qualis est, sistam illam in sua nuditate. In hac talis est –

Quod Deus Pater iratus contra genus humanum, rejecerit illud a Se, et ex justitia statuerit vindicare per ejus damnationem aeternam; et quod dixerit ad Filium, Descende, imple Legem, ac damnationem illis destinatam in Te suscipe, et tunc forte miserebor. Quare descendit, et implevit Legem, et passus Se suspendi cruce, et immaniter occidi; quo facto, rediit ad Patrem et dixit, Damnationem generis humani in Me suscepi; nunc misericors esto – intercedens pro illis. At responsum tulit, Non possum erga illos, sed quia Te vidi super cruce, et tunc sanguinem Tuum, factus sum misericors; at usque non condonabo illis, sed imputabo illis Tuum meritum, verum non aliis quam qui hoc agnoscunt. Hoc erit fides per quam salvari possunt.

45   Haec est fides illa in sua nuditate. Quisnam, cui aliqua ratio illustrata est, in illa non videt paradoxa quae contra ipsam Divinam essentiam sunt? Ut, quod Deus, qui est ipse Amor et ipsa Misericordia, potuerit ex ira et inde vindicta damnare homines, et devovere illos inferno; tum, quod velit ad misericordiam moveri per damnationem Filio impositam, et per intuitionem Ejus passionis super cruce et Ejus sanguinis. Quis, cui aliqua ratio illustrata est, non videt quod Deus ad Deum aequalem non dicere potuerit, Non condono illis, sed imputo illis Tuum meritum – ut et – Nunc vivant sicut velint, modo illud credant, et salvabuntur? Praeter plura.

46   Sed causa quod haec non visa sint, est quia induxerunt fidem caecam, et per illam occluserunt oculos et obturaverunt

The nature of faith separate from the love of others

44   For it to be seen what the nature is of faith separate from the love of others I am going to lay bare that faith. When laid bare it is this –

God the Father was angry with the human race, cast it away from Himself, and out of a demand for justice to be done decided to take vengeance by damning it for ever. So He said to the Son, Go down, fulfil the Law, and take upon Yourself the damnation meant for them; then, perhaps, I will take pity on them. He therefore went down and fulfilled the Law, and allowed Himself to be hung up on a cross and savagely put to death. After He had done this He returned to the Father and said, I have taken upon Myself the damnation of the human race; now take pity on them – interceding for them. But He received the reply, I am unable to do that; however, because I beheld You up on the cross, and Your blood shed then, I have been moved to pity. Yet I will not pardon them but will impute Your merit to them, though to none other than those who acknowledge that merit. This has to be the faith through which they can be saved.

45   This is that faith when laid bare. Is there anyone possessing some degree of enlightened reason who does not see in it notions inconsistent with the essential nature of God Himself? For instance, the notion that God, who is Love itself and Mercy itself, could in anger and consequent vengeance damn human beings and consign them to hell; also the notion that He was willing to be moved to pity by laying the sentence of damnation on the Son, and by beholding His suffering on the cross and His blood. Who with some degree of enlightened reason fails to see that in no way could God have said to a God equal to Himself, I do not pardon them, but I impute Your merit to them; now let them live as they please, provided they believe in Your merit, and they will be saved? And more notions in addition to these.

46   The reason why these notions have not been seen for what they are is that they have led to blind faith, through which people's

aures. Occlude oculos et obtura aures, hoc est, fac ut non cogitent ex aliquo intellectu, et dic illis quibus aliqua idea de vita aeterna impressa est, quicquid velis, et credent; imo, si dixeris quod Deus possit irasci et vindictam spirare; quod Deus possit alicui damnationem aeternam inferre; quod Deus velit ad misericordiam moveri per sanguinem Filii; ac id pro merito imputare et adscribere homini ut ejus; ac salvare per solum cogitare. Ut et, quod unus Deus cum altero Deo unius essentiae potuerit talia stipulari, et Illi injungere; praeter similia alia. Sed aperi oculos et reclude aures, hoc est, cogita de illis ex intellectu, ac videbis discordantiam illorum cum ipsa veritate.

47 Occlude oculos et obtura aures, et fac ut non cogitent ex aliquo intellectu, annon poteris inducere fidem quod Deus dederit omnem Suam potestatem homini, ut sit pro Deo in terris? Annon poteris inducere fidem quod homines mortui invocandi sint, quod nudandum sit caput et flectenda sint genua pro simulachris eorum, quodque cadavera eorum, ossa eorum, et sepulchra illorum, sancta sint et veneranda? Sed si aperis oculos et recludis aures, hoc est, de illis ex aliquo intellectu cogitas, annon videbis enormia quae ratio humana abominabitur?

48 Cum talia et similia alia recipiuntur ab homine cui ex religione occlusus est intellectus, annon tunc templum in quo cultum agit, comparari potest speluncae seu cavernae sub terris, ubi quae videt nescit quid sunt, ac religio ejus comparari potest habitationi in domo in qua non sunt fenestrae, et vox cultus ejus sono, et non loquelae? Cum tali homine non potest angelus caeli loqui, quia unus non intelligit loquelam alterius.

eyes have become closed and their ears blocked. If you close people's eyes and block their ears – that is, prevent them from thinking in any way with their understanding – and then tell anything you like to the ones who have received some conception of eternal life they will believe it. Indeed, were you to tell them that God is able to be angry and wreak vengeance, that God is able to subject someone to eternal damnation, that God is willing to be moved to pity through the blood of the Son, to impute this as merit and credit it to people as theirs, and to save them through their doing no more than thinking this to be so they would believe it. They would also believe it were you to tell them that one God could set out such conditions with another God of one essence with Himself and impose them on Him; and other inconsistent notions like these. But open your eyes and unblock your ears, that is, think about those notions with your understanding, and you will see their confliction with the truth.

47 If you close people's eyes and block their ears, and prevent them from thinking with any degree of understanding, will you not then be able to lead people to believe that God has given all His power to a human being to act on earth in place of God? Will you not be able to lead them to believe that they are to invoke dead human beings, bare their head and kneel before images of these, consider their dead bodies, bones, and tombs to be sacred, and venerate them? But if you open your eyes and unblock your ears, that is, think about these notions with any degree of understanding, will you not then see them to be monstrous, and offensive to human reason?

48 When such notions and others like them are accepted by people whose power of understanding has been shut down by their religion, is not the temple they perform worship in comparable to a cave or cavern underground in which they see objects but do not know what they are; and is not their religion comparable to life in a house with no windows, and their audible worship to sound, not speech? An angel of heaven cannot talk to a person such as this, because the one does not understand the other's speech.

Quod illi qui in fide separata a charitate sunt, in Verbo repraesentati sint per Philisthaeos

49   In Verbo per omnia nomina gentium et populorum, tum personarum et locorum, significantur res ecclesiae – ipsa ecclesia per Israelem et Jehudam, quia apud illos fuit instituta, et varia religiosa per gentes et populos circum illos; religiosa concordantia per gentes bonas et religiosa discordantia per gentes malas. Sunt duo religiosa mala in quae omnis ecclesia successu temporis degeneratur, unum quod adulterat bona ejus et alterum quod falsificat vera ejus. Illud religiosum quod adulterat bona ecclesiae trahit suum ortum ex amore imperandi, et alterum religiosum quod falsificat vera ecclesiae trahit suum ortum ex fastu propriae intelligentiae. Religiosum quod trahit ortum ex amore imperandi, in Verbo intelligitur per Babyloniam, et religiosum quod trahit ortum ex fastu propriae intelligentiae, in Verbo intelligitur per Philisthaeam. Notum est quinam ex Babylonia hodie sunt, sed non notum quinam ex Philisthaea. Ex Philisthaea sunt qui in fide et non in charitate.

50   Quod illi ex Philisthaea sint qui in fide et non in charitate, constare potest ex variis quae de illis in Verbo dicuntur, in spirituali sensu intellectis; tam ex altercationibus illorum cum Abrahami et Isaci servis, de quibus Gen.21 et 26, quam ex bellis illorum cum filiis Israelis, de quibus in Libro Judicium ac in Libris Samuelis et Regum, omnia enim bella in Verbo descripta in sensu spirituali involvunt et significant bella spiritualia. Et quia hoc religiosum, quod est fidei separatae a charitate, continue vult invadere ecclesiam, ideo Philisthaei manserunt in terra Canaane, et filios Israelis crebro infestarunt.

51   Quoniam Philisthaei repraesentabant illos qui in fide separata charitate sunt, ideo vocati sunt **Praeputiati**; et per

People who adhere to faith separate from the love of others are represented in the Word by the Philistines

49 In the Word all names of nations and peoples, of persons and places too, serve to mean things connected with the church. The church itself is meant by Israel and Judah, because it was they among whom it was established, while varieties of religion are meant by the nations and peoples round about them, compatible varieties by good nations and incompatible by bad ones. There are two bad kinds of religion that every church in the course of time degenerates into, one which adulterates the forms of goodness it possesses and the other which falsifies the truths it knows. The kind of religion which adulterates the forms of goodness the church possesses derives its origin from the love of exercising control over others, and the other kind that falsifies the truths the church knows derives its origin from the arrogance of self-intelligence. The kind of religion deriving its origin from the love of exercising control is meant in the Word by Babylon, and the kind deriving its origin from the arrogance of self-intelligence is meant in the Word by Philistia. Who they are who belong to Babylon at the present day is well known, but not those who belong to Philistia. To Philistia belong those who are adherents of faith and not the love of others.

50 The fact that they belong to Philistia who are adherents of faith and not the love of others becomes clear from the meaning in the spiritual sense of various accounts in the Word involving them, both from their disputes with the servants of Abraham and Isaac, dealt with in Genesis 21 and 26, and from their wars with the children of Israel, in the Book of Judges and the Books of Samuel and Kings. For in the spiritual sense all conflicts described in the Word embody and serve to mean spiritual conflicts. And because this kind of religion – namely that of faith separate from the love of others – constantly wishes to invade the church, the Philistines remained in the land of Canaan and frequently attacked the children of Israel.

51 Since the Philistines represented those who adhere to faith separate from the love of others they were called the **Uncircumcised**;

Praeputiatos intelliguntur qui absque amore spirituali sunt, et inde in solo amore naturali – amor spiritualis est charitas. Causa quod hi Praeputiati dicti sint, est quia per **Circumcisos** intelliguntur qui in amore spirituali sunt. Quod Philisthaei Praeputiati dicti sint, videatur 1 Sam.17:26,36; 2 Sam.1:20; et alibi.

52 Quod illi qui in fide separata a charitate sunt per Philisthaeos repraesentati sint, constare potest non modo ex bellis eorum cum filiis Israelis sed etiam ex pluribus aliis quae de illis in Verbo memorantur, ut ex illis quae de Dagone idolo eorum, de haemorrhoidibus et muribus, quibus propter arcam in fano idoli eorum positam percussi et infestati sunt, et ex reliquis quae tunc evenerunt, de quibus, 1 Sam.5 et 6; similiter quae de Goliatho, qui Philisthaeus erat, a Davide interfecto, de quo 1 Sam.17. Dagon enim idolum eorum, erat superius sicut homo, inferius sicut piscis, per quod repraesentabatur religio eorum, quod ex fide esset sicut spiritualis, ex nulla charitate autem esset mere naturalis. Per haemorrhoides quibus percussi erant significabantur spurci eorum amores; per mures quibus infestati erant significabatur devastatio ecclesiae per falsificationes veri; et per Goliathum a Davide percussum repraesentabatur fastus propriae intelligentiae illorum.

53 Quod illi qui in fide separata a charitate sunt repraesentati sint per Philisthaeos, patet etiam ex propheticis Verbi ubi de illis agitur, ut ex sequentibus his –

Apud Jeremiam,

Contra Philisthaeos: Ecce aquae ascendentes ex septentrione quae fient in flumen inundans, et inundabunt terram et plenitudinem ejus, urbem et habitantes in ea, ut clament homines et ejulet omnis habitator terrae. Vastabit Jehovah Philisthaeos. 47:1,2,4.

Aquae ascendentes e septentrione sunt falsa ex inferno; quae fient in flumen inundans, et inundabunt terram et plenitudinem ejus significat per illa devastationem omnium ecclesiae; urbem et habitantes in ea significat devastationem omnium doctrinae

and by the Uncircumcised are meant those who are devoid of spiritual love and therefore possess only natural love – spiritual love being the love of others. The reason why these people were referred to as the Uncircumcised is that those who do possess spiritual love are meant by the **Circumcised**. For references to the Philistines as the Uncircumcised, see 1 Sam.17:26,36; 2 Sam.1:20; and elsewhere.

52   The representation by the Philistines of those adhering to faith separate from the love of others is evident not only from their wars with the children of Israel but also from many other details mentioned in the Word concerning them, from for instance the details relating to Dagon their idol, the haemorrhoids they were afflicted with and the mice they were pestered by, on account of their placing the ark in the temple of their idol, and from all else that happened then, described in 1 Sam.5 and 6; and in a similar way from the details mentioned concerning David's slaying of Goliath, who was a Philistine, described in 1 Sam.17. For the upper part of Dagon their idol resembled a human being, the lower part a fish; and this was a representation of their religion, in that because there was faith this religion was seemingly spiritual, but because there was no love of others it was wholly natural. The haemorrhoids they were afflicted with stood for their foul kinds of love; the mice they were pestered by stood for the laying waste of the church by falsifications of what is true; and Goliath whom David struck down represented the arrogance of their self-intelligence.

53   The representation by the Philistines of those adhering to faith separate from the love of others is also evident from places they are referred to in the prophetical parts of the Word, for instance the following –

In Jeremiah,

Against the Philistines: Behold, waters rising out of the north which will become a deluging stream, and they will deluge the land and all that fills it, the city and those who dwell in it, so that people will cry out and every inhabitant of the land will wail. Jehovah will lay waste the Philistines. 47:1,2,4.

Waters rising out of the north stand for false notions that come from hell. They will become a deluging stream and will deluge the land and all that fills it means the devastation by those false notions of everything composing the church; the city and those who dwell in it means the devastation by them of everything constituting the

ejus; ut clament homines et ejulet omnis habitator terrae significat defectum omnis veri et boni in ecclesia; vastabit Jehovah Philisthaeos significat interitum eorum.

Apud Esaiam,

Ne laeteris, Philisthaea tota, quod fracta sit virga percutiens te, nam e radice serpentis exibit basiliscus, cujus fructus prester volans. 14:29.

Ne laeteris, Philisthaea tota, significat ne gaudeant qui in fide separata a charitate sunt, quod adhuc maneant; nam e radice serpentis exibit basiliscus significat ex fastu propriae intelligentiae destructionem omnis veri apud illos; cujus fructus prester volans significat ratiocinia ex falsis mali contra vera et bona ecclesiae.

54 Quod per circumcisionem repraesentata sit purificatio a malis quae sunt amoris mere naturalis, patet ex his –

Circumcidite cor vestrum et removete praeputia cordis vestri, ne exeat ira Mea propter malitiam operum vestrorum. Jer.4:4.
Circumcidite praeputium cordis vestri, et cervicem vestram non indurate amplius. Deut.10:16.

Circumcidere cor aut praeputium cordis est purificare se a malis. Inde vicissim, per incircumcisum seu praeputiatum intelligitur qui a malis amoris mere naturalis non purificatus, ita qui non in charitate est. Et quia immundus corde per praeputiatum intelligitur, dicitur, Nullus praeputiatus corde, et praeputiatus carne, intrabit in sanctuarium, Ezech.44:9; Nullus praeputiatus comedet Pascha, Exod.12:48; et quod damnatus sit, Ezech.28:10; 31:18; 32:19.

---

6   See pages vii-viii above regarding the chapter-and-verse numbering of this

teaching of the church; so that people will cry out and every inhabitant will wail means the lack within the church of everything true and good. Jehovah will lay waste the Philistines means their destruction.

In Isaiah,

Rejoice not, all Philistia, that the rod which smites you has been broken, for from the serpent's root will come forth a basilisk, and its fruit will be a flying fiery serpent. 14:29.

Rejoice not, all Philistia, means let not those adhering to faith separate from the love of others feel glad that they still remain; for from the serpent's root will come forth a basilisk means that from the arrogance of self-intelligence comes the destruction of everything true with them; and its fruit will be a flying fiery serpent means reasonings – based on false notions that are a product of evil – which are directed against the truth and goodness composing the church.

54 Circumcision represented purification from the evil desires that go with merely natural love, as is evident from the following places,

Circumcise your heart,[1] and remove the foreskin of your heart, lest My anger goes forth on account of the wickedness of your works. Jer.4:4. Circumcise the foreskin of your heart, and be stiff-necked no longer. Deut.10:16.

Circumcising the heart or the foreskin of the heart means purifying oneself from evil desires. Conversely therefore, being uncircumcised or possessing a foreskin serves to mean those who have not been purified from the evil desires that go with wholly natural love, and so those who are not governed by the love of others. And because uncleanness in heart is meant by possessing a foreskin, it says at Ezek.44:9 that no one uncircumcised in heart and uncircumcised in flesh shall enter the sanctuary, at Exod.12:48 that no one uncircumcised shall eat the Passover, and at Ezek.28:10; 31:18; 32:19 that such a person is damned.

---

1 The Hebrew here means *Circumcise yourselves to Jehovah*. To judge from what Swedenborg wrote in *AC* 2039:3 and 4462 he had in mind, here in *FI* 54, Deut.30:6 as well as Jer.4:4 and Deut.10:16

Quod illi qui in fide separata a charitate sunt intelligantur per Draconem in Apocalypsi

55 Dictum est supra quod omnis ecclesia successu temporis abeat in duo communia religiosa mala – in unum ex amore imperandi et in alterum ex fastu propriae intelligentiae – et quod prius religiosum in Verbo intelligatur et describatur per **Babyloniam**, et posterius per **Philisthaeam**. Nunc quia in Apocalypsi agitur de statu Ecclesiae Christianae, imprimis qualis in fine est, ideo de binis illis religiosis malis, in genere et in specie ibi agitur. Religiosum quod per Babyloniam intelligitur, describitur in cap. 17-19, quod ibi est meretrix sedens super bestia coccinea; ac religiosum quod per Philisthaeam intelligitur describitur in capitibus 12-13, quod ibi est draco, tum bestia ex mari, ac bestia ex terra ascendens. Quod hoc religiosum per draconem et ejus binas bestias intellectum sit, hactenus non sciri potuit; causa est quia sensus spiritualis Verbi non prius apertus fuit, et inde Apocalypsis non intellecta est, et imprimis quia religiosum de fide separata a charitate in Christiano orbe tantum invaluit ut nemo id videre posset. Omne enim religiosum malum occaecat oculos.

56 Quod religiosum fidei separatae a charitate intelligatur et describatur in Apocalypsi per draconem et per binas ejus bestias, non modo e caelo mihi dictum est sed etiam in mundo spirituum, qui sub caelo est, ostensum est. Visi mihi sunt illi qui in fide separata erant, in caetu sicut magnus draco cum extensa cauda versus caelum; et visi sunt alii, qui tales, separati, in apparentia sicut dracones. Sunt enim in illo mundo hujuscemodi apparentiae ex correspondentia spiritualium cum naturalibus, quare etiam illi ab angelis caeli vocantur draconici. Sed plura illorum genera sunt; quidam

Those who adhere to faith separate from the love of others are meant by the Dragon in the Book of Revelation

55   It was mentioned above that in the course of time every church goes off into two general bad kinds of religion – one that has its origin in the love of exercising control over others, the other in the arrogance of self-intelligence – and that in the Word the former is meant and described by **Babylon**, the latter by **Philistia**. Now because in the Book of Revelation the state of the Christian Church is dealt with, especially what it is like towards the end of it, both of those bad kinds of religion are dealt with there in general and in particular. The kind of religion meant by Babylon is described in chapters 17-19, where it is a prostitute sitting on a scarlet beast; and the kind of religion meant by Philistia is described in chapters 12-13, where it is a dragon, also a beast coming up out of the sea, and a beast rising out of the earth. Up to now it had not been possible for people to know that this kind of religion was meant by the dragon and its two beasts. This was because the spiritual sense of the Word had not yet been opened up and there had not consequently been any understanding of the Book of Revelation, and especially because in the Christian world the religion of faith separate from the love of others had grown so strong that no one was able to see the description of it there. For every form of bad religion brings blindness to the eyes.

56   Not only have I been told from heaven that the religion of faith separate from the love of others is what is meant and described in the Book of Revelation by the dragon and its two beasts; I have also had it demonstrated to me in the world of spirits, which is underneath heaven. There I saw adherents of faith separate, in a group resembling a large dragon with its tail reaching up towards heaven or the sky; and I saw some others – similar to, yet separate from, those in this group – who looked like dragons. For in the world of spirits manifestations such as these occur because of the correspondence of spiritual realities with natural things, and this also is why the angels in heaven call those people dragonists. But there are

eorum constituunt draconis caput, quidam illius corpus, et quidam ejus caudam. Illi qui constituunt ejus caudam sunt qui omnia vera Verbi falsificaverunt, quare dicitur de dracone in Apocalypsi quod cauda sua detraxerit tertiam partem stellarum caeli. Per stellas caeli significantur cognitiones veri, et per tertiam partem omnes.

57   Nunc quia per draconem in Apocalypsi intelliguntur qui in fide separata a charitate sunt, et hoc hactenus ignoratum fuit, et quoque occultum ex non cognitione sensus spiritualis Verbi, ideo dabitur hic explicatio generalis super illa quae in cap.12 ibi de dracone dicuntur.

58   De dracone haec dicuntur in capite 12, in Apocalypsi –

Et signum magnum visum est in caelo: Mulier circumdata sole, et luna sub pedibus ejus, et super capite ejus corona stellarum duodecim. Et in utero habens clamavit parturiens, et cruciata parere. Et visum est aliud signum in caelo, et ecce draco magnus rufus, habens capita septem, et cornua decem, et super capitibus suis diademata septem. Et cauda sua traxit tertiam partem stellarum caeli, et projecit illas in terram. Et draco stetit coram muliere paritura, ut postquam pepererat, faetum ejus devoraret. Et peperit filium masculum, qui pasturus est omnes gentes virga ferrea; et raptus est faetus ejus ad Deum et thronum Ipsius. Et mulier fugit in desertum, ubi habet locum praeparatum a Deo, ut ibi alant eam diebus mille ducentis sexaginta. Et factum est bellum in caelo. Michael et angeli ejus pugnarunt cum dracone, et draco pugnavit et angeli ejus, et non praevaluerunt; et non locus inventus illorum amplius in caelo. Et cum vidit draco quod projectus in terram, persequutus est mulierem quae peperit filium. Et datae mulieri duae alae aquilae magnae, ut volaret in desertum in locum suum, ubi aleretur ibi tempus et tempora et dimidium temporis, a facie serpentis. Et ejecit serpens post mulierem ex ore suo aquam tanquam flumen, ut illam a flumine absorptam faceret. Et adjuvit terra mulierem, et aperuit terra os suum et deglutivit flumen

17   decem: septem *FI*
30   temporis: tempus *FI*

very many kinds of these, some composing the head of the dragon, some its body, and some its tail. The ones composing its tail are those who have falsified all the truths in the Word, which is why it says of the dragon in the Book of Revelation that its tail dragged down one third of the stars in the sky. By the stars in the sky are meant items of knowledge of what is true, and by one third is meant all.

57 Now because those who adhere to faith separate from the love of others are meant by the dragon in the Book of Revelation, and this is something that has been unknown up to now and also something hidden from view because there has not been any awareness of the spiritual sense of the Word, a general explanation of the things said in chapter 12 of that book regarding the dragon will therefore be presented here.

58 The things said in the Book of Revelation, chapter 12, regarding the dragon are these –

And a great sign appeared in heaven: A woman clothed with the sun, and the moon under her feet, and a crown of twelve stars on her head. And being with child she cried out in labour, and in pain to give birth. And another sign appeared in heaven, and, behold, a great fiery-red dragon, having seven heads and ten horns, and on its heads seven jewels[1]. And its tail dragged down a third of the stars of heaven and cast them to the earth. And the dragon stood before the woman about to give birth, so that after she had given birth it would devour her infant. And she gave birth to a male child, who would shepherd all nations with a rod of iron; and her infant was caught up to God and His throne. And the woman fled into the wilderness, where she has a place prepared by God, so that they may feed her there for one thousand two hundred and sixty days. And war broke out in heaven; Michael and his angels fought against the dragon, and the dragon fought and his angels, and did not prevail. And no place was found for them any longer in heaven. And when the dragon saw that it had been cast to the earth it persecuted the woman who gave birth to a son. And the woman was given two wings of a great eagle, so that she might fly into the wilderness to her place – where she would be nourished for a time and times and half a time – from the presence of the serpent. And the serpent poured out of its mouth water like a river after the woman, so that it might cause her to be swallowed up by the river. And the earth helped the woman, and the earth opened its mouth and

---

1   The ordinary meaning of the Latin word is *diadems, crowns*, but it is clear from the exposition at *AR* 540 that here it must be taken to mean *precious stones, jewels*

quod ejecit draco ex ore suo. Et iratus est draco contra mulierem, et abivit facere bellum cum reliquis seminis ejus, observantibus mandata Dei et habentibus testimonium Jesu Christi.

59   Haec illorum explicatio est:

Signum magnum visum est in caelo significat revelationem a Domino de futura ecclesia, et de receptione doctrinae ejus, et a quibus impugnabitur. Mulier circumdata sole, et luna sub pedibus ejus significat ecclesiam quae a Domino in amore, et in fide est. Et super capite ejus corona stellarum duodecim significat sapientiam ac intelligentiam ex Divinis veris apud illos. Et in utero habens significat nascentem doctrinam. Clamavit parturiens, et cruciata parere, significat resistentiam ab illis qui in fide separata a charitate sunt. Et visum est aliud signum in caelo significat iterum revelationem. Et ecce draco magnus rufus significat fidem separatam a charitate, qui rufus dicitur ab amore mere naturali. Habens capita septem significat falsum intellectum Verbi. Et cornua decem significat potentiam ex receptione a multis. Et super capitibus suis diademata septem significat falsificata vera Verbi. Et cauda sua traxit tertiam partem stellarum caeli, et projecit illas in terram, significat destructionem omnium cognitionum veri. Et draco stetit coram muliere paritura, ut postquam pepererat, faetum ejus devoraret, significat odium illorum et animum destruendi doctrinam ecclesiae in suo ortu. Et peperit filium masculum significat doctrinam. Qui pasturus omnes gentes virga ferrea significat quae ex potentia veri naturalis ex spirituali convincet. Et raptus est filius ejus ad Deum et thronum Ipsius significat tutationem ejus a Domino e caelo. Et mulier fugit in desertum significat ecclesiam inter paucos. Ubi habet locum praeparatum a Deo significat statum ejus, ut interea provideatur inter plures. Ut ibi alant illam diebus mille ducentis sexaginta significat usque dum crescit ad suum statutum. Et factum est bellum in caelo, Michael et angeli ejus pugnarunt cum dracone, et draco pugnavit et angeli ejus, significat dissensionem et pugnam illorum qui in fide separata a charitate sunt contra illos qui in doctrina ecclesiae de

26   mulier *FP*: om *FP*, *FP*

swallowed the river which the dragon had poured out of its mouth. And the dragon was angry with the woman, and went off to make war with the rest of her offspring, with those who keep God's commandments and hold to the testimony of Jesus Christ.

59   Here is the explanation of these things:

A great sign appeared in heaven means a revelation from the Lord concerning the future church, the acceptance of its teaching, and those who will stand opposed to it. A woman clothed with the sun, and the moon under her feet, means a church which from the Lord possesses love and faith. And a crown of twelve stars on her head means the wisdom and intelligence derived from the Divine truths present with those belonging to that church. And being with child means the teaching coming to birth. She cried out in labour, and in pain to give birth, means opposition to it on the part of those who adhere to faith separate from the love of others. And another sign appeared in heaven means a second revelation. And, behold, a great fiery-red dragon means faith separate from the love of others, which is described as being fiery-red on account of a wholly natural love. Having seven heads means a false understanding of the Word. And ten horns means the power gained from the acceptance of things from many sources. And on its heads seven jewels means truths of the Word which have been falsified. And its tail dragged down a third of the stars of heaven and cast them to the earth means the destruction of all items of knowledge of what is true. And the dragon stood before the woman about to give birth, so that after she had given birth it would devour her infant, means their hatred and intention to destroy the teaching of the church as soon as it came into existence. And she gave birth to a male child means that teaching. Who would shepherd all nations with a rod of iron means that this teaching will, with the power that natural truth derived from spiritual possesses, be convincing. And her infant was caught up to God and His throne means the Lord's protection, coming from heaven, of that teaching. And the woman fled into the wilderness means the church existing among few. Where she has a place prepared by God means the state of the church, that provision may be made in the meantime for its existence among many. So that they may feed her there for one thousand two hundred and sixty days means until it increases in size to its appointed state. And war broke out in heaven; Michael and his angels fought against the dragon, and the dragon fought and his angels, means the disagreement and conflict between those who adhere to faith separate from a love of others and those who adhere to the teaching of the church concerning the Lord and to the life of love towards others. And

Domino et de vita charitatis sunt. Et non praevaluerunt significat quod succubuerint. Et non locus inventus eorum amplius in caelo significat dejectionem illorum. Cum vidit draco quod projectus sit in terram, persequutus est mulierem quae peperit masculum significat infestationem ecclesiae ab illis qui in fide separata a charitate, propter doctrinam ejus. Et datae mulieri duae alae aquilae magnae, ut volaret in desertum in locum suum, significat circumspectionem dum adhuc inter paucos est. Ubi aleretur tempus et tempora et dimidium temporis, a facie serpentis significat usque dum ecclesia crescit ad suum statutum. Et ejecit serpens post mulierem ex ore suo aquam tanquam flumen, ut illam a flumine absorptam faceret, significat ratiocinationes illorum ex falsis in copia ad destruendum ecclesiam. Et adjuvit terra mulierem, et aperuit terra os suum et deglutivit flumen quod ejecit draco ex ore suo, significat quod ratiocinationes, quia ex falsis, a se ipsis deciderint. Et iratus est draco contra mulierem, et abivit facere bellum cum reliquis seminis ejus, significat perstans odium illorum. Observantibus mandata Dei et habentibus testimonium Jesu Christi significat contra illos qui vivunt vitam charitatis et credunt in Dominum.

60   In capite 13 sequente in Apocalypsi agitur de binis bestiis draconis, de una quae visa est ex mari ascendisse, et de altera quae visa est ex terra ascendisse. De priore agitur a versu 1 ad 10, et de posteriore a versu 11 ad 18, quae quod sint bestiae draconis, patet a versibus 2,4,11, ibi. Per primam bestiam significatur fides separata a charitate quoad confirmationes ejus ex naturali homine, et per alteram significatur fides separata a charitate quoad confirmationes ejus ex Verbo, quae etiam sunt falsificationes veri. Sed praetereo illa explicare, quia continent argumentationes eorum quae prolixius diducendae forent; solum ultimum hoc,

Habens intelligentiam computet numerum bestiae, numerus enim hominis est; et numerus ejus sexcenta sexaginta sex. Vers.18.

Habens intelligentiam computet numerum bestiae significat qui in illustratione sunt inquirant quale confirmationum istius

did not prevail means that they were overcome. And *no place was found for them any longer in heaven* means that they were cast out. *When the dragon saw that it had been cast to the earth it persecuted the woman who had given birth to the male child* means attacks made on the church, because of its teaching, by those adhering to faith separate from the love of others. *And the woman was given two wings of a great eagle, so that she might fly into the wilderness to her place,* means vigilance while it still exists among few. *Where she would be nourished for a time and times and half a time, from the presence of the serpent,* means until the church increases in size to its appointed state. *And the serpent poured out of its mouth water like a river after the woman, to cause her to be swallowed up by the river,* means their reasonings in abundance that are based on false notions and are intended to destroy the church. *And the earth helped the woman, and the earth opened its mouth and swallowed the river which the dragon had poured out of its mouth,* means that the reasonings, because they were based on false notions, fell by their very nature to the ground. *And the dragon was angry with the woman, and went off to make war with the rest of her offspring,* means their continual hatred. *With those who keep God's commandments and hold to the testimony of Jesus Christ* means directed against those who lead the life of the love of others and believe in the Lord.

60   Chapter 13 that follows in the Book of Revelation refers to the dragon's two beasts, one of which was seen rising up out of the sea, the other rising up out of the earth. The former is the subject in verses 1-10, the latter in verses 11-18; and the fact that they are the dragon's beasts is evident in verses 2,4,11. The first beast means ideas produced on a natural level of human thought that are used to support faith separate from the love of others, while the second means ideas derived from the Word, which are in fact falsifications of what is true, that are used to support it. But I am going to pass over an explanation of the verses in this chapter because they contain lines of argument which would be too tedious to set out, except just the final one –

Let anyone having understanding calculate the number of the beast, for it is the number of a person; and its number is six hundred and sixty-six. Verse 18.

Let anyone having understanding calculate the number of the beast means that anyone who is enlightened may, to see what they are like, examine the ideas derived from the Word that are used in support of

fidei ex Verbo. Numerus enim hominis est significat quod sit quale propriae intelligentiae. Et numerus ejus sexcenta sexaginta et sex significat omne verum Verbi falsificatum.

that faith. For it is the number of a person means that they are seen to be the product of self-intelligence. And its number is six hundred and sixty-six means that every truth in the Word has been falsified.

Quod illi qui in fide separata a charitate sunt, intelligantur per hircos apud Danielem et Matthaeum

61 Quod per hircum apud Danielem 8, et per hircos apud Matthaeum 25, intelligantur illi qui in fide separata a charitate sunt, constare potest ex eo quod opponantur arieti et ovibus ibi; et per arietem et per oves intelliguntur qui in charitate sunt. Dominus enim in Verbo vocatur Pastor; ecclesia ovile; et homines ecclesiae in genere vocantur grex, et in specie oves; et quia oves sunt illi qui in charitate sunt, ideo hirci sunt illi qui non in charitate.

62 Quod illi qui in fide separata a charitate sunt, per hircos intelligantur, demonstrabitur,

i Ab experientia in mundo spirituali
ii Ab Ultimo Judicio, super quos peractum est
iii Ex descriptione pugnae inter arietem et hircum apud Danielem
iv Et demum ex omissione charitatis illorum de quibus apud Matthaeum

63 i **Quod illi qui in fide separata a charitate sunt intelligantur in Verbo per hircos, ab experientia in mundo spirituali.** In mundo spirituali apparent omnia quae in mundo naturali. Apparent domus et palatia, apparent paradisi et horti, et in illis arbores omnis generis, apparent agri et novalia, tum campi et vireta, et quoque armenta et greges. Omnia in tali similitudine in qua super nostra tellure; nec alia intercedit differentia quam quod haec sint ex origine naturali, et illa ex origine spirituali. Quare angeli, quia spirituales sunt, vident illa quae ex origine spirituali sunt, similiter ut homines illa quae ex origine naturali sunt.

Omnia quae apparent in mundo spirituali sunt correspondentiae, correspondent enim affectionibus angelorum et spirituum. Haec causa est quod illi qui in affectione

Those who adhere to faith separate from the love of others are meant by the goats in Daniel and Matthew

61 The he-goat in Daniel 8 and the goats in Matthew 25 mean those who adhere to faith separate from the love of others. This is evident from their being opposed in those chapters to a ram and to sheep, and the ram and the sheep stand for those who possess the love of others. For in the Word the Lord is called the Shepherd, the church the sheepfold; and members in general of the church are called the flock, in particular the sheep. And since the sheep are those who possess the love of others, the goats are therefore those who do not.

62 The fact that those who adhere to faith separate from the love of others are meant by goats will be made clear from the following –

i   Experience in the spiritual world
ii   The Last Judgment, on whom it was accomplished
iii   The fight between the ram and the he-goat that is described in Daniel
iv   And lastly, the disregarding of the love of others by those meant by the goats in Matthew

63   **i Those who adhere to faith separate from the love of others are meant in the Word by goats. This becomes clear from experience in the spiritual world.** All things existing in the natural world appear in the spiritual world. Houses and palaces appear; parks and gardens appear, with every kind of tree in them; fields and newly ploughed areas appear, as well as lowlands and meadows, and herds and flocks too. All things that appear there resemble those on our planet; there is no difference between them apart from the latter having a natural origin, the former a spiritual origin. Angels therefore, being spiritual, see those things which have a spiritual origin, in the same way as people see those that have a natural origin.

All things appearing in the spiritual world are correspondences, because they correspond to angels' and spirits' desires. This

boni et veri sunt, et inde in sapientia et intelligentia, habitent in palatiis magnificis, circum quae sunt paradisi pleni arboribus, quae correspondent, et circum illos agri et campi in quibus cubant greges, qui sunt apparentiae. Correspondentiae autem oppositae sunt apud illos qui in affectionibus malis sunt. Hi vel sunt in infernis inclusi ergastulis quae sunt absque fenestris, in quibus tamen est lumen sicut ex igne fatuo, vel sunt in desertis et habitant in mapalibus, circum quae omnia sterilia sunt, et ibi serpentes, dracones, ululae, et plura, quae malis illorum correspondent.

Inter caelum et infernum est locus medius, qui vocatur mundus spirituum. In hunc venit omnis homo statim post mortem, et ibi simile commercium est unius cum altero, sicut hominum inter se super tellure; ibi etiam omnia quae apparent correspondentiae sunt. Apparent etiam ibi horti, luci, sylvae cum arboribus et virgultis, ut et campi floridi et virides, et simul varii generis bestiae, mites et immites, omnia secundum correspondentiam affectionum illorum. Ibi saepius vidi oves et hircos, et quoque pugnas inter illos, similes illi pugnae quae describitur apud Danielem 8.

Vidi hircos cum cornibus antrorsum et retrorsum flexis, ac illos cum furore irruentes in oves. Vidi hircos cum duobus cornibus, quibus cum vehementia ferierunt oves. Et cum aspexi quid esset, vidi aliquos rixantes inter se de charitate et fide, ex quo patuit quod fides separata a charitate esset quae appareret sicut hircus, et quod charitas ex qua fides esset quae appareret sicut ovis. Quia haec saepius vidi, datum est pro certo scire quod illi qui in fide separata a charitate sunt, in Verbo per hircos intelligantur.

64 ii **Quod illi qui in fide separata a charitate sunt intelliguntur in Verbo per hircos; ex Ultimo Judicio, super quos peractum est.** Ultimum Judicium non super alios factum est quam qui in externis fuerunt morales, ac in internis non spirituales, aut parum spirituales. Illi autem qui tam in externis quam in internis fuerunt mali, longe ante Ultimum Judicium in infernum conjecti sunt; et illi qui in externis et simul in internis spirituales fuerunt, longe ante Ultimum Judicium in caelum elevati sunt. Nam judicium non factum

being so, those with a desire for what is good and true, who therefore possess wisdom and intelligence, live in corresponding magnificent palaces surrounded by parks full of trees, and the parks surrounded by fields and clearings with flocks lying down in them. These are appearances. But the correspondences that occur among those with evil desires are an utter contrast. These people either exist in the hells, imprisoned in windowless workhouses, in which however there is poor light like that emitted by a will-o'-the-wisp, or they exist in desert places, dwelling in huts around which everything is barren, and where there are serpents, poisonous snakes, screeching owls, and many more things corresponding to their evil desires.

3   Between heaven and hell there is a middle region, called the world of spirits. Everyone enters this immediately after death, where there is a similar interaction of one being with another, like that which goes on among people on earth. Also, all things that appear in that world are correspondences. Also appearing in it there are gardens, groves, woodlands with trees and bushes, as well as green and flowery clearings, and at the same time various kinds of gentle and fierce animals, all in accord with spirits' desires. I have often seen sheep and goats there, and also fights between them, like that which is described in Daniel 8.

4   I have seen goats with horns bent forwards and backwards, and those rushing furiously against sheep. I have seen goats with two horns, which they have violently butted the sheep with. And when I turned to see what was going on I noticed some spirits violently quarrelling with one another about the love of others and faith, from which it was evident that faith separate from the love of others was what would manifest itself as a goat, and the love of others from which faith emanates was that which would manifest itself as a sheep. Since I have seen this rather often I have been allowed to know for certain that people who adhere to faith separate from the love of others are meant in the Word by goats.

64   **ii Those who adhere to faith separate from the love of others are meant in the Word by goats. This becomes clear from the Last Judgment, on whom it was accomplished.** The Last Judgment was carried out on no one else than those who in respect of their outward self were moral and in respect of their inward self were not spiritual or barely so. But those who in respect of both their outward self and their inward self were bad had been cast into hell long before the Last Judgment, and those who in respect of their outward self and at the same time inward self were spiritual had been raised to heaven long before the Last Judgment. For the judgment was not

est super illos qui in caelo erant nec super illos qui in inferno, sed super illos qui in medio inter caelum et infernum fuerunt, et ibi sibi fecerunt sicut caelos. Quod Ultimum Judicium super illos et non super alios factum sit, videri potest in opusculo **De Ultimo Judicio**, n.59 et 70, et videbitur ulterius in **Continuatione de Ultimo Judicio**, et ibi super Reformatos; ex quibus tunc illi qui in fide separata a charitate non modo doctrina sed etiam vita fuerunt, in infernum conjecti sunt, ac illi qui in eadem fide solum quoad doctrinam sed usque in charitate quoad vitam fuerunt, in caelum elevati sunt. Ex quibus patuit quod non alii per hircos et per oves a Domino – apud Matthaeum 25, ubi loquitur de Ultimo Judicio – intellecti sint.

65 iii **Quod illi qui in fide separata a charitate sunt intelligantur in Verbo per hircos, ex descriptione pugnae inter arietem et hircum apud Danielem.** Omnia quae in Daniele sunt, in spirituali sensu agunt de rebus caeli et ecclesiae, sicut omnia in universa Scriptura Sacra, ut in **Doctrina Novae Hierosolymae** de illa, n.5-26, ostensum est. Ita quoque illa in Daniele quae de pugna arietis et hirci ibi, cap. 8, dicuntur, quae talia sunt –

In visione vidi arietem cui duo cornua alta, sed altius ascendens posterius; et quod cornu feriret versus occidentem, septentrionem, et meridiem, et magnum se faceret. Dein vidi hircum venientem ab occidente super facies totius terrae, cui esset cornu inter oculos, et quod cucurrerit ad arietem cum furore roboris sui, et fregerit duo cornua ejus, et projecerit eum in terram, et conculcaverit eum; at quod fractum sit cornu magnum hirci, et loco ejus ascenderint quatuor cornua; et quod ex uno eorum exiret cornu exiguum, quod crevit valde versus meridiem, versus ortum, et versus decus, et usque ad exercitum caelorum, et dejecit in terram de exercitu, et de stellis, et conculcavit ea. Imo extulit se ad Principem exercitus, et ab Eo sublatum est juge, et projectum habitaculum sanctuarii Ejus; quin projecit veritatem in terram. Et audivi unum sanctum

34 quin: quia *FI*

carried out on those who were in heaven, not on those in hell either, but on those in the middle region between heaven and hell, where they had established pseudo-heavens for themselves. That the Last Judgment was carried out on these and no one else can be seen in the small work concerning **The Last Judgment**, §§59 and 70; and there will be more to see in **A Continuation concerning the Last Judgment**, where the carrying out of it on the Reformed is dealt with. Those of the Reformed who at that time adhered to faith separate from the love of others not only in the teaching they knew but also in the lives they led were cast into hell, and those who adhered to the same faith solely because it was the teaching they knew but nevertheless in life adhered to the love of others were raised to heaven. From all this it was evident that the Lord meant none other than these two kinds of people by the goats and the sheep in Matthew 25, where He is speaking about the Last Judgment.

2

65 iii **Those who adhere to faith separate from the love of others are meant in the Word by goats. This becomes clear from the description in Daniel of the fight between the ram and the he-goat.** Everything in Daniel refers in the spiritual sense to the realities of heaven and the church, as everything does throughout Sacred Scripture, which was shown to be so in **Teaching of the New Jerusalem concerning Sacred Scripture**, §§5-26. Thus the same applies to the details in Daniel of the fight between the ram and the he-goat described in chapter 8, which go like this –

In the vision I saw a ram that had two high horns, the higher one rising up later than the other; and he was butting[1] towards the west, the north, and the south, and became great[2]. Then I saw a he-goat coming from the west across the face of the whole earth, who had a horn between his eyes; and he ran at the ram with all his might and broke his two horns, and threw him to the ground, and trampled on him. But the large horn of the he-goat was broken and four horns came up in place of it; and out of one of them there came forth a little horn, which grew exceedingly towards the south, towards the east, and towards the glorious land. It grew even towards the host of heaven, and cast down to earth some of the host, and of the stars, and trampled on them. He even set himself up as high as the Prince of the host, and from Him was the regular offering taken away, and the place of His sanctuary thrown down; or rather, he threw truth down to the ground. And I heard a holy one saying, For how

---

1 lit. *striking with horn*
2 lit. *made himself great* or *magnified himself*

dicentem, Quousque visio haec, juge et praevaricatio vastans, ut detur sanctum et exercitus conculcatio? Et dixit, Usque ad vesperam mane; tunc justificabitur sanctum. 8:2-14.

66   Quod visio illa praedicat status ecclesiae futuros, patet manifeste, nam dicitur quod a Principe exercitus sublatum sit juge, projectum habitaculum sanctuarii Ejus, et quod hircus projecerit veritatem in terram; tum quod sanctus dixerit, Quousque visio haec, juge et praevaricatio vastans, ut detur sanctum et exercitus conculcatio? Et quod hoc esset ad vesperam mane, quando justificabitur sanctum; per vesperam enim intelligitur finis ecclesiae quando nova erit. Simile postea in eo capite per reges Mediae et Persiae intelligitur quod per arietem, et simile per regem Graeciae quod per hircum, nam nomina regnorum, gentium, et populorum, tum personarum et locorum, in Verbo significant res caeli et ecclesiae.

67   Explicatio illorum haec est:

Aries cui duo cornua alta, quorum altius ascendit posterius, significat illos qui in fide ex charitate sunt. Quod cornu feriret versus occidentem, septentrionem, et meridiem, significat dissipationem mali et falsi. Quod magnum se faceret significat incrementum. Hircus veniens ab occidente super facies totius terrae significat illos qui in fide separata a charitate sunt, ac invasionem ecclesiae ab illis; occidens est malum naturalis hominis. Cui cornu inter oculos significat propriam intelligentiam. Quod cucurrerit ad arietem cum furore roboris significat quod vehementer impugnaverit charitatem et ejus fidem. Quod fregerit duo cornua ejus, projecerit eum in terram, et conculcaverit eum, significat quod prorsus disperserit et charitatem et fidem, nam qui unam etiam alteram dispergit, unum enim faciunt. Quod fractum sit cornu magnum hirci significat non apparentiam propriae intelligentiae. Quod loco ejus ascenderint quatuor cornua significat applicationes sensus literae Verbi ad confirmandum. Quod ex uno eorum exiret cornu exiguum significat argumentationem quod nemo possit implere legem et facere bonum a se ipso. Quod id cornu creverit versus meridiem, versus ortum, et versus decus, significat per id insurrectionem in omnia ecclesiae. Et

long is this vision going to last concerning the regular offering and the desolating transgression, the giving over of the sanctuary and of the host to be trampled on? And he said, Up to the evening when it is becoming morning, at which time the sanctuary will be restored[1]. 8:2-14.

66 Most plainly this vision foretells the future states of the church, for it tells of the regular offering being taken away from the Prince of the host, the place of His sanctuary being thrown down, and the he-goat throwing truth down to the ground. It also tells of a holy one saying, How long is this vision going to last concerning the regular offering and the desolating transgression, the giving over of the sanctuary and of the host to be trampled on? And of the reply that it will last up to the evening when it is becoming morning, when the sanctuary will be restored, evening being used to mean the end of the church when there will be a new one. Much the same is meant further on in that chapter by the kings of Media and Persia as is meant by the ram, and much the same by the king of Greece as is meant by the he-goat; for in the Word the names of kingdoms, nations, and peoples, also of persons and places, stand for the realities of heaven and the church.

67 The explanation of these descriptions is this:

The ram that had two high horns, the higher one of which rose up later than the other, means those who adhere to faith emanating from the love of others. His butting towards the west, the north, and the south means the dispelling of what is evil and false. His becoming great means growth. The he-goat's coming from the west over the face of the whole earth means those who adhere to faith separate from the love of others, and the invasion of the church by them, the west meaning the evil in natural-minded people. Who had a horn between his eyes means self-intelligence. His running at the ram with all his might means violent aggression against the love of others and the faith that goes with it. His breaking the ram's two horns, throwing him to the ground, and trampling on him, means the total dispersion of both love of others and of faith, for those who disperse the one disperse the other as well, since the two form a single entity. The he-goat's large horn was broken means the non-appearance of self-intelligence. Four horns came up in place of it means usages of the literal sense of the Word to give support. Out of one of them a little horn came forth means the line of argument that none are able, of themselves, to fulfil the law and do what is good. The growth of that horn towards the south, towards the east, and towards the glorious land, means an uprising by means of it against

---

1 lit. *will be justified* or *will be made correct*

usque ad exercitum caelorum, et dejecit de exercitu, et de stellis, et conculcavit illa, significat sic destructionem omnium cognitionum boni et veri quae charitatis et fidei essent. Quod extulerit se ad Principem exercitus, et ab Eo sublatum est juge, et habitaculum sanctuarii Ejus, significat quod sic depopulatus sit omnia cultus Domini et ecclesiae Ipsius. Quod veritatem projecerit in terram significat quod vera Verbi falsificaverit. Per vesperam mane, quando justificabitur sanctum significatur finis ecclesiae istius et principium novae.

68   iv **Quod illi qui in fide separata a charitate sunt intelligantur per hircos, ex omissione charitatis eorum apud Matthaeum.** Quod non alii per hircos ac per oves intelligantur apud Matthaeum 25:31-46 quam qui per hircum et per arietem apud Danielem, patet ex eo quod ad oves enumerentur opera charitatis et dicatur quod illa fecerint; et quod ad hircos enumerentur eadem opera charitatis et dicatur quod illa non fecerint, et quod hi ideo damnentur. Est enim apud eos qui in fide separata a charitate sunt, omissio operum, ex negatione quod nihil salutis et ecclesiae in illis sit. Et cum removetur ita charitas, quae consistit in operibus, cadit etiam fides, quoniam fides est ex charitate; et cum non charitas et fides, est damnatio. Si omnes mali per hircos ibi intellecti fuissent, non opera charitatis quae non fecerunt, sed mala quae fecerunt, enumerata fuissent. Similes per hircos etiam intelliguntur apud Sachariam,

Super pastores exarsit ira Mea, et super hircos visitabo. 10:3.

Et apud Ezechielem,

Ecce Ego judicans inter pecudem et pecudem, inter arietes et inter hircos. Num parum vobis – pascuum bonum depascitis, etiam reliquum pascuorum conculcatis pedibus vestris? Cornibus vestris feritis omnes oves infirmas, donec disperseritis illas. Ideo salvabo gregem Meum, ut non sit amplius in praedam. 34:17,18,21,22,seq.

everything constituting the church. Its growth even towards the host of heaven, its casting down some of the host, and of the stars, and its trampling on them, means that in this way all recognitions of what is good and true which should go with love of others and faith were destroyed. It set itself up as high as the Prince of the host, and from Him the regular offering was taken away, and the place of His sanctuary, means that in this way everything composing worship of the Lord and His church was wiped out. It threw truth to the ground means that it falsified the truths of the Word. The evening when it is becoming morning, at which time the sanctuary will be restored, means the end of that church and the beginning of a new one.

68 iv **Those who adhere to faith separate from the love of others are meant by goats. This becomes clear from the disregarding of the love of others by those meant by the goats in Matthew.** No others are meant by the goats and sheep in Matthew 25:31-46 than those meant by the he-goat and ram in Daniel. This is evident from the fact that the sheep are said to have performed the list of works that flow from the love of others, and that the goats are said not to have performed those same works, and are therefore damned. For those who adhere to faith separate from the love of others disregard works; they deny that anything of salvation and the church resides in them. And when the love of others, which consists in works, is banished in this way, faith too falls away, since faith is rooted in the love others; and when there is no love of others and no faith, the result is a state of damnation. If all people who were wicked had been meant by the goats in those verses, there would have been no listing of the works flowing from the love of others which they failed to perform but of the wicked deeds which they did perform. People like these are also meant by the goats in Zechariah,

My anger has blazed out against the shepherds, and I will visit the goats. 10:3.

And in Ezekiel,

Behold, I am judging between member of the flock and member of the flock[1], between rams and he-goats. Is this to you a small thing – you feed off the good pasture, you also tread down with your feet the rest of the pastures? You butt with your horns all the weak sheep till you have scattered them. Therefore I will save My flock, that it will no longer be a prey. 34:17,18,21,22, and following verses.

   1   ie *between good ones and bad ones*

Quod fides separata a charitate ecclesiam et omnia ejus destruat

69 Fides separata a charitate nulla est fides, quoniam charitas est vita fidei, est anima ejus, et est essentia ejus; et ubi nulla fides est quia nulla charitas, ibi nulla ecclesia est. Quare dicit Dominus,

Filius Hominis cum venerit, num inveniet fidem super terra? Luc.18:8.

70 Audivi hircos et oves aliquoties de eo colloquutos, num illis qui se confirmaverunt in fide separata a charitate, ulla veritas sit; et quia dixerunt quod multa sit, lis illa in examen missa est. Et tunc interrogati sunt num sciant quid amor, quid charitas, et quid bonum; et quia haec erant quae separaverunt, non potuerunt aliter respondere quam quod non scirent. Interrogati sunt, quid peccatum, quid paenitentia, et quid remissio peccatorum; et quia responderunt quod qui justificati sunt per fidem, illis remissa peccata sint, ut non amplius appareant, dictum est illis, Haec non veritas sunt. Interrogati quid regeneratio, responderunt quod vel sit baptismus, vel quod sit remissio peccatorum per fidem. Dictum illis quod id non veritas sit. Interrogati quid spiritualis homo, responderunt quod sit qui justificatus est per fidem confessionis nostrae. Sed dictum illis quod haec non veritas sit. Interrogati de redemptione, de unione Patris et Domini, deque unitate Dei, et responderunt quae non veritates erant; praeter plura. Post interrogationes et responsa lis ad judicium venit, quod erat quod illi qui confirmaverunt se in fide separata a charitate non habeant ullam veritatem.

Faith separate from the love of others destroys the church and everything that constitutes it

69   Faith separate from the love of others is no faith at all, because the love of others is the life, soul, and essence of faith; and where there is no faith because there is no love of others there is no church. This is why the Lord says,

When the Son of Man comes is He going to find faith on the earth? Luke 18:8.

70   I have several times heard goats and sheep discussing with one another whether those who have adhered firmly to faith separate from the love of others were in possession of any truth at all; and because these said that they did possess much truth, the whole matter was subjected to examination. They were asked whether they knew what love is, what charity or the love of others is, and what goodness is; and because they had separated these from faith, they could do no other than reply that they did not know. They were asked what sin is, what repentance is, and what the forgiveness of sins is; and because they replied that the sins of anyone who has been justified or made righteous by faith stand forgiven so that those sins are no longer seen, they were told, There is no truth in that. Asked what is regeneration they replied that either it is baptism or that it is the forgiveness of sins received through faith. They were told that that is not the truth. Asked what is a spiritual person they replied it is one who has been justified or made righteous through the faith our church confesses. But they were told this is not the truth. When asked about redemption, the union of the Father and the Lord, and the oneness of God, their replies contained no truth in them. And there were further questions and replies. After questions and replies a verdict was reached, which was that people who have adhered firmly to faith separate from the love of others do not possess any truth at all.

71 Quod ita sit, non credi potest ab illis in mundo, quoniam qui in falsis sunt non vident aliter quam quod falsa sint vera, et quod plura scire quam quae fidei eorum sunt, tanti non sit. Et fides illorum est separata ab intellectu, est enim fides caeca, et ideo non inquirunt; et hoc non aliter inquiri potest quam ex Verbo media illustratione intellectus; quare vera quae ibi sunt vertunt in falsa, cogitando fidem ubi vident amorem, paenitentiam, remissionem peccatorum, et plura quae facti erunt.

72 Verum enim vero, tales sunt illi qui se in sola fide et doctrina et vita confirmaverunt, sed non illi qui, tametsi audiverunt et crediderunt quod sola fides salvet, usque mala ut peccata fugerunt.

71 This is not something such people are capable of believing while they are in the world, because those who are immersed in falsities inevitably see falsities as truths; and knowing anything more than what has regard to their faith is of no importance to them. Also their faith is separated from their power of understanding, for it is a blind faith, and therefore they make no enquiries relating to it. And such enquiries can be made from nowhere else than the Word, and doing so with an enlightened power of understanding. Consequently those with that blind faith turn the truths there into falsities, because they think of faith wherever they see references to love, repentance, forgiveness of sin, and the many ways in which people ought to act.

72 For such is indeed what those people are like who have adhered firmly to faith alone in both what they have been taught and in the life they have led, but not those who, although they have learned and believed that faith alone saves, have nevertheless shunned evil ways as sins.

TABLE OF PARALLEL PASSAGES

FI	34-36	AR 67
		SE 116
		VR 2
	37	AR 67

DOCTRINA
NOVAE HIEROSOLYMAE
DE DOMINO

AB
EMANUEL SWEDENBORG

EDITED BY JOHN ELLIOTT

LONDON
THE SWEDENBORG SOCIETY
2019

**DOCTRINA NOVAE HIEROSOLYMAE
DE DOMINO /
TEACHING OF THE NEW JERUSALEM
CONCERNING THE LORD**

TEACHING OF THE NEW JERUSALEM CONCERNING THE LORD

BY

EMANUEL SWEDENBORG

TRANSLATED BY JOHN ELLIOTT

LONDON
THE SWEDENBORG SOCIETY
2019

Published by the Swedenborg Society
Swedenborg House, 20-21 Bloomsbury Way, London WC1A 2TH

© Swedenborg Society 2019

Cover artwork: Stephen McNeilly
Typeset in Palatino at Swedenborg House
Printed and bound in Great Britain
at TJ International, Padstow

ISBN 978-0-85448-210-8

British Library Cataloguing-in-Publication Data
A catalogue record for this book
is available from the British Library

CONTENTS

Editor and Translator's Introduction	page vii
Abbreviations	xv
Doctrina Novae Hierosolymae de Domino	2
Teaching of the New Jerusalem concerning the Lord	3
Table of Parallel Passages	213

EDITOR AND TRANSLATOR'S INTRODUCTION

The five *opuscula* or *small works* which Emanuel Swedenborg mentions at the beginning of his Preface to **Doctrina Novae Hierosolymae de Domino** (**DD**) were printed and published while he was in London during the second half of 1758. In one of these five – **De Ultimo Judicio** – he expresses his intention to publish in the next couple of years *Explicatio super Apocalypsin*,[1] a long work which he seems to have been writing during, perhaps even before, his stay in London, as well as after his arrival back home in Stockholm in July 1759. For about two or three years he was making a rough draft, also a fair copy for the printer, of what came to be entitled **Apocalypsis Explicata** (**AE**); but he did not complete this work, which was already amounting to quite a few volumes, and so never published it. However, **AE** is of great importance, because it lies behind the publications Swedenborg saw through the press in Amsterdam during the summer, autumn, and winter of 1763-4, that is, the publications also mentioned by him in his Preface to **DD**. A brief description of that lengthy unpublished work is therefore called for here.

Apocalypsis Explicata

In this work Swedenborg's principal aim was to disclose the inner or spiritual meaning of the last book of the Bible, which he did in much the same way as previously in **Arcana Coelestia** (**AC**) he had presented the spiritual content of the first two books, Genesis and Exodus. As in that earlier *magnum opus*, comprising eight volumes published in London 1749-56, he dealt with the biblical text in detail, section by section, verse by verse, and phrase by phrase; and to aid this exposition of the spiritual sense of the text he regularly brought in other parts of Scripture. In many instances, as in **AC**, he did no more than quote or merely refer to one or more verses, while in others he went on to show their inner meaning, sometimes in considerable

---

[1] **De Ultimo Judicio**, §42. See also §§50,60,61,72

detail. Another feature of the earlier published work which occurs, though slightly differently, in **AE**, is the author's departure from his exposition of the biblical text to write separate sections on specific subjects. In **AC** Swedenborg placed these sections before and after chapters expounding Genesis and Exodus, but in the work on the Book of Revelation, beginning at Chapter 15, they appear at intervals below the exposition of the spiritual meaning of that book. The contents of the seven publications which were to appear in 1763-4 are in effect re-workings of themes contained in these separate sections in **AE**. For instance, the subject matter spread out in the latter below the expository material of §§932-1028 is much the same as that to be found in **Doctrina Vitae pro Nova Hierosolyma** published in 1763. And a forerunner of what Swedenborg presented in **DD** may be seen at various points under §§1091-1191.

Why Swedenborg did not expound the final three and a half chapters of the Book of Revelation and so complete **AE**, a work which would then have been almost as long as **AC**, is not at all clear. One reason may have been that in November 1760 he had to lay aside what he was doing and, as a member of the Swedish diet or parliament, give his full attention to a national crisis. For about four months he was engaged in writing documents relating principally to the Swedish metallic currency. After this short period of political activity he appears to have concentrated primarily on the production of the seven works which, two years later, were published by him in Amsterdam. There is evidence to show, however, that even before that period of political activity he was already contemplating the composition and publication of small works on subjects he had dealt with in the separate sections of **AE**. This evidence lies in two manuscripts no longer extant which were found among Swedenborg's possessions after his death in 1772.

Two Manuscripts

Before these two manuscripts became lost, transcriptions of them were made in 1788 'under the superintendence of A Nordenskjöld'. Known as **De Athanasii Symbolo (AT)**[2] and **De Domino (DO)**,[3] they are each a series of notes on Christian teaching concerning the Lord. The transcriptions made in 1788 contain, it is true, numerous copyist's errors, which later editors have sought to emend. But in spite of these errors Swedenborg's intentions are quite clear; he wished to write and publish a small work on that subject.

2 See **RB** 59/03
3 See **RB** 59/04

He appears to have begun compiling notes on the wording and understanding of the Athanasian Creed while he remained in London for a few months after the publication of his five *opuscula* there during the latter part of 1758. While making these notes constituting **AT** he was still intending to publish **AE**, for the notes contain several references to this long work, that is, to places in it where further information on particular matters could be found. In **DO** however, composed towards the end of 1759 or perhaps a little later, **AE** is mentioned only once. But whatever Swedenborg's intentions may have been in the years 1759-60 regarding **AE** – the lengthy, still-unfinished explanation of the Book of Revelation, with additional sections on particular subjects – it is clear that the sections dealing with the Athanasian Creed, together with the notes in the two manuscripts **AT** and **DO**, were forerunners to **DD**, the first of the works published in 1763-4. To these two a third may be added, which was found, as they were, among his possessions after his death, though this particular manuscript has survived to the present day, whereas they, after being transcribed, became lost.

Prophets and Psalms

Having completed his four-month (or more) engagement in the affairs of his country, that is, by the spring of 1761, Swedenborg was able to resume his preparatory work on the themes he was intending to write about and publish. He was now led to read systematically the whole of that part of the Old Testament containing the books often referred to as the Major and Minor Prophets, ie from Isaiah right through to Malachi, and after this to read the whole Book of Psalms. As he went along he made brief notes on the spiritual level of meaning in everything he read there. The manuscript containing these notes has come to receive a lengthy Latin title which is generally shortened in English to **Prophets and Psalms (PP)**.[4] From even a cursory examination of these notes it can be seen that their subject is essentially the same as that presented in §3 and §4 of **DD**, where Swedenborg indicates that the Person and Work of Him who came into the world was the real message of everything in Isaiah to Malachi, and in the Psalms. His quotations from these books and any other in the Sacred Scriptures are drawn mainly from the Latin translation of Sebastian Schmidt, published in 1696 in Strasbourg, a copy of which was found among Swedenborg's possessions after he died.[5]

 4 See **RB** 61/04
 5 See **LS** page 583 for *Note to the Latin Bible of Sebastian Schmidt*

Scriptural Quotations

When quoting from the Schmidt Latin Bible Swedenborg does not always reproduce the exact wording there. Sometimes he uses a different, yet synonymous, expression; sometimes he omits a word, whole phrase, or entire sentence; and occasionally his choice of words seems to spring from a different understanding of the original Hebrew or Greek from Schmidt's. Generally Swedenborg follows the system of versification he found in Schmidt, which differs in quite a number of places, especially the Book of Psalms, from that in English and other translations of Scripture. In this two-language edition of **DD** the placement of Latin and English alongside each other clearly reveals the chapter-and-verse variations.

Divine Name

The Divine name in the Hebrew Bible which was never uttered – known as the Tetragrammaton, because it consists of four consonants – may be transliterated as YHWH or JHVH. But in copies of the Old Testament in which the Hebrew letters are pointed – that is, have points and other marks to indicate vowel sounds – the Tetragrammaton is pointed with vowel signs that belong to another Divine name, usually those of **Adonai** (Lord), which has led Christians to write and pronounce the sacred name as **Jehovah**. But if the Tetragrammaton is immediately preceded by **Adonai**, then it is pointed with the vowel signs of **Elohim** (God), which gives rise to the spelling **Jehovih**. In this case Schmidt rendered the two Divine names standing together in the Hebrew Scriptures as **Adonai Jehovih**, but Swedenborg in his quotations from them preferred **Dominus Jehovih**. Most English versions of the Bible employ the two names *the Lord God*, but in the translation below of **DD** the unusual *the Lord Jehovih* has been adopted.

Athanasian Creed

In §1091 of **AE**, where Swedenborg quotes the whole of the Athanasian Creed, he explains that he is relying on the English version of it, which he would have found in **The Book of Common Prayer** (**BCP**) immediately after *The Order for Evening Prayer*.[6] But his knowledge of the content of the creed extended beyond the

---

6   The list of books from Swedenborg's own library that went on sale in November 1772 included a copy of The Book of Common Prayer, printed in London in 1711 – see *Contents of Swedenborg's Library*, pages 469-482 of **BB**. Possibly Swedenborg obtained this copy when a young man, during his first residence in London

English version, for in both of his quotations of it he indicates alternative words or phrasings of *others*, by whom he must have meant Christians, probably members of Lutheran churches, in other parts of Europe.

It seems that Swedenborg was not acquainted with the traditional Latin version of this creed until the late 1760s, so we must assume that what he set out in **AE**, and repeated in **DD** (see below on pages 184-189), is his own translation into Latin of the English version in **BCP**. The historic Latin creed *Symbolum Athanasii* is often referred to by the first two words of its opening phrase *Quicunque vult salvus esse*, but Swedenborg's Latin version of the English reads *Qui vult salvari*. Thus he never speaks, as others may do, of the *Quicunque Vult*; and although in certain places he refers to *Symbolum Athanasii* or else *Symbolum Athanasianum*, he employs in **DD**, and in the other works published in 1763-4, such phrases as *Doctrina fidei Athanasianae* and *Doctrina fidei quae Athanasiana vocatur*.

Modern scholarship shows that although the Athanasian Creed or *Quicunque Vult* dates back to the sixth century, if not earlier, it was not until the thirteenth century that it began to be called a *symbolum*, that is, a credal statement standing alongside the Apostles' and Nicene Creeds. Up to then it was generally called a *fides*, which *symbolum* was perhaps a virtual synonym of. But Swedenborg's preference for *fides* in **DD** does not lie in the fact that it was the term used in the earlier medieval centuries but in the very presence of the term in the initial statements of the creed itself. He saw the whole of the latter as an embodiment of current Christian teaching and belief concerning the Incarnation and the Trinity.

In the first Latin edition of **DD**, at §56, the actual *symbolum* or *fides* is printed in larger type, yet the text is not set out, as it is in **BCP** and elsewhere, as 41 separate statements, one below another. One possible explanation for this may have been that space could be saved, and printing costs therefore reduced, by 'running on' the text, while the larger type served to set the creed apart. Below on pages 184-189, however, the traditional 'versified' arrangement has been adopted in both Latin text and English version (the English version being transcribed - with a couple of minor modifications of spelling and punctuation - from the 1662 edition of **BCP** printed by John Bill and Christopher Barker, printers to the king, in London).

Latin Text

The first Latin edition of **DD** was published in Amsterdam in 1763; a second appeared in Tübingen in 1834, and a third in New York in

1889.[7] Thus the publication now of a fourth edition comes exactly 130 years after the third and over 250 years since the first.

As regards the spelling of words, use of capitals and italics, punctuation, etc., in this fourth edition, the policy adopted has been the same as that stated in my Editor's Preface to the fourth edition of another of the Latin works first published in 1763, namely this –

The present edition does not retain Swedenborg's use of punctuation, capital letters, italics, and so on; but his Neo-Latin spellings have been preserved, with one exception. In the works published in London during the years 1749-58, the *oe* diphthong appears in such words as *coelum* or *poenitentia*; but in those printed in Amsterdam 1763-1771 we find *caelum*, *paenitentia*, and so on. In indexes which Swedenborg himself compiled for his works these words stand in *coe-/poe-* columns, but presumably the use of *cae-/pae-* by the printer in Amsterdam was quite acceptable to him, since the pronunciation of *oe* and *ae* was identical. The *ae* of his Dutch printer has therefore been preserved in the present edition...[8]

Most of the Roman numerals in the Latin text of not only the first edition but also the second and third have been changed to Arabic. And Swedenborg's practice of 'highlighting' one or more words within certain scriptural quotations or references, which was not repeated in the third Latin edition and consequently does not feature in translations based on this, has been followed here in the fourth. Numerals beside the English translation, in the right-hand margin, belong to the system devised by J F Potts by which paragraphs numbered by Swedenborg himself were divided into subsections.

Translations

There have been only three or four fresh translations of **DD** into English since the publication of the first in 1784, but there have been many revisions and a great number of reprints. Other languages into which the work is known to have been translated are Czech, Danish, Dutch, French, German, Ilokano, Japanese, Russian, Swedish, Welsh and Zulu. Detailed information concerning these translations, and any revisions or reprints, will be found in the bibliographical volumes which the Swedenborg Society is in the midst of publishing.

---

7   See **RB** 63/02
8   **Continuatio de Ultimo Judicio**, published 2007, page vii

Acknowledgements

The first three volumes of **A Descriptive Bibliography of the Works of Emanuel Swedenborg**, compiled and edited by Revd Norman Ryder, have already been published, and the fourth is about to be. I am greatly indebted to Norman – friend for more than half a century, and ministerial colleague for almost that amount of time – for providing me with bibliographical information included in his as yet unpublished volumes, as well as for his advice on various other matters.[9] To my appointed consultant, Revd Robert Gill, also a long-time friend and colleague, I wish to express my gratitude for his careful scrutiny of the Latin text, and for his many helpful observations and suggestions regarding the translation. Stephen McNeilly and James Wilson must be thanked too, for laying out the printed page and presenting the whole work in a neat and attractive format; and so must Judy, my wife, for her love and support here in our home where the task of editing and translating the Latin text has been carried out. Above all let our thanks rise up to our Lord for all the teaching held within that text concerning Him.

London 2013   *John Elliott*

---

[9] Norman Ryder sadly passed away in July 2018 having submitted the files for volumes four and five of **RB** for publication. These volumes are forthcoming, to be published by the Swedenborg Society

ABBREVIATIONS

Works published by the Swedenborg Society which are cited in the Editor and Translator's Introduction and in English footnotes

BB　Swedenborg's Secret
　　A biography by Lars Bergquist, 2005
BCP　Book of Common Prayer
　　Edition of 1662 printed by John Bill and Christopher Barker, London
LS　A Lexicon to the Latin Text of the Theological Writings of Emanuel Swedenborg (1688-1772)
　　Edited by John Chadwick and Jonathan S Rose, 2008
RB　A Descriptive Bibliography of the Works of Emanuel Swedenborg (1688-1772)
　　edited and compiled by Norman Ryder;
　　published by the Swedenborg Society
　　Volume One 2010 (repr. 2017); Volume Two 2012;
　　Volume Three 2015; Volume Four in preparation
STWL　Small Theological Works and Letters of Emanuel Swedenborg
　　A volume of edited Latin and Swedish texts translated by various persons; general editor John Elliott, 1975

Works cited in Critical Apparatus to the Latin text

AR　Apocalypsis Revelata
　　All editions
AR^1　Apocalypsis Revelata
　　First edition, 1766
AR^2　Apocalypsis Revelata
　　Second edition, 1881, editor Samuel H Worcester
DD　Doctrina Novae Hierosolymae de Domino
　　All editions
DD^1　Doctrina Novae Hierosolymae de Domino
　　First edition, 1763

DD^2	**Doctrina Novae Hierosolymae de Domino**
	Second edition, 1834, editors L Hofaker and G Werner
DD^3	**Doctrina Novae Hierosolymae de Domino**
	Third edition, 1889, editor Samuel H Worcester
VR	**Vera Christiana Religio**
	All editions
VR^1	**Vera Christiana Religio**
	First edition, 1771
VR^2	**Vera Christiana Religio**
	Second edition, 1857, editor JFI Tafel
VR^3	**Vera Christiana Religio**
	Third edition, 1889, editor Samuel H Worcester

DOCTRINA NOVAE HIEROSOLYMAE
DE DOMINO /
TEACHING OF THE NEW JERUSALEM
CONCERNING THE LORD

Praefatio

Ante aliquot annos edita sunt quinque opuscula, quae sunt –

i **De Caelo et Inferno**
ii **Doctrina Novae Hierosolymae**
iii **De Ultimo Judicio**
iv **De Equo Albo**
v **De Planetis et Telluribus in Universo**

in quibus manifestata sunt plura quae hactenus ignota fuerunt. Nunc ex mandato Domini, qui mihi revelatus est, publico sistenda sunt sequentia –

Doctrina Novae Hierosolymae de Domino
Doctrina Novae Hierosolymae de Scriptura Sacra
Doctrina Vitae pro Nova Hierosolyma ex Praeceptis Decalogi
Doctrina Novae Hierosolymae de Fide
Continuatio de Ultimo Judicio
Sapientia Angelica de Divina Providentia
Sapientia Angelica de Divina Omnipotentia, Omni-
   praesentia, Omniscientia, Infinitate et Aeternitate
Sapientia Angelica de Divino Amore et de Divina Sapientia
Sapientia Angelica de Vita

Dicitur Doctrina Novae Hierosolymae, ac intelligitur Doctrina pro Nova Ecclesia, quae hodie a Domino instauranda est, vetus

Preface

A few years ago five small works were published, namely these –

i   **Heaven and Hell**
ii   **The New Jerusalem**
iii   **The Last Judgment**
iv   **The White Horse**
v   **The Worlds in Space**[1]

In these works very many things were disclosed that had remained unknown up to then; and now the Lord, who has revealed Himself to me, requires the following to be presented to everyone –

Teaching of the New Jerusalem concerning the Lord
Teaching of the New Jerusalem concerning Sacred Scripture
Teaching for the New Jerusalem concerning Life drawn from the Ten Commandments
Teaching of the New Jerusalem concerning Faith
A Continuation concerning the Last Judgment
Angelic Wisdom concerning Divine Providence
Angelic Wisdom concerning Divine Omnipotence, Omnipresence, Omniscience, Infinity, and Eternity
Angelic Wisdom concerning Divine Love and concerning Divine Wisdom
Angelic Wisdom concerning Life[2]

The phrase 'Teaching of the New Jerusalem' is being used to mean the teaching for a new church which is to be established at the

---

1   The title adopted by John Chadwick for his translation, published in 1997, of the work previously known to English readers as **The Earths in the Universe**
2   Only seven of the nine themes listed here became actual publications that appeared in 1763-4, ie the first six and the eighth

enim Ecclesia ad finem suum pervenit, ut constare potest ex illis quae in opusculo **De Ultimo Judicio**, n.33-39, dicta sunt, et quae in sequentibus opusculis mox nominatis ulterius dicenda sunt. Quod per Novam Hierosolymam, quae in
5 Apocalypsi 21 praedicitur ventura post judicium, intelligatur Nova Ecclesia, videatur hic infra in ultimo articulo.

present day by the Lord, because the old one has come to an end, as is made evident by the things already stated in §§33-39 of the small work **The Last Judgment**, and in more that is to be stated in the coming small works that have just been mentioned. As for the New Jerusalem – which the twenty-first chapter of the Book of Revelation foretells the arrival of after the judgment – and its meaning a new church, see the final section below of this small work.

Doctrina Novae Hierosolymae de Domino

Quod universa Scriptura Sacra sit de Domino et quod Dominus sit Verbum

1   Legitur apud Johannem,

In principio erat Verbum, et Verbum erat apud Deum, et Deus erat Verbum. Hoc erat in principio apud Deum. Omnia per Ipsum facta sunt et sine Ipso factum est nihil quod factum est. In Ipso vita erat, et vita erat lux hominum; et lux in tenebris apparet, sed tenebrae illam non comprehenderunt. Caeterum Verbum caro factum est et habitavit inter nos, et vidimus gloriam Ipsius, gloriam sicut Unigeniti a Patre, plenus gratia et veritate. 1:1-5,14.

Apud eundem,

Lux venit in mundum, sed dilexerunt homines magis tenebras quam lucem, erant enim opera eorum mala. 3:19.

Et alibi apud eundem,

Quousque lucem habetis, credite in lucem, ut filii lucis sitis. Ego lux in mundum veni, ut omnis qui credit in Me, in tenebris non maneat. 12:36,46.

Ex his patet quod Dominus sit ab aeterno Deus, et quod Ipse ille Dominus sit qui natus est in mundo, dicitur enim Verbum erat apud Deum, et Deus erat Verbum, tum, Sine Ipso factum est nihil quod factum est; et postea, quod Verbum caro factum sit, et viderint Ipsum. Quod Dominus dicatur Verbum, parum in ecclesia intelligitur, sed dicitur Verbum quia Verbum significat Divinum Verum seu Divinam Sapientiam,

Teaching of the New Jerusalem concerning the Lord

The whole of Sacred Scripture has to do with the Lord and the Lord is the Word

1   We read in John,

In the beginning was the Word, and the Word was with God, and the Word was God. He was in the beginning with God. All things were made through Him, and without Him nothing was made that was made. In Him was life, and the life was the light of men; and the light appears in the darkness, but the darkness has not overcome it. Furthermore[1] the Word became flesh and dwelt among us, and we have seen His glory, glory as the Only-begotten from the Father, full of grace and truth. 1:1-5,14.

In the same gospel,

The light came into the world, but people loved darkness rather than the light, because their deeds were evil. 3:19.

And in another place in the same gospel,

As long as you have the light, believe in the light, so that you may be children of light. I the light have come into the world so that everyone who believes in Me may not remain in darkness. 12:36,46.

From these places it is evident that the Lord is God, from eternity, and that God Himself is the Lord who was born in the world. For the gospel says, The Word was with God, and the Word was God; also, Without Him nothing was made that was made, and, in a later verse, that the Word became flesh and people saw Him. In the church there is little understanding of why the Lord is called the Word, but He is called this because Word means Divine Truth or Wisdom, and the

---

[1] Swedenborg is following the Latin version of Sebastian Schmidt, who appears to regard the conjunction *kai* at this point in the original Greek to be more than a simple *and*

et Dominus est ipsum Divinum Verum seu ipsa Divina Sapientia, quare etiam vocatur lux, de qua etiam dicitur quod in mundum venerit. Quia Divina Sapientia et Divinus Amor unum faciunt, et in Domino unum ab aeterno fuerant, ideo etiam dicitur, **In Ipso vita erat, et vita erat lux hominum** – vita est Divinus Amor, et lux est Divina Sapientia. Hoc unum est quod intelligitur per quod **in principio esset Verbum apud Deum, et quod Deus esset Verbum** – apud Deum est in Deo, nam sapientia est in amore et amor in sapientia. Similiter alibi apud Johannem,

Glorifica Me Tu, Pater, apud Te Ipsum, gloria quam habui, antequam mundus esset, apud Te. 17:5.

Apud Te Ipsum est in Te Ipso, quare etiam dicitur, Et Deus erat Verbum; et alibi, quod Dominus sit in Patre et Pater in Ipso, tum quod Pater et Ipse unum sint. Nunc quia Verbum est Divina Sapientia Divini Amoris, sequitur quod sit Ipse Jehovah, ita Dominus, a quo omnia facta sunt quae facta, nam ex Divino Amore per Divinam Sapientiam omnia creata sunt.

2 Quod sit idem Verbum quod manifestatum est per Mosen et Prophetas, et per Evangelistas, quod hic in specie intelligitur, manifeste constare potest ex eo quod illud sit ipsum Divinum Verum ex quo omnis sapientia est angelis, et intelligentia spiritualis hominibus. Est enim idem hoc Verbum quod est apud homines in mundo, etiam apud angelos in caelis, at in mundo apud homines est illud naturale, in caelis autem est spirituale; et quia est Divinum Verum, est etiam Divinum procedens, et hoc non modo est a Domino sed etiam est Ipse Dominus. Quia illud est Ipse Dominus, ideo omnia et singula Verbi de solo Ipso scripta sunt; ab Esaia usque ad Malachiam non datur aliquid quod non de Domino aut in opposito sensu contra Dominum.

Quod ita sit, nemo adhuc viderat, sed usque omnis id videre potest, modo id scit, et dum legit, id cogitat, ac insuper scit quod in Verbo non modo sit sensus naturalis sed etiam spiritualis, et quod in hoc sensu per nomina personarum et locorum significetur aliquid Domini, et inde aliquid caeli et ecclesiae ab Ipso, aut aliquod oppositum. Quoniam omnia et

Lord is Divine Truth or Wisdom itself. For this reason He is also called the light, which, the gospel also says, came into the world. Since Divine Wisdom and Divine Love make one, and in the Lord have from eternity existed as one, it also says therefore, **In Him was life, and the life was the light of men,** the life being Divine Love, and the light Divine Wisdom. This oneness is what is meant by **In the beginning the Word was with God, and the Word was God.** With God implies within God, for wisdom exists within love, and love within wisdom. Something similar to this occurs in another place in John,

Glorify Me, Father, with Yourself, with the glory I had with You before the world was. 17:5.

With Yourself implies within Yourself, and this too explains why it says, And the Word was God, and elsewhere that the Lord is within the Father, and the Father within Him, as well as that the Father and He are one. Now seeing that the Word is Divine Wisdom which exists together with Divine Love, it follows that it is Jehovah Himself – that is, the Lord – by whom all things were made that have been made, for all things have been created by Divine Love through Divine Wisdom.

2 The same Word as was made known through Moses and the Prophets, and through the writers of the Gospels, is what is meant specifically here. This becomes perfectly clear from the consideration that it is Divine Truth itself, the source of all wisdom that angels possess and all spiritual understanding that people possess. For this same Word which resides among people on earth does so as well among angels in the heavens, though among people on earth it is natural whereas in the heavens it is spiritual. And being Divine Truth it is also the Divine going forth, which not only goes forth from the Lord but also is the Lord Himself. Because it is the Lord Himself, every single thing written in the Word has to do solely with Him; from Isaiah right through to Malachi not a thing is there which does not relate to the Lord or in the contrary sense to that which stands against Him.

No one up to now has been seeing this, yet any can do so provided that they have come to know of it and have it in mind as they read, and above all have come to know that in the Word there is not only a natural but also a spiritual level of meaning, and that on this level the names of people and places serve to mean some aspect of the Lord, and therefore of heaven and the church which derive from Him, or else something which is the opposite of Him or them.

singula Verbi de Domino sunt, et Verbum est Dominus quia est Divinum Verum, patet cur dicitur, **Et Verbum caro factum est, et habitavit inter nos, et vidimus gloriam Ipsius**, tum cur dicitur, **Quousque lucem habetis, credite in lucem, ut filii lucis sitis. Ego lux in mundum veni; qui credit in Me, in tenebris non manet.** Lux est Divinum Verum, ita Verbum. Propter hoc, omnis, etiam hodie, qui Dominum solum adit, dum legit Verbum et orat ad Ipsum, illustratur in eo.

3 Paucis hic etiam dicetur quid de Domino apud omnes Prophetas Veteris Testamenti, ab Esaia usque ad Malachiam in genere et in specie agitur –

i Quod Dominus in mundum venerit in plenitudine temporum, quae erat quando Ipse non amplius a Judaeis cognoscebatur, et ex eo quando non aliquid ecclesiae supererat. Et nisi tunc Dominus in mundum venisset et Se revelavisset, homo morte aeterna periisset. Dicit Ipse apud Johannem,

Nisi credideritis quod Ego sim, moriemini in peccatis vestris. 8:24.

ii Quod Dominus in mundum venerit ut ultimum judicium faceret, et per id inferna tunc dominantia subjugaret – quod factum est per pugnas, seu per tentationes in humanum Suum a Matre, admissas, et per continuas tunc victorias – quae nisi subjugata fuissent, nullus homo potuisset salvari.

iii Quod Dominus in mundum venerit ut glorificaret Humanum, hoc est, uniret illud Divino, quod in Ipso ex conceptione erat.

iv Quod Dominus in mundum venerit ut novam ecclesiam instauraret quae Ipsum agnosceret Redemptorem et Salvatorem, ac per amorem et fidem in Ipsum redimeretur et salvaretur.

v Quod simul tunc ordinaret caelum, ut unum faceret cum ecclesia.

vi Quod passio crucis fuerit ultima pugna seu tentatio, per quam plene vicit inferna et plene glorificavit Humanum Suum.

Quod Verbum non de aliis rebus agat, videbitur in sequente opusculo **De Scriptura Sacra**.

Since every single thing in the Word relates to the Lord, and the Lord is the Word because He is the Divine Truth, it is plain to see why it says, **And the Word became flesh and dwelt among us, and we have seen His glory,** and also why it says, **As long as you have the light, believe in the light, so that you may be children of light. I the light have come into the world; whoever believes in Me does not remain in darkness.** The light is Divine Truth, thus the Word. For this reason everyone, even this very day, who goes to the Lord alone while reading the Word and praying to Him receives enlightenment there.

3   At this point a short statement must also be made, setting out what those matters relating to the Lord are which are dealt with in general and in detail in the Old Testament Prophets, from Isaiah right through to Malachi –

i   The Lord came into the world in the fullness of time, that is, when the Jews no longer recognized Him and consequently nothing of the church existed any more. And if at that point the Lord had not come into the world and revealed Himself people would have been lost in everlasting death. The Lord Himself says in John,

If you do not believe that I am, you will die in your sins. 8:24.

ii   The Lord came into the world to carry out a last judgment and through this to subdue the hells dominating then. This was accomplished by means of conflicts – that is, by means of temptations He underwent in the human He derived from Mary – and by means of His being continually victorious in them. Had the hells not been subdued no one at all could have been saved.

iii   The Lord came into the world to glorify His Human, that is, unite it to the Divine that was within Him from when He was conceived.

iv   The Lord came into the world to establish a new church that would recognize Him as Redeemer and Saviour, and that would be redeemed and saved through loving and believing in Him.

v   At the same time heaven would be set in order, to make one with the church.

vi   The passion on the cross was the final conflict or temptation through which He completely overcame the hells and completely glorified His Humanity.

The fact that the Word deals with no other matters than these will be seen in the coming small work concerning **Sacred Scripture**.

4   Ad confirmandum quod ita sit, velim in primo hoc articulo solum adducere loca e Verbo ubi dicitur **dies ille**, in **die illo**, inque **tempore illo**, in quibus per **diem** et per **tempus** intelligitur Adventus Domini. Apud Esaiam,

5   Fiet in **posteritate dierum**, stabilis erit mons Jehovae in capite montium. Exaltabitur Jehovah solus in **die illo**. **Dies Jehovae** Zebaoth super omnem magnificum et altum. In **die illo** projiciet homo idola argenti et auri sui. 2:2,11,12,20.
In **die illo** removebit Dominus ornatum. 3:18.
10 In **die illo** erit germen Jehovae in decus et gloriam. 4:2.
Fremet contra eum in **die illo** ac despiciet in terram, quae ecce tenebrae, anxietas; et lux obtenebrescet in ruinis. 5:30.
Fiet in **die illo**, sibilabit Jehovah muscae in extremitate fluviorum Aegypti. In **die illo** detondebit Dominus in transitibus fluvii. In **die**
15 **illo** vivificabit. Erit in **die illo** omnis locus in senticetum et vepretum. 7:18,20,21,23.
Quid facietis in **die** visitationis qui veniet? In **die illo** Israel innitetur Jehovae, Sancto Israelis, in veritate. 10:3,20.
Fiet in **die illo**, radicem Jischaji, quae stans in signum populorum,
20 gentes quaerent; et erit quies Ipsius gloria. Imprimis in **die illo** Dominus requiret reliquias populi Sui. 11:10,11.
Dices in **die illo**, Confitebor Tibi, Jehovah. Dicetis in **die illo**, Confitemini Jehovae, invocate nomen Ipsius. 12:1,4.
Propinquus est **dies Jehovae**, sicut devastatio a Schaddai veniet. Ecce
25 **dies Jehovae** venit crudelis, et indignationis, et excandescentiae, et irae. Commovebo caelum, et trepidabit terra e loco suo, in **die** excandescentiae irae Ipsius. Propinquum est **tempus** Ipsius, et veniet, et dies non extrahentur. 13:6,9,13,22.

9   Dominus: Dominus Jehovih *DD*

4 In support of all this I wish in this first section to do no more than draw from the Word places where the expressions **that day**, **on that day**, and **at that time** occur, and in which **day** and **time** serve to mean the Lord's Coming. In Isaiah,

> It will happen **in the latter days**, that the mountain of Jehovah will be firmly established as the head of the mountains. Jehovah alone will be exalted **on that day**. **The day of Jehovah** Zebaoth will be against everyone that is magnificent and high. **On that day** people will throw away their idols of silver and gold. 2:2,11,12,20.
> **On that day** the Lord[1] will take away the finery. 3:18.
> **On that day** the branch of Jehovah will be beauty and glory. 4:2.
> He will roar against him **on that day** and look down onto the earth, which, behold, is darkness and distress; and the light will turn to darkness in the ruins[2]. 5:30.
> It will happen **on that day**, that Jehovah will whistle for the fly in the farthest part of the rivers of Egypt. **On that day** the Lord will shave at the crossing-places of the river. **On that day** [a man] will keep alive [a young cow and two sheep]. It will be **on that day**, that every place will become briers and brambles. 7:18,20,21,23.
> What will you do on **the day** of visitation that will come? **On that day** they will lean on Jehovah, the Holy One of Israel, in truth. 10:3,20.
> It will happen **on that day**, that the root of Jesse, which is standing as an ensign of the peoples, the nations will seek, and His rest will be glory. Especially **on that day** the Lord will search out the remnant of His people. 11:10,11.
> You will say **on that day**, I will praise You, O Jehovah. You will say **on that day**, Praise Jehovah, call on His name. 12:1,4.
> **The day of Jehovah** is near, like devastation from Shaddai will it come. Behold, **the day of Jehovah** comes – cruel, and of indignation, and of wrath, and of anger. I will make heaven quake, and the earth will be shaken out of its place on **the day** of His fierce anger. His **time** is near, and it will come; and the days will not be prolonged. 13:6,9,13,22.

---

1   The first and both later Latin editions have two Divine names in this quotation of Isa.3:18, but the original Hebrew has only one – **Adonai** – which Latin versions of the Bible either transliterate or else render as **Dominus** (*Lord*). Regarding **Jehovih**, the second name in the quotation, see above, page x
2   The meaning in the original Hebrew of the word rendered *in the ruins* here is uncertain

Fiet in **die illo**, attereetur gloria Jacobi. In **die illo** respiciet homo ad Factorem suum, et oculi ad Sanctum Israelis. In **die illo** erunt urbes refugii in derelicta sylvae. 17:4,7,9.
In **die illo** erunt quinque civitates in terra Aegypti, loquentes labia Canaanis. In **die illo** erit altare Jehovae in medio Aegypti, et cognoscent Aegyptii Jehovam in **die illo**. In **die illo** erit semita ex Aegypto in Aschurem, et in **die illo** Israel erit in medio terrae. 19:18,19,21,23,24.
Dicet habitator insulae in **die illo**, Ecce exspectatio nostra. 20:6.
Dies tumultus, et conculcationis, et perplexitatis, Domino Jehovih Zebaoth. 22:5,12.
In **die illo** visitabit Jehovah super exercitum altitudinis et super reges terrae. Post multitudinem **dierum** visitabuntur; tunc erubescet luna, et pudefiet sol. 24:21-23.
Dicet in **die illo**, Ecce Deus noster hic, quem exspectavimus ut liberet nos. 25:9.
In **die illo** cantabitur canticum hoc in terra Jehudae, Urbs valida nobis. 26:1.
In **die illo** visitabit Jehovah gladio Suo. In **die illo** respondete illi, Vinea meri. 27:1,2,12,13.
In **die illo** erit Jehovah Zebaoth in coronam ornatus et in cidarim. 28:5.
Tunc audient in **die illo** surdi verba libri, eque tenebris oculi caecorum videbunt. 29:18.
Erunt ductus aquarum in **die** caedis magnae, cum cadent turres, et lux lunae sicut lux solis, in **die** quo obligabit Jehovah fracturam populi Sui. 30:25,26.
In **die illo** rejicient vir idola argenti et auri sui. 31:7.
Dies vindictae Jehovae, **annus** retributionum Ipsius. 34:8.
Venient tibi duo illa in uno **die**, orbitas et viduitas. 47:9.
Cognoscet populous Meus nomen Meum, et in **die illo** Ego Ille qui loquens. Ecce Me. 52:6.
Unxit Jehovah me ad proclamandum **annum** beneplaciti Jehovae et **diem** vindictae Deo nostro, ad consolandum omnes lugentes. 61:1,2.
Dies vindictae in corde Meo, et **annus** redemptorum meorum venit. 63:4.

4-9 In **die illo** erunt quinque civitates ... 20:6 DD³: Dicet habitator insulae in **die illo**, ecce exspectatio nostra. In **die illo** erunt quinque civitates in terra Aegypti, loquentes labia Canaanis. In **die illo** erit Altare Jehovae in medio Aegypti. In **die illo** erit semita ex Aegypto in Aschurem, et Israel erit in medio terrae. 20:6,18,21,24. DD¹, DD²
14 21-23 DD³: 21,23 DD¹, DD²
15 Dicet in **die illo**: Jehovah dicet in **die illo** DD
17 Jehudae DD³: Jehovae DD¹, DD²

It will happen **on that day**, that the glory of Jacob will be diminished. **On that day** people will look to their Maker, and their eyes to the Holy One of Israel. **On that day** there will be cities of refuge in the abandoned places of the forest. 17:4,7,9.

On that day there will be five cities in the land of Egypt speaking the language of Canaan. **On that day** there will be an altar to Jehovah in the midst of Egypt, and the Egyptians will know Jehovah **on that day**. **On that day** there will be a highway from Egypt to Assyria, and **on that day** Israel will be in the midst of the earth. 19:18,19,21,23,24.

The inhabitant of an island will say **on that day**, Behold, here is our expectation. 20:6.

The Lord Jehovih Zebaoth has a **day** of tumult and of trampling and of confusion. 22:5.

On that day Jehovah will visit[1] the host of the height and the kings of the earth. After a great number of **days** they will be visited, at which time the moon will blush and the sun be ashamed. 24:21-23.

It will be said **on that day**, Behold, this is our God, whom we have waited for to deliver us. 25:9.

On that day this song will be sung in the land of Judah, Ours is a strong city. 26:1.

On that day Jehovah will visit with His sword. **On that day** answer it with, This is a vineyard of unmixed wine. 27:1,2,12,13.

On that day Jehovah Zebaoth will be a crown of adornment and a tiara. 28:5.

On that day the deaf will hear the words of a book, and out of darkness the eyes of the blind will see. 29:18.

There will be streams of water on **the day** of the great slaughter, when the towers will fall, and the light of the moon will be as the light of the sun, on **the day** when Jehovah will bind up the hurt of His people. 30:25,26.

On that day a man will spurn his idols of silver and gold. 31:7.

The day of Jehovah's vengeance, **the year** of His retributions. 34:8.

These two things will come to you in one **day**, the loss of children and widowhood. 47:9.

My people will know My name, and **on that day** that I am the one who is speaking. Behold, it is I. 52:6.

Jehovah has anointed me to proclaim **the year** of Jehovah's good pleasure, and **the day** of vengeance for our God, to comfort all that mourn. 61:1,2.

The day of vengeance was in My heart, and **the year** of My redeemed has come. 63:4.

---

1   ie *come to judge*

Apud Jeremiam,

In **diebus illis** non dicetis amplius, Arca faederis Jehovae. In **tempore** illo vocabunt Hierosolymam thronum Jehovae. In **diebus illis** ibunt domus Jehudae ad domum Israelis. 3:16-18. In **die illo** peribit cor regis et cor principum, et obstupescent sacerdotes, et prophetae admirabuntur. 4:9. Ecce **dies venientes**, quibus in vastitatem evadet terra. 7:32,34. Cadent inter cadentes in **tempore** visitationis eorum. 8:12. Ecce **dies venientes**, visitabo omnem circumcisum in praeputio. 9:24. In **tempore** visitationis eorum peribunt. 10:15. Reliquiae non erunt eis; adducam malum super illos **anno** visitationis illorum. 11:23. Ecce **dies venientes** quibus non dicetur amplius. 16:14. Cervice et non faciebus respiciam eos in **die** exitii illorum. 18:17. Ecce **dies venientes**, quibus non nomen dabitur loco huic amplius Thopheth. 19:6. Ecce **dies venientes**, quum suscitabo Davidi germen justum qui regnet Rex. In **diebus Illius** salvabitur Jehudah, et Israel habitabit secure. Quare ecce **dies venientes**, quibus non dicent amplius ... Adducam super illos malum **anno** visitationis illorum. In **extremitate dierum** intelligetis intelligentiam. 23:5-7,12,20. Ecce **dies venientes** quibus conversurus. Heu! magnus **dies hic**, et non erit sicut ille. Fiet in **die illo**, frangam jugum, et vincula avellam. 30:3,7,8. **Dies** erit, quo clamabant custodes in monte Ephraim, Surgite, ascendamus Sionem, ad Jehovam Deum nostrum. Ecce **dies venientes**, dictum Jehovae, quibus seminabo domum Israelis et domum Jehudae. Ecce **dies venientes** quibus pangam faedus novum. Ecce **dies venientes** quibus aedificabitur urbs Jehovae. 31:6,27,31,38. Ecce **dies venientes** quibus stabiliam verbum bonum. In **diebus illis**, et in **tempore illo** germinare faciam Davidi germen justum. In **diebus illis** salvabitur Jehudah. 33:14-16.

6   admirabuntur DD³: *om* DD¹, DD²
8   **tempore**: die DD
15-16   non nomen dabitur loco huic amplius Thopheth: dabo locum hunc in devastationem DD
17   quum: quibus DD
18   **Illius**: Illis DD
26-28   *om* Ecce **dies venientes**, dictum Jehovae, quibus seminabo domum Israelis et domum Jehudae DD
31   *om* Ecce DD

In Jeremiah,

In **those days** you will no longer say, The ark of the covenant of Jehovah. **At that time** they will call Jerusalem the throne of Jehovah. In **those days** the house of Judah will go to the house of Israel. 3:16-18.
On **that day** the heart of the king and the heart of the princes will perish, and the priests will be dumbfounded and the prophets left wondering. 4:9.
Behold, **the days are coming** in which the land will become a waste. 7:32,34.
They will fall among those who fall **at the time** of their visitation. 8:12.
Behold, **the days** are coming; I will visit everyone circumcised in the foreskin. 9:25.
At the time of their visitation they will perish. 10:15.
There will not be any remnant of them. I will bring evil to them **in the year** of their visitation. 11:23.
Behold, **the days are coming** in which it will no longer be said. 16:14.
I will look them in the neck and not in the face on **the day** of their calamity. 18:17.
Behold, **the days are coming** in which the name given to this place will not be Topheth any more. 19:6.
Behold, **the days are coming** when I will raise up for David a righteous branch who will reign as King. **In His days** Judah will be saved and Israel will dwell securely. Therefore, behold, **the days are coming** in which they will say no longer, ... I will bring evil upon them in **the year** of their visitation. In **the latter days** you will fully understand. 23:5-7,12,20.
Behold, **the days** are coming in which I will turn things around. Alas! Great is this **day**, and there will be none like it. It will happen **on that day**, that I will break the yoke and pull away bonds. 30:3,7,8.
There will be **a day** when watchmen will cry on mount Ephraim, Arise, let us go up to Zion, to Jehovah our God. Behold, **the days are coming**, said Jehovah, in which I will sow the house of Israel and the house of Judah. Behold, **the days are coming** in which I will make a new covenant. Behold, **the days are coming** in which the city of Jehovah will be built. 31:6,27,31,38.
Behold, **the days are coming** in which I will perform the good thing. **In those days** and **at that time** I will cause a righteous branch to grow for David. **In those days** Judah will be saved. 33:14-16.

Adducam verba contra urbem hanc in malum in **die illo**. Te autem eripiam in **die illo**. 39:16,17.
Dies ille Domino Jehovih Zebaoth **dies** ultionis, vindictam sumet de hostibus Suis. **Dies** exitii venit super eos, **tempus** visitationis eorum. 46:10,21.
Propter **diem venientem** ad vastandum. 47:4.
Adducam super illum **annum** visitationis. Reducam tamen captivitatem ejus in **extremitate dierum**. 48:44,47.
Exitium adducam super eos **tempore** visitationis eorum. Cadent juvenes ejus in plateis, et omnes viri belli exscindentur in **die illo**. In **extremitate dierum** reducam captivitatem illorum. 49:8,26,39.
In **diebus illis** et in **tempore illo** venient filii Israelis et filii Jehudae simul, et Jehovam Deum suum quaerent. In **diebus illis** et in **tempore illo** quaeretur iniquitas Israelis, et non illa. Vae illis, quia venit **dies** illorum, **tempus** visitationis illorum. 50:4,20,27,31.
Vanitas illa, opus errorum, in **tempore** visitationis illorum peribunt. 51:18.

Apud Ezechielem,

Finis venit, venit finis, venit mane super te, venit **tempus**, propinquus est **dies** tumultus. Ecce **dies**, ecce venit, exivit mane, effloruit virga, germinavit insolentia. Venit **tempus**, advenit **dies** super omni multitudine ejus. Non argentum et aurum eripient illos in **die** irae Jehovae. 7:6,7,10,12,19.
Dicebant de propheta, Visio quam ille videns, fiet post dies multos; in **tempora longinqua** ille prophetans. 12:27.
Non stabunt in bello in **die** Jehovae. 13:5.
Tu confossus impius, princeps Israelis, cujus venit **dies**, in **tempore** iniquitatis finis. 21:30,34.
Urbs effundens sanguinem in medio sui, ut veniat **tempus** ejus; et appropinquare fecisti **dies**, ut venias ad annos tuos. 22:3,4.
Nonne in **die** quo abstulero ab iis robur? In **die illo** veniet ereptus ad te ad informationem aurium. In **die illo** aperietur os tuum cum erepto. 24:25-27.

21 insolentia: violentia *DD*
21 Venit **tempus**, advenit **dies**: Advenit **dies**, advenit **tempus** *DD*
26 in **die** Jehovae: in **die** irae Jehovae *DD*
29 sui *DD³*: tui *DD¹*, *DD²*
30 annos *DD²*, *DD³*: amores *DD¹*

I will fulfil My words against this city for evil **on that day**. I will however deliver you **on that day**. 39:16,17.
That day is to the Lord Jehovih Zebaoth **a day** of vengeance; He will take revenge on His adversaries. **The day** of their ruin has come upon them, **the time** of their visitation. 46:10,21.
On account of **the day coming** to lay waste. 47:4.
I will bring upon him **the year** of visitation. Yet I will bring back his captives **in the latter days**. 48:44,47.
I will bring ruin upon them **at the time** of their visitation. Her young men will fall in the streets, and all the men of war will be cut down **on that day**. **In the latter days** I will bring back their captives. 49:8,26,39.
In those days and **at that time** the children of Israel will come, and together with them the children of Judah, and they will seek Jehovah their God. **In those days** and **at that time** the iniquity of Israel will be sought, but there will be none. Woe to them, for their **day** has come, **the time** of their visitation. 50:4,20,27,31.
Worthless, a work of errors, **at the time** of their visitation they will perish. 51:18.

In Ezekiel,

An end has come, the end has come; the morning has come upon you, **the time** has come, **a day** of tumult is near. Behold, **the day**; behold, it comes. The morning has gone forth, the rod has blossomed, pride has budded. **The time** has come, **the day** has arrived – on the whole multitude of it. Silver and gold will not deliver them **on the day** of Jehovah's anger. 7:6,7,10,12,19.
They said of the prophet, The vision that he sees will take place after many days; he prophesies of **times far ahead**. 12:27.
They will not stand in war **on the day** of Jehovah. 13:5.
O you slain wicked one, prince of Israel, whose **day** has come, **at the time** of the iniquity of the end. 21:25,31.
A city that sheds blood in her midst, so that her **time** may come; and you have brought **the days** near, so that you come to your years. 22:3,4.
Will it not be **on the day** in which I take away from them their strength? **On that day** the rescued one will come to you with information for your ears. **On that day** your mouth will be opened to the rescued. 24:25-27.

In **die illo** crescere faciam cornu domui Israelis. 29:21.
Ejulate, heu **diem**, nam propinquus **dies**, propinquus **dies Jehovae**, **dies** nubis; **tempus** gentium erit. In **die illo** exibunt nuntii a Me. 30:2,3,9.
In **die** quo descensurus est in infernum. 31:15.
Ego quaeram gregem Meum, in **die** quo erit in medio gregis sui, et eripiam eos ex omnibus locis quo dispersi fuerunt, in **die** nubis et caliginis. 34:11,12.
In **die** quo mundavero vos ab omnibus iniquitatibus vestris. 36:33.
Propheta et dic, Nonne in **die illo**, quo sedebit populus Meus Israel secure, cognosces? In **posteritate dierum** deducam te in terram meam. In **die illo**, in **die** quo veniet Gog super terram. In zelo Meo, in igne indignationis Meae, si non in **die hoc** fuerit terrae motus magnus super terra Israelis. 38:14,16,18,19.
Ecce venit; **hic dies** de quo loquutus sum. Fiet in **die illo**, dabo Gogo locum sepulchro in Israele; ut cognoscat domus Israelis quod Ego Jehovah Deus illorum ex **die illo** et deinceps. 39:8,11,22.

Apud Danielem,

Deus in caelis revelavit arcana, quid futurum in **posteritate dierum**. 2:28.
Tempus advenit, ut regnum confirmarent sancti. 7:22.
Attende, quia ad **tempus finis** visio. Dixit, Ecce ego notum faciam tibi, quod futurum in **extremitate** irae, quia ad statum **tempus finis**. Visio vesperae et mane veritas est; tu, reconde visionem, quia in **dies multos**. 8:17,19,26.
Veni ad faciendum te intelligere, quid obveniet populo tuo in **extremitate dierum**, quia adhuc visio in dies. 10:14,15.
Intelligentes probabuntur ad purgandum et mundandum, usque ad **tempus finis**, nam adhuc ad statum **tempus**. 11:35.
In **tempore illo** surget Michael princeps magnus, qui stat pro filiis populi tui, et erit **tempus** angustiae, quale non fuit, ex quo gens. In **tempore hoc** tamen eripietur populus tuus, omnis qui invenietur scriptus in libro. 12:1.

2	nam propinquus **dies**: nam propinquus **dies Jehovae** *DD*	
5	est: es *DD*	
6	sui: tui *DD*	
13	igne *DD³*: die *DD¹*, *DD²*	
16	in Israele: in terra Israelis *DD*	

On that day I will make a horn grow up for the house of Israel. 29:21.
Wail, alas for **the day**! For **the day** is near, **the day of Jehovah** is near, **a day** of cloud; it will be **a time** of the nations. **On that day** messengers will go forth from Me. 30:2,3,9.
On the day in which he will go down into hell. 31:15.
I will look for My sheep, **on the day** in which [a shepherd] will be in the midst of his flock, and I will rescue them from all the places where they have been scattered, on **a day** of cloud and thick darkness. 34:11,12.
On the day in which I will cleanse you from all your iniquities. 36:33.
Prophesy and say, **On the day** in which My people Israel sit securely will you not know? **In the latter days** I will bring you into My land. **On that day, on the day** in which Gog comes over the land. In My zeal, in My fierce indignation, there will surely be **on that day** a great earthquake over the land of Israel. 38:14,16,18,19.
Behold, it is coming; **this is the day** which I have spoken about. It will happen **on that day**, that I will give to Gog a place for a burial in Israel; so that the house of Israel may know that I am Jehovah their God from **that day** and onwards. 39:8,11,22.

In Daniel,

God in heaven has revealed mysteries, what is to be **in the latter days**. 2:28.
The time arrived for the saints to establish firmly the kingdom. 7:22.
Pay attention, for the vision is for **the time of the end**. He said, Behold, I will make known to you what will be **at the latter end** of the anger, because it refers to the appointed **time of the end**. The vision of the evening and the morning is the truth; you, conceal the vision, for it refers to **many days** from now. 8:17,19,26.
I came to make you understand what is to happen to your people **in the latter days**, for the vision is for days to come. 10:14,15.
Those with understanding will be tested, to purge and cleanse them, up to **the time of the end**, for it is still for an appointed **time**. 11:35.
At that time Michael the great prince will arise, who stands up for the children of your people, and there will be **a time** of distress like never before since there was a nation. Yet **at that time** your people will be rescued, every one who is found written in the book. 12:1.

Tu, Daniel, occlude verba, et obsigna librum usque ad **tempus finis**. Abi, Daniel, quoniam occlusa et obsignata verba usque ad **tempus finis**. **A tempore** vero, quo removebitur juge, et dabitur abominatio devastans, dies mille ducenti nonaginta. Surges in sortem tuam sub **finem dierum**. 12:4,9,11,13.

Apud Hoscheam,

Finem faciam regni domus Israelis. In **die illo** frangam arcum Israelis. Magnus **dies** Jisreelis. 1:4,5,11.
In **die illo** vocabis, Marite mi. Feriam illis faedus in **die illo**. In **die illo** exaudiam. 2:16,18,21.
Revertentur filii Israelis, et quaerent Jehovam Deum, et Davidem regem suum, in **extremitate dierum**. 3:5.
Ite et revertemur ad Jehovam, vivificabit nos post biduum, et in **die tertio** eriget nos, et vivemus coram Ipso. 6:1,2.
Venerunt **dies** visitationis, venerunt **dies** retributionis. 9:7.

Apud Joelem,

Heu **dies**! quia propinquus **dies Jehovae**, et sicut devastatio a Schaddai veniet. 1:15.
Venit **dies Jehovae**, propinquus **dies** tenebrarum et caliginis, **dies** nubis et obscuritatis. Magnus **dies Jehovae** et terribilis valde, et quis sustinebit illum? 2:1,2,11.
Super servos et ancillas in **diebus illis** effundam spiritum Meum. Sol vertetur in tenebras et luna in sanguinem, antequam venit **dies Jehovae** magnus et terribilis. 3:2,4.
In **diebus illis**, et in **tempore illo** congregabo omnes gentes. Propinquus est **dies Jehovae**. Fiet in **die illo** stillabunt montes mustum. 4:1,2,14,18.

Apud Obadiam,

In **die illo** perdam sapientes ex Edomo. Ne laeteris super illis in **die** interitus eorum, in **die** angustiae eorum. Propinquus namque **dies Jehovae** super omnes gentes. Vers.8,12-15.

2-3 *om* Abi, Daniel, quoniam occlusa et obsignata verba usque ad **tempus finis** *DD*
8 Jisreelis: Israelis *DD*
12 **extremitate dierum**. 3:5. : **extremitate dierum**. 3:5. Ecce in **diebus illis**, et in tempore illo, quibus reducam. 4:1. *DD*
13 revertemur: revertamur *DD*

You, Daniel, shut up the words and seal the book until **the time of the end**. Go your way, Daniel, for the words have been shut up and sealed until **the time of the end**. But from **the time** in which the regular burnt offering is taken away and the devastating abomination is brought in there will be a thousand two hundred and ninety days. You will rise up into your allotted place **at the end of the days**. 12:4,9,11,13.

In Hosea,

I will put **an end** to the kingdom of the house of Israel. **On that day** I will break the bow of Israel. Great will be **the day** of Jezreel. 1:4,5,11.
On that day you will call Me, My husband. I will make for them a covenant **on that day**. **On that day** I will hearken. 2:16,18,21.
The children of Israel will return and seek Jehovah their God, and David their king, **in the latter days**. 3:5.[1]
Come and we will return to Jehovah. He will revive us after two days, and **on the third day** He will raise us up, and we will live before Him. 6:1,2.
The days of visitation have come, **the days** of recompense have come. 9:7.

In Joel,

Alas for **the day**! For **the day of Jehovah** is near, and as destruction from Shaddai it will come. 1:15.
The day of Jehovah is coming, **a day** of darkness and thick darkness is near, **a day** of cloud and gloom. **The day of Jehovah** is great and extremely terrifying, and who will endure it? 2:1,2,11.
On your menservants and maidservants **in those days** I will pour out My spirit. The sun will be turned into darkness and the moon into blood, before the great and terrifying **day of Jehovah** comes. 2:29,31.
In those days and **at that time** I will gather all the nations. **The day of Jehovah** is near. It will happen **on that day** that the mountains will drip new wine. 3:1,2,14,18.

In Obadiah,

On that day I will destroy the wise men out of Edom. Do not rejoice over them **on the day** of their destruction, **on the day** of their distress. For **the day of Jehovah** is near upon all the nations. Verses 8,12-15.

1   At this point among the quotations from Hosea, the first, second, and third editions of the Latin text include what appears to be an incomplete quotation of a verse in Joel. (In the Latin version of Joel the verse is the first of chapter 4, but in the English it is the first of chapter 3.)

Apud Amosum,

Fortis corde suo fugiet nudus in **die illo**. 2:16.
In **die** quo visitaturus praevaricationes Israelis super illum. 3:14.
Intelligens in **die illo** silebit, quia **tempus** malum erit. Vae desi-
derantibus **diem Jehovae**! Quid vobis **dies Jehovae**? ille tenebrarum
et non lucis. Nonne tenebrae erit **dies Jehovae**, et non lux? et caligo,
non autem splendor illi? 5:13,18,20.
Ejulabunt cantica templi in **die illo**. In **die illo** occidere faciam solem
in meridie, et obtenebrabo terram in die lucis. In **die illo** deficient
virgines pulchrae et juvenes siti. 8:3,9,13.
In **die illo** erigam tentorium Davidis collapsum. Ecce **dies venientes**
ut stillent montes mustum. 9:11,13.

Apud Micham,

In **die illo** lamentabitur, Vastando vastati sumus. 2:4.
In **extremitate dierum** erit mons domus Jehovae constitutus in caput
montium. In **die illo** colligam claudum. 4:1,6.
In **illo die** exscindam equos tuos et perdam currus tuos. 5:9.
Dies speculatorum tuorum, visitatio tua venit. **Dies** adest ad aed-
ificandum macerias. **Dies** hic, usque ad te venient. 7:4,11,12.

Apud Habakuk,

Adhuc visio in **tempus** constitutum, et effatur in finem; si morabitur,
exspecta illud, quia veniendo veniet, nec procrastinabitur. 2:3.
Jehovah, in **medio annorum** fac opus tuum; in **medio annorum**
notum facias. Deus veniet. 3:2.

Apud Zephaniam,

Propinquus est **dies Jehovae**. In **die** sacrificii Jehovae visitabo
super principes, et super filios regis. Visitabo etiam super omnem
salientem super limen, in **die illo**. In **die illo** erit vox clamoris. In
tempore illo perscrutabor Hierosolymam lucernis. Propinquus **dies
Jehovae** magnus. **Dies** excandescentiae **dies hic**; **dies** angustiae et
coarctationis; **dies** vastationis et devastationis; **dies** tenebrarum et

---

4		om Intelligens in **die illo** silebit, quia **tempus** malum erit *DD*
17		om perdam *DD*
19		venient: veniet *DD*
27-28		om Visitabo etiam super omnem salientem super limen, in **die illo** *DD*

In Amos,

The stout in heart will flee naked **on the day**. 2:16.
On the day in which I will visit Israel for his transgressions. 3:14.
The prudent will keep silent **on that day**, for it will be an evil **time**. Woe to you desiring **the day of Jehovah**! What will **the day of Jehovah** be for you? It will be one of darkness and not light. Will not **the day of Jehovah** be darkness and not light, and thick darkness having no brightness in it? 5:13,18,20.
The songs of the temple will be wailing **on that day**. **On that day** I will make the sun go down at noon, and I will darken the earth in broad daylight. **On that day** the beautiful virgins and the young men will faint for thirst. 8:3,9,13.
On that day I will raise up the tent of David that is fallen down. Behold, **the days are coming** when the mountains will drip new wine. 9:11,13.

In Micah,

On that day one will say lamentingly, We have been utterly ruined. 2:4.
In the latter days it will be that the mountain of the house of Jehovah is established as the head of the mountains. **On that day** I will assemble the lame. 4:1,6.
On that day I will cut off your horses from your midst and destroy your chariots. 5:10.
The day of your watchmen, your visitation, has come. **The day** is present for building walls. This is **the day**; they will come all the way to you. 7:4,11,12.

In Habakkuk,

The vision is yet for an appointed **time**, and speaks at the end; if it tarries, wait for it, because it will surely come and not delay. 2:3.
O Jehovah, **in the midst of the years** do your work, **in the midst of the years** make it known. God will come. 3:2.

In Zephaniah,

The day of Jehovah is near. **On the day** of Jehovah's sacrifice I will visit the chief men and the king's sons. I will also visit everyone leaping over the threshold **on that day**. **On that day** there will be the sound of a cry. **At that time** I will search Jerusalem with lamps. The great **day of Jehovah** is near. **A day** of wrath is **this day**; **a day** of distress and oppression; **a day** of vastation and desolation; **a day** of darkness and thick darkness; **a**

caliginis; **dies** nubis et obnubilationis; **dies** buccinae et clangoris. In **die** excandescentiae Jehovae comedetur tota terra; et consummationem festinatam faciet cum omnibus habitatoribus terrae. 1:7-10,12,14-16,18. Cum nondum venit super vos **dies** irae Jehovah. Forte abscondemini in **die** irae Jehovae. 2:2,3.
Exspectate Me usque ad **diem** surgere Meum ad praedam, nam judicium Meum. In **die illo** non pudefies ab operibus tuis. In **die illo** dicetur Hierosolymae, Ne time. Conficiam oppressores tuos in **tempore illo**. In **tempore illo** adducam vos; in **tempore illo** congregabo vos, quia dabo vos in nomen et in laudem. 3:8,11,16,19,20.

Apud Sachariam,

Tunc adhaerebunt gentes multae Jehovae in **die illo**. 2:15.
Removebo iniquitatem terrae in **die uno**. In **die illo** clamabitis vir ad socium suum, sub vitem et sub ficum. 3:9,10.
In **diebus illis** apprehendent decem viri alam viri Judaei. 8:23.
Servabit illos Jehovah Deus illorum in **die illo**, sicut gregem populum Suum. 9:16.
Faedus Meum ruptum est in **die illo**. 11:11.
In **die illo** ponam Hierosolymam lapidem oneris omnibus populis. In **die illo** percutiam omnem equum stupore. In **die illo** ponam duces Jehudae sicut fornacem ignis in lignis. In **die illo** proteget Jehovah habitatores Hierosolymae. In **die illo** quaeram perdere omnes gentes. In **die illo** crescet planctus in Hierosolyma. 12:3,4,6,8,9,11.
In **die illo** fons erit apertus domui Davidis et habitatoribus Hierosolymae. Fiet in **die illo** exscindam nomina idolorum in terra. In **die illo** pudefient prophetae. 13:1-4.
Ecce **dies veniens** Jehovae. Stabunt pedes Ipsius in **die illo** super Monte Olivarum. In **die illo** non erit lux et splendor. **Dies unus** qui notus erit Jehovae, non dies, non nox; circa tempus vesperae erit lux. In **die illo** exibunt aquae vivae ex Hierosolyma. In **die illo** erit Jehovah unus, et nomen Ipsius unum. In **die illo** erit tumultuatio Jehovae magna. In **die illo** erit super tintinnabulis equorum, Sanctitas Jehovae. Non erit amplius Cananaeus in domo Jehovae in **die illo**. 14:1,4,6-9,13,20,21.

Apud Malachiam,

---

2   comedetur DD^2, DD^3 : commedetur DD^1
4   vos DD^3 : nos DD^1, DD^2

day of cloud and clouding over; **a day** of trumpet sound and blast. **On the day** of Jehovah's wrath the whole earth will be consumed, and He will bring to a hasty end all the inhabitants of the earth. 1:7-10,12,14-16,18. Before there comes upon you **the day** of Jehovah's anger. Perhaps you will be hidden **on the day** of Jehovah's anger. 2:2,3. Wait for Me until **the day** I rise up for the prey, for it is My judgment. **On that day** you will not be put to shame by your works. **On that day** it will be said to Jerusalem, Do not be afraid. I will deal with your oppressors **at that time**. **At that time** I will lead you onwards; **at that time** I will gather you together, for I will give you fame and praise. 3:8,11,16,19,20.

In Zechariah,

Then many nations will cling to Jehovah **on that day**. 2:11.
I will remove the iniquity of the land **in a single day**. **On that day** you will shout, each to his companion, under his vine and under his fig tree. 3:9,10.
In those days ten men will take hold of the hem of a man of Judah. 8:23. Jehovah their God will save them **on that day**, as a flock His people. 9:16. My covenant was broken **on that day**. 11:11.
On that day I will make Jerusalem a heavy stone for all the peoples. **On that day** I will strike every horse with panic. **On that day** I will make the leaders of Judah like a furnace of fire within wood. **On that day** Jehovah will protect the inhabitants of Jerusalem. **On that day** I will seek to destroy all the nations. **On that day** the mourning in Jerusalem will increase. 12:3,4,6,8,9,11.
On that day there will be a fountain opened for the house of David and the inhabitants of Jerusalem. It will happen **on that day**, that I will cut off the names of the idols in the land. **On that day** the prophets will be ashamed. 13:1-4.
Behold **the day is coming for Jehovah**. His feet will stand **on that day** upon the Mount of Olives. **On that day** there will be no light and brightness. It will be **one day** which will be known to Jehovah; not day, not night; around evening time there will be light. **On that day** living waters will go out from Jerusalem. **On that day** there will be one Jehovah, and His name one. **On that day** there will be a great tumult from Jehovah. **On that day** there will be on the horse-bells, Holiness to Jehovah. No longer will the Canaanite be in the house of Jehovah **on that day**. 14:1,4,6,9,13,20,21.

In Malachi,

Quis sustinet **diem** adventus Ipsius, et quis consistet cum apparuerit? Ut sint Mihi in **die** quem facio, in peculium. Ecce **dies veniens**, ardens sicut clibanus. Ecce Ego mitto vobis Eliam Prophetam, antequam venit **dies Jehovae** magnus et terribilis. 3:2,17,19,23.

Apud Davidem,

Florebit in **diebus Ipsius** justus, et multa pax; et dominabitur a mari ad mare, et a fluvio usque ad fines terrae. Ps.72:7,8. Praeter alibi.

5   In his locis per **diem** et per **tempus** intelligitur Adventus Domini. Per **diem** aut **tempus** tenebrarum, caliginis, obscuritatis, non lucis, devastationis, iniquitatis finis, interitus, intelligitur Adventus Domini, quando non amplius cognoscebatur et inde quando non amplius aliquid ecclesiae supererat. Per **diem** crudelem, terribilem, excandescentiae, irae, tumultus, visitationis, sacrificii, retributionis, angustiae, belli, clamoris, intelligitur Adventus Domini ad judicium. Per **diem** quo exaltabitur Jehovah solus, quo unus erit et nomen Ipsius unum, quo erit germen Jehovae in decus et gloriam, quo florebit justus, quo vivificabit, quo quaeret gregem Suum, quo feriet faedus novum, quo stillabunt montes mustum, quo exibunt aquae vivae ex Hierosolyma, quo respicient ad Deum Israelis, et plura similia, intelligitur Adventus Domini ad instaurandam ecclesiam novam quae Ipsum agnoscet Redemptorem et Salvatorem.

6   His adjicere licet aliqua loca quae apertius de Adventu Domini loquuntur, quae sunt –

Dat Dominus Ipse vobis signum: Ecce virgo concipiet et pariet Filium, et vocabit nomen Ipsius **Deus nobiscum**. Esai.7:14; Matt.1:22,23.
Puer natus est nobis, Filius datus est nobis, super cujus humero principatus; et vocabit nomen Ipsius, Mirabilis, Consiliarius, Deus, Heros, Pater aeternitatis, Princeps pacis. Multiplicanti principatum et pacem non erit finis, super throno Davidis et super regno ejus, ad stabiliendum illud in judicio et justitia, a nunc et usque in aeternum. Esai.9:5,6.

Who will endure **the day** of His coming, and who will stand when He appears? That they may be Mine **on the day** I make them My special treasure. Behold, **the day is coming**, burning like an oven. Behold, I am sending you Elijah the prophet before the great and terrifying **day of Jehovah** comes. 3:2,17; 4:1,5.

In David,

In his days the righteous will flourish, and much peace; and He will have dominion from sea to sea, and from the river to the ends of the earth. Ps.72:7,8. And elsewhere in addition to this.

5   In all these places **day** and **time** serve to mean the coming of the Lord. The Lord's Coming when He was no longer recognized and as a consequence nothing of the church existed any more is meant by a **day** or **time** of darkness, thick darkness, gloom, no light, desolation, iniquity of the end, or destruction. The Lord's Coming to execute judgment is meant by a **day** that is cruel, terrifying, one of wrath, anger, tumult, visitation, sacrifice, retribution, distress, war, or a cry. The Lord's Coming to establish a new church which will recognize Him as Redeemer and Saviour is meant by a **day** in which Jehovah alone will be exalted, in which He will be one and His name one, in which the branch of Jehovah will be beauty and glory, in which the righteous will flourish, in which He will cause to live, in which He will look for His flock, in which He will make a new covenant, in which mountains will drip new wine, in which living waters will go out from Jerusalem, in which people will look to the God of Israel, and many more predictions like these.

6   To these places let me add some others which speak more plainly about the Coming of the Lord –

The Lord Himself will give you a sign: Behold, a virgin will conceive and bear a Son, and will call His name **God with us**. Isa.7:14; Matt.1:22,23. To us a Boy is born, to us a Son is given, on whose shoulder will be the government. And He will call His name, Wonderful, Counsellor, God, Hero[1], Father of Eternity, Prince of Peace. Of the increase of His government and of peace there will be no end upon the throne of David and over His kingdom, to establish it in judgment and righteousness, from now and even for evermore. Isa.9:6,7.

---

1   *Hero* is used in its original sense of *a man of superhuman strength*

Exibit virga de trunco Jischaji, et surculus e radicibus ejus fructum feret. Quiescet super Eo spiritus Jehovae, spiritus sapientiae et intelligentiae, spiritus consilii et virtutis. Erit justitia cingulum lumborum Ejus, et veritas cingulum feminum Ejus. Fiet ergo in die illo, radicem Jischaji, quae stans in signum populorum, gentes quaerent; et erit quies Ejus gloria. Esai.11:1,2,5,10.

Mittite Agnum Dominatoris terrae de petra versus desertum, ad montem filiae Zionis. Firmatus est per misericordiam thronus, et sedit super eo in veritate in tabernaculo Davidis, judicans et quaerens judicium, et festinans justitiam. Esai.16:1,5.

Dicetur in die illo, Ecce Deus noster Hic, quem exspectavimus ut liberet nos. **Hic Jehovah**, quem exspectavimus; exsultemus et laetemur in salute Ipsius. Esai.25:9.

Vox clamantis in deserto, Parate viam **Jehovae**, complanate in solitudine semitam **Deo nostro**. Revelabitur enim gloria **Jehovae**, et videbunt omnis caro simul. Ecce **Dominus Jehovih** in forti venit, et brachium Ipsius dominabitur Ipsi; ecce merces Ipsius cum Ipso. Sicut pastor gregem Suum pascet. Esai.40:3,5,10,11.

Electus Meus, in quo beneplacitum habet anima Mea. Ego **Jehovah** vocavi Te in justitia, et dabo Te in faedus populo, in lucem gentium; ad aperiendum oculos caecos, ad educendum e carcere vinctum, e domo claustri sedentes in tenebris. Ego **Jehovah**, hoc nomen Meum; gloriam Meam non alteri dabo. Esai.42:1,6-8.

Quis credidit verbo nostro, et brachium Jehovae super quo revelatum est? Non forma Ipsi; vidimus Ipsum, sed non aspectus. Morbos nostros Ille tulit, et dolores nostros portavit. Esai.53:1 ad fin.

Quis Hic qui venit ex Edom, conspersus vestes ex Bozra, incedens in multitudine roboris Sui? Qui loquor in justitia, magnus ad salvandum. Nam dies vindictae in corde Meo, et annus redemptorum Meorum venit. Ideo factus est illis in Salvatorem. Esai.63:1,4,8.

Ecce dies venientes cum suscitabo Davidi germen justum, qui regnet Rex, et prosperetur, facietque judicium et justitiam in terra. Et hoc nomen Ipsius quod vocabunt Ipsum, **Jehovah Justitia nostra**. Jer.23:5,6; 33:15,16.

Exulta valde, filia Zionis; clange, filia Hierosolymae. Ecce Rex tuus venit tibi; justus et servatus Ille. Loquetur pacem gentibus; dominari Ipsius a mari ad mare et a flumine usque ad fines terrae. Sach.9:9,10.

---

26 53:1 ad fin: 53 ad fin DD^1, DD^2; 53:1,2,4 DD^3
30 63:1,4,8 DD^3: 63:1-8 DD^1, DD^2
32 facietque: faciatque DD

There will come forth a shoot from the trunk of Jesse, and a branch from his roots will bear fruit. The spirit of Jehovah will rest upon Him, the spirit of wisdom and understanding, the spirit of counsel and strength. Righteousness will be the girdle of His loins, and truth the girdle of His thighs. It will happen therefore on that day, that the root of Jesse, which is standing as an ensign of the peoples, the nations will seek, and His rest will be glorious. Isa.11:1,2,5,10.

Send the Lamb of the Ruler of the land from the rock towards the wilderness, to the mountain of the daughter of Zion. In compassion a throne was established, and on it there sat in truthfulness in the tent of David one who judges and seeks judgment, and moves swiftly to righteousness. Isa.16,1,5.

It will be said on that day, Behold, this is our God, whom we have waited for to deliver us. **This is Jehovah**, whom we have waited for; let us be glad and rejoice in His salvation. Isa.25:9.

The voice of one crying in the wilderness, Prepare the way of **Jehovah**; make plain in the lonely place a highway for **our God**. For the glory of **Jehovah** will be revealed, and all flesh will see it together. Behold, **the Lord Jehovih** comes with might, and His arm will exercise dominion for Him; behold, His reward is with Him. He will pasture His flock like a shepherd. Isa.40:3,5,10,11.

My chosen, in whom My soul is well pleased. I **Jehovah** have called You in righteousness, and I will give You to be a covenant for the people, a light of the nations, to open the blind eyes, to bring the bound out of prison, out of the dungeon house those sitting in darkness. I am **Jehovah**, this is My name; and My glory I will not give to another. Isa.42:1,6-8.

Who has believed our report, and to whom has the arm of Jehovah been revealed? He has no form; we have seen Him, but He has no beauty. He has borne our sicknesses and carried our sorrows. Isa.53:1-end.

Who is This who is coming from Edom, with spattered clothes from Bozra, marching in the vast numbers of His strength? I who speak in righteousness, mighty to save. For the day of vengeance was in My heart, and the year of My redeemed has come. Therefore He became their Saviour. Isa.63:1,4,8.

Behold, the days are coming when I shall raise up for David a righteous branch, who is going to reign as King and prosper, and will execute judgment and righteousness in the land. And this is His name which they will call Him, **Jehovah our Righteousness**. Jer.23:5,6; 33:15,16.

Exult greatly, O daughter of Zion! Make a noise, O daughter of Jerusalem! Behold, your King comes to you; righteous and having salvation is He. He will speak peace to the nations; His rule will be from sea to sea, and from the river right to the ends of the earth. Zech.9:9,10.

Jubila et laetare, filia Zionis; ecce Ego venio ut habitem in medio tui. Tunc adhaerebunt gentes multae **Jehovae** in die illo, et erunt Mihi in populum. Sach.2:14,15.

Tu, Bethlechem Ephrataea, parum est ut sis inter millenas Jehudae; ex te Mihi exibit, qui erit Dominator in Israele, et cujus exitus ab antiquo a diebus aeternitatis. Stabit et pascet in robore **Jehovae**. Mic.5:1,3.

Ecce Ego mitto angelum Meum, qui parabit viam ante Me, et subito veniet ad templum suum **Dominus**, quem vos quaeritis, et angelus faederis, quem vos desideratis; ecce venit. Quis sustinet diem adventus Ipsius? Ecce Ego mitto vobis Eliam prophetam, antequam venit dies Jehovae magnus et terribilis. Mal.3:1,2,23.

Vidi, et ecce cum nubibus caelorum sicut Filius Hominis veniens fuit. Huic datum est dominium, et gloria, et regnum; et omnes populi, gentes, et linguae Ipsum colent. Dominium Ipsius dominium saeculi quod non transibit, et regnum Ipsius quod non peribit. Et omnia dominia colent Ipsum et obedient Ipsi. Dan.7:13,14,27.

Septimanae septuaginta decisae sunt super populum tuum, et super urbem sanctitatis tuam, ad consummandum praevaricationem, et ad obsignandum visionem et prophetam, et ad ungendum sanctum sanctorum. Scito ergo et percipito, ab exitu Verbi usque ad restituendum et ad aedificandum Hierosolymam, usque ad Messiam Principem, septimanae septem. Dan.9:24,25.

Ponam in mari manum Ipsius et in fluviis dextram Ipsius. Ille vocabit Me, Pater meus Tu, Deus meus, et Petra salutis meae. Etiam Ego Primogenitum dabo Ipsum, altum regibus terrae. Ponam in aeternum semen Ipsius, et thronum Ipsius sicut dies caelorum. Ps.89:26-28,30.

Dictum **Jehovae** ad **Dominum** meum, Sede ad dextram Meam usque dum posuero inimicos Tuos scabellum pedum Tuorum. Sceptrum roboris Tui mittet **Jehovah** e Zione; dominare in medio inimicorum Tuorum. Tu Sacerdos in aeternum juxta modum Malchizedechi. Ps.110:1,2,4; Matt.22:42; Luc.20:42,43.

Ego inunxi Regem Meum super Zionem, montem sanctitatis Meae. Annuntiabo de statuto: **Jehovah** dixit ad Me, Filius Meus Tu, Ego hodie genui Te. Dabo gentes haereditatem Tuam, et possessionem tuam fines terrae. Osculamini Filium ne irascatur, et pereatis in via. Beati omnes confidentes in Ipso. Ps.2:6-8,12.

---

33 Matt.22:42; Luc.20:42,43: Matt.22:44; Luc.20:41 DD^1, DD^2; Matt.22:44; Luc.20:42 DD^3

37 et DD^3: ne DD^1, DD^2

Rejoice and be glad, O daughter of Zion! Behold, I am coming to dwell in the midst of you. Then many nations will cling to **Jehovah** on that day, and they will be My people. Zech.2:10,11.

You, Bethlehem Ephrath, it is little that you are among the thousands of Judah; from you will come forth for Me one who will be Ruler in Israel; and His origins are from of old, from the days of eternity. He will stand and feed [His flock] in the strength of **Jehovah**. Mic.5:2,4.

Behold, I am sending My angel, who will prepare the way before Me; and suddenly there will come to His temple **the Lord** whom you are seeking, and the angel of the covenant, in whom you delight. Behold, He is coming. Who will endure the day of His coming? Behold, I am sending you Elijah the prophet before the great and terrifying day of Jehovah comes. Mal.3:1,2; 4:5.

I looked, and behold, with the clouds of heaven One like the Son of Man was coming. To Him was given dominion and glory and kingdom; and all peoples, nations, and languages will worship Him. His dominion is an everlasting dominion which will not pass away, and His kingdom one that will not perish. And all dominions will worship Him and obey Him. Dan.7:13,14,27.

Seventy weeks have been decreed concerning your people and your holy city to bring transgression to a close, and to seal up vision and prophet, and to anoint the holy of holies. Know therefore and perceive that from the going forth of the Word to restore and to build Jerusalem until the Messiah, the Prince, there will be seven weeks. Dan.9:24,25.

I will set His hand in the sea and His right hand in the rivers. He will cry to Me, You are my Father, my God, and the Rock of my salvation. I will also make Him the Firstborn, supreme over the kings of the earth. I will establish His seed for ever, and His throne as the days of the heavens. Ps.89:25-27,29.

Jehovah said to my **Lord**, Sit at My right hand until I make Your enemies Your footstool. **Jehovah** will send the rod of Your strength from Zion; have dominion in the midst of Your enemies. You are a priest for ever after the manner of Melchizedek. Ps.110:1,2,4; Matt.22:44; Luke 20:42,43.

I have anointed My King over Zion, the mountain of My holiness. I will tell of the statute: **Jehovah** has said to Me, You are My Son, today I have begotten You. I will make the nations Your inheritance, and the ends of the earth Your possession. Kiss the Son lest He be angry, and you perish on the way. Blessed are all putting their trust in Him. Ps.2:6-8,12.

Carere quidem Ipsum fecisti paululum prae angelis; sed gloria et honore coronasti Ipsum. Dominari fecisti Ipsum super opera manuum Tuarum; omnia posuisti sub pedes Ipsius. Ps.8:6,7.

Memento, **Jehovah**, Davidis, qui juravit **Jehovae**, vovit forti Jacobi, Si intravero intra tentorium domus meae, si ascendero super spondam strati mei, si dedero somnum oculis meis, usque dum invenero locum **Jehovae**, habitacula forti Jacobi. Ecce audivimus de Eo in Ephrata, invenimus Eum in agris sylvae. Intrabimus in habitacula Ejus, incurvabimus nos scabello pedum Ejus. Sacerdotes tui induantur justitia, et sancti Tui jubilent. Ps.132:1-9.

Sed haec pauca sunt quae allata.

7   Quod universa Scriptura Sacra de solo Domino scripta sit, plenius ex sequentibus constabit, imprimis ex illis quae in opusculo **De Scriptura Sacra** afferenda sunt. Inde et non aliunde est sanctitas Verbi; hoc quoque intelligitur per haec in Apocalypsi –

Testimonium Jesu est spiritus prophetiae. 19:10.

Yet You have made Him a little lower than the angels, but crowned Him with glory and honour. You have given Him dominion over the works of Your hands; You have put all things under His feet. Ps.8:5,6.

O Jehovah, remember David, who swore to **Jehovah**, made the vow to the Mighty One of Jacob, Surely I will not enter the tent of my house, get up onto my bed, give sleep to my eyes until I find a place for **Jehovah**, dwelling places for the Mighty One of Jacob. Behold, we heard of Him in Ephratah, we found Him in the fields of the forest. We will enter His dwelling places, we will bow down at His footstool. Let Your priests be clothed with righteousness and Your saints shout for joy. Ps.132:1-9.

But these are just a few of the places that could be quoted.

7   The truth that what has been written in the whole of Sacred Scripture has reference to the Lord alone will be established more fully in what is to follow, especially in what is to be presented in the small work concerning **Sacred Scripture**. It is the one and only reason for the holiness of the Word; and it is also what is meant by these words in the Book of Revelation,

The testimony of Jesus is the spirit of prophecy. 19:10.

Quod Dominus impleverit omnia Legis sit quod impleverit omnia Verbi

8   Creditur a multis hodie quod ubi dicitur de Domino quod impleverit Legem, intelligatur quod impleverit omnia praecepta Decalogi, et quod sic Justitia factus sit, ac justificaverit homines mundi etiam per illud fidei. Attamen non intelligitur illud, sed quod impleverit omnia quae de Ipso scripta sunt in Lege et Prophetis, hoc est, in universa Scriptura Sacra, quia haec de solo Ipso agit, ut in superiore articulo dictum est. Quod multi aliter crediderint, est causa quia non scrutati sunt Scripturas et viderunt quid per Legem ibi intelligitur. Per Legem ibi intelliguntur in stricto sensu decem praecepta Decalogi, in latiori sensu omnia quae a Mose in quinque ejus libris scripta sunt, et in latissimo sensu omnia Verbi. **Quod per Legem in stricto sensu intelligantur decem praecepta Decalogi,** notum est.

9   **Quod per Legem in latiori sensu intelligantur omnia quae a Mose in quinque ejus libris scripta sunt,** patet ex his sequentibus – Apud Lucam,

Abraham dixit ad divitem in inferno, Habent **Mosen et Prophetas**; audiunto illos. Si **Mosen et Prophetas** non audiunt, neque si quis ex mortuis resurrexerit, persuadebuntur. 16:29,31.

Apud Johannem,

Philippus dixit ad Nathanaelem, Quem scripsit **Moses in Lege, et Prophetae,** invenimus. 1:46.

Apud Matthaeum,

Nolite putare quod venerim ad solvendum **Legem et Prophetam**; non veni ad solvendum sed ad implendum. 5:17,18.

21   audiunt *DD²*, *DD³*: audiant *DD¹*

The Lord's fulfilment of everything in the Law means His fulfilment of everything in the Word

8   Many at the present day think that where it speaks of the Lord's having fulfilled the Law the meaning is that He fulfilled all the commands of the Decalogue, and that by doing this He became Righteousness and made righteous or justified people in the world too through their belief in that accomplishment. But this is not what is meant; rather, the meaning is that He fulfilled everything written about Him in the Law and Prophets, that is, in the whole of Sacred Scripture, for He alone is the subject there, as stated in the previous section. The reason why many believe anything different from this is that they have not examined the Scriptures carefully to see what is meant there by the Law. There the Law is used in a restricted sense to mean the ten commands within the Decalogue, in a broader sense to mean everything Moses wrote in his five books, and in the broadest sense to mean everything in the Word. **The Law is used in a restricted sense to mean the ten commands in the Decalogue.** This is something well known.

9   **The Law is used in a broader sense to mean everything Moses wrote in his five books.** This is evident from the following – In Luke,

Abraham said to the rich man in hell, They have **Moses and the Prophets**; let them hear them. If they do not hear **Moses and the Prophets**, neither will they be persuaded if someone rose from the dead. 16:29,31.

In John,

Philip said to Nathanael, We have found the one of whom **Moses in the Law, and the Prophets**, wrote. 1:45.

In Matthew,

Do not think that I came to destroy **the Law and the Prophets**; I did not come to destroy but to fulfil. 5:17,18.

Apud eundem,

Omnes **Prophetae et Lex** usque ad Johannem prophetarunt. 11:13.

Apud Lucam,

Lex et Prophetae usque ad Johannem; abhinc regnum Dei evangelizatur. 16:16.

Apud Matthaeum,

Omnia quaecunque volueritis ut faciant vobis homines, sic et vos facite illis; haec est **Lex et Prophetae**. 7:12.

Apud eundem,

Jesus dixit, Amabis Dominum Deum tuum ex toto corde tuo, et in tota anima tua, et amabis proximum tuum ut teipsum. Ex his duobus mandatis **Lex et Prophetae** pendent. 22:35,37,38.

In illis locis per Mosen et Prophetas, tum per Legem et Prophetas, intelliguntur omnia quae in libris Mosis et in libris Prophetarum scripta sunt.
Quod per Legem in specie intelligantur omnia quae per Mosen scripta sunt, patet adhuc ex his – Apud Lucam,

Impleti sunt dies purificationis juxta **Legem Mosis**. Deduxerunt Jesum Hierosolymam ut sisterent Domino – quemadmodum scriptum est in **Lege Domini**, quod omnis masculus aperiens uterum, sanctum Domino vocandus esset – ac ut darent sacrificium juxta quod dictum est in **Lege Domini**, par turturum et duos pullos columbarum. Et adducebant parentes Jesum in templum ut facerent juxta consuetum **Legis** pro Ipso. Cum perfecissent omnia quae juxta **Legem Domini**. 2:22-24,27,39.

Apud Johannem,

In **Lege** Moses praecepit tales lapidare. 8:5.

Apud eundem,

Lex per Mosen data est. 1:17.

In the same gospel,

> All **the Prophets and the Law** prophesied until John. 11:13.

In Luke,

> **The Law and the Prophets** were until John; since that time the kingdom of God is proclaimed. 16:16.

In Matthew,

> All things whatever you wish people to do to you, do also to them; this is **the Law and the Prophets**. 7:12.

In the same gospel,

> Jesus said, You shall love the Lord your God with all your heart, and with all your soul, and you shall love your neighbour as yourself. On these two commandments **the Law and the Prophets** depend. 22:37,39,40.

In these places Moses and the Prophets, as well as the Law and the Prophets, are used to mean everything that has been written in the books of Moses and those of the Prophets.

The fact that the Law is used in particular to mean everything written through Moses is plainer still in the following – In Luke,

> The days of purification according to **the Law of Moses** were completed. They brought Jesus to Jerusalem to present Him to the Lord – as it has been written in **the Law of the Lord**, that every male opening the womb should be called holy to the Lord – and to offer a sacrifice according to what has been stated in **the Law of the Lord**, A pair of doves and two young pigeons. And the parents brought Jesus into the temple, to do for Him according to the custom of **the Law**. When they had performed everything according to **the Law of the Lord**. 2:22-24,27,39.

In John,

> In **the Law** Moses commanded us to stone such [women]. 8:5.

In the same gospel,

> **The Law** was given **through Moses**. 1:17.

Inde patet quod nunc Lex nunc Moses nominetur ubi agitur de talibus quae in libris ejus scripta sunt, ut quoque Matt.8:4; Marc.10:2-4; 12:19; Luc.20:28,37; Joh.3:14; 7:19,51; 8:17; 19:7. Plura etiam a Mose dicuntur **Lex**, quae mandata sunt, ut
5 de holocaustis, Lev.6:2; 7:37; de sacrificiis, Lev.6:18; 7:1-11; de mincha, Lev.6:7; de lepra, Lev.14:2; de zelotypia, Num.5:29,30; de Naziraeatu, Num.6:13,21. Et ipse Moses vocat libros suos **Legem**,

Scripsit Moses **Legem hanc**, et dedit eam sacerdotibus, filiis Levi, portantibus arcam faederis Jehovae; et dixit illis, Accipiendo **Librum**
10 **Legis** hujus, ponite eum a latere arcae faederis Jehovae. Deut.31:9,11,26.

A latere positus est, intus enim in arca erant tabulae lapideae, quae in stricto sensu sunt Lex. Libri Mosis vocantur Liber Legis postea,

Dixit Chilkia sacerdos magnus ad Schaphanem scribam, **Librum**
15 **Legis** inveni in domo Jehovae. Cum audivit Rex verba **Libri Legis**, rupit vestes suas. 2 Reg.22:8,11; 23:24.

10   **Quod omnia Verbi per Legem in latissimo sensu intelligantur,** constare potest ex his locis,

Jesus dixit, Nonne scriptum est in **Lege vestra**, Ego dixi, Dii estis?
20 Joh.10:34.

Hoc scriptum est, Ps.82:6.

Respondit turba, Nos audivimus ex **Lege** quod Christus maneat in aeternum. Joh.12:34.

Hoc scriptum est, Ps.89:30; Ps.110:4; Dan.7:14.

25 Ut impleretur verbum scriptum in **Lege illorum**, Odio habuerunt Me sine causa. Joh. 15:25.

Hoc scriptum est, Ps.35:19.

Dixerunt Pharisaei, Num quis ex principibus credidit in Ipsum? Sed turba haec quae non novit **Legem**, maledicti sunt. Joh.7:48,49.

29   maledicti sunt *DD³: om DD¹, DD²*

These verses show that at one time the Law, at another Moses, is mentioned where reference is made to those kinds of things that were written in his books, as the following also show, Matt.8:4; Mark 10:2-4; 12:19; Luke 20:28,37; John 3:14; 7:19,51; 8:17; 19:7.

Also, very many instructions that are given are called **the Law** by Moses, for example, those relating to burnt offerings, Lev.6:9; 7:37; sacrifices, Lev.6:25; 7:1-11; the grain offering, Lev.6:14; leprosy, Lev.14:2; jealousy, Num.5:29,30; Naziriteship, Num.6:13,21. And Moses himself calls his books **the Law**,

Moses wrote **this Law** and gave it to the priests, the sons of Levi, carrying the ark of the covenant of Jehovah; and he said to them, Take **the Book** of this **Law** and place it by the side of the ark of the covenant of Jehovah. Deut.31:9,11,26.

It was placed by the side because the inside of the ark contained the stone tablets, which are the Law in a restricted sense. Later on the Books of Moses are called the Book of the Law,

Hilkiah the high priest said to Shaphan the scribe, I have found **the Book of the Law** in the house of Jehovah. When the king heard the words of **the Book of the Law** he tore his clothes. 2 Kings 22:8,11; 23:24.

10   **The Law is used in the broadest sense to mean everything in the Word**. This can be seen in the following places –

Jesus said, Is it not written in **your Law**, I said, You are gods. John 10:34.

This is written in Ps.82:6.

The crowd replied, We have heard from **the Law** that the Christ remains for ever. John 12:34.

This is written in Ps.89:30; Ps.110:4; Dan.7:14.

That the word written in **their Law** might be fulfilled: They hated Me without a cause. John 15:25.

This is written in Ps.35:19.

The Pharisees said, Has any of the leaders believed in Him? But this crowd which does not know **the Law** is accursed. John 7:48,49.

Facilius est caelum et terram transire quam **Legis** unum apicem cadere. Luc.16:17.

Per Legem ibi intelligitur tota Scriptura Sacra.

11 Quod Dominus impleverit omnia Legis sit quod impleverit omnia Verbi, patet a locis ubi dicitur quod ab Ipso impleta sit Scriptura, et quod omnia consummata sint, ut ex his –

Jesus intravit in synagogam et surrexit ad legendum. Tunc traditus est Ipsi liber Esaiae prophetae, et evolvit librum et invenit locum scriptum, Spiritus Domini super Me, propter quod unxit Me; ad evangelizandum pauperibus misit Me, ad sanandum contritos corde, ad evangelizandum vinctis remissionem, et caecis visum, ad praedicandum annum Domini acceptum. Postea convolvens librum, et dixit, **Hodie impleta est Scriptura haec** in auribus vestries. Luc.4:16-21.

Scrutamini **Scripturas**, atque illae testantur de Me. Joh.5:39.

Ut **Scriptura impleretur**, Qui comedit Mecum panem, sustulit super Me calcaneum. Joh.13:18.

Nemo ex illis periit, nisi filius perditionis, ut **Scriptura impleretur**. Joh.17:12.

Ut **impleretur verbum** quod dixit, Quos dedisti Mihi, non perdidi ex illis unum. Joh.18:9.

Dixit Jesus Petro, Absconde tuum gladium in loco; quomodo ergo **implerentur Scripturae**, quod sic oporteat fieri? Hoc totum factum est ut **implerentur Scripturae Prophetarum**. Matt.26:52,54,56.

Filius Hominis abit, sicut scriptum est de Ipso, ut **impleantur Scripturae**. Marc.14:21,49.

Sic **impleta est Scriptura** quae dixit, Cum impiis reputatus est. Marc.15:28; Luc.22:37.

Ut **Scriptura impleretur**, Diviserunt vestimenta mea sibi, et super tunicam meam jecerunt sortem. Joh.19:24.

Post hoc, sciens Jesus quod omnia jam consummata essent, ut **impleretur Scriptura**. Joh.19:28.

Cum accepisset acetum Jesus, dixit, **Consummatum est**, hoc est, **impletum**. Joh.19:30.

Facta haec sunt ut **Scriptura impleretur**, Os non confringetis Ipsius. Et rursus **alia Scriptura dicit**, Videbunt quem transfoderunt. Joh.19:36,37.

16 illae *DD*³: illi *DD*¹, *DD*²
30 mea *DD*³, *VR*³: sua *DD*¹, *DD*², *VR*¹, *VR*²

It is easier for heaven and earth to pass away than for one tittle of **the Law** to fall. Luke 16:17.

In these places the Law is used to mean the entire Sacred Scripture.

11   The truth that the fulfilment by the Lord of everything in the Law means His fulfilling everything in the Word is evident from places where it says that the Scripture was fulfilled by Him and everything finished, for example, from these –

Jesus went into the synagogue and got up to read. Then the book of Isaiah the prophet was handed to Him, and He unrolled the book and found the place where it was written, The Spirit of the Lord is upon Me, because He has anointed Me. He has sent Me to preach good news to the poor, to heal the crushed at heart, to preach good news of forgiveness to the bound, and of sight to the blind, to preach the acceptable year of the Lord. After this He rolled up the book and said, **Today this scripture has been fulfilled** in your ears. Luke 4:16-21.

You search **the Scriptures**; and they testify of Me. John 5:39.

That **the Scripture might be fulfilled**, He who eats bread with Me has lifted up his heel against Me. John 13:18.

None of them has been lost except the son of perdition, that **the Scripture might be fulfilled**. John 17:12.

That **the word** which He had spoken **might be fulfilled**: Those whom you have given Me, I have lost not one of them. John 18:9.

Jesus said to Peter, Put away your sword in its place. How therefore should **the Scriptures be fulfilled**, that it must be so? All this has taken place that **the Scriptures of the Prophets might be fulfilled**. Matt.26:52,54,56.

The Son of Man goes away as it has been written of Him, that **the Scriptures may be fulfilled**. Mark 14:21,49.

So **the Scripture was fulfilled** which said, He was reckoned with the wicked. Mark 15:28; Luke 22:37.

That **the Scripture** might be fulfilled: They divided my garments among them, and for my tunic they cast lots. John 19:24.

After this, Jesus knowing that everything had now been accomplished ... that **the Scripture might be fulfilled**. John 19:28.

When Jesus had taken the vinegar, He said, **It has been accomplished** (that is, **fulfilled**). John 19:30.

These things took place in order that **the Scripture** might be fulfilled: You shall not break a bone of His. And again **another Scripture says**, They will see the one whom they pierced. John 19:36,37.

Praeter alibi, ubi loca Prophetarum adducuntur et non simul dicitur quod Lex seu Scriptura impleta sit.

Quod omne Verbi de Ipso scriptum sit, et quod in mundum venerit ut illud impleret, docuit etiam discipulos antequam abivit, his verbis –

Jesus ad discipulos. Stulti et tardi corde ad credendum omnibus quae loquuti sunt Prophetae! Nonne hoc oportebat pati Christum et ingredi in gloriam? Incipiens porro **a Mose et ab omnibus Prophetis**, interpretatus est illis in **omnibus Scripturis de Ipso**. Luc.24:25-27.

Porro,

Jesus dixit discipulis, Haec sunt verba quae loquutus sum ad vos cum adhuc essem vobiscum, **quod oporteret impleri omnia quae scripta sunt in Lege Mosis et Prophetis et Psalmis de Me**. Luc.24:44,45.

Quod Dominus in mundo impleverit omnia Verbi, usque ad singularissima ejus, patet ab his Ipsius verbis –

Amen dico vobis, Usque dum praetereat caelum et terra, **jotha una aut unum corniculum non praeteribit de Lege, donec omnia fiant**. Matt.5:18.

Ex his nunc clare videri potest quod per id quod Dominus impleverit omnia Legis non intelligatur quod impleverit omnia praecepta Decalogi sed quod omnia Verbi.

---

16   jotha una *DD*[1]: **jotha unum** *DD*[2]; **iota unum** *DD*[3]

There are in addition other verses in which places in the Prophets are quoted but without any mention at the same time of the fulfilment of the Law or Scripture.

That all of the written Word had reference to Himself, and that He came into the world to fulfil it all, is also what the Lord told the disciples, in these words, before He departed from them –

Jesus said to the disciples, O foolish ones and slow of heart to believe all that the Prophets have spoken! Ought not the Christ to have suffered this and to enter into glory? Then beginning **at Moses and all the Prophets** He explained to them in **all the Scriptures things concerning Himself.** Luke 24:25,27.

And then,

Jesus said to the disciples, These are the words which I spoke to you when I was still with you, **that everything written about Me in the Law of Moses and the Prophets and the Psalms must be fulfilled.** Luke 24:44,45.

That the Lord in the world fulfilled everything in the Word, right down to the smallest detail there, is evident from these words of His,

Truly I say to you, Even until heaven and earth pass away, **one jot or one small part of a letter will not pass from the Law till all things are done.** Matt.5:18.

From all this it may now be seen clearly that fulfilment by the Lord of everything in the Law does not mean that He fulfilled every command in the Decalogue but everything in the Word.

Quod Dominus in mundum venerit ut subjugaret inferna et glorificaret Humanum, et quod passio crucis fuerit ultima pugna, per quam plene vicit inferna et plene glorificavit Humanum Suum

12   Notum est in ecclesia quod Dominus vicerit mortem, per quam intelligitur infernum, et quod postea cum gloria ascenderit in caelum; sed nondum notum est quod Dominus per pugnas, quae sunt tentationes, vicerit mortem seu infernum, et simul per illas glorificaverit Humanum Suum, et quod passio crucis fuerit ultima pugna seu tentatio per quam vicit et glorificavit. De his, multis agitur apud Prophetas et apud Davidem sed non ita multis apud Evangelistas. Apud hos, tentationes, quas a pueritia sustinuit, in summa descriptae sunt per tentationes Ipsius in deserto, et postea a diabolo, ac ultimae per illa quae passus est in Gethsemane et super cruce. De tentationibus Ipsius in deserto, et postea a diabolo, videatur apud Matthaeum 4:1-11, apud Marcum 1:12,13, et apud Lucam 4:1-13. Sed per illas intelliguntur omnes usque ad ultimas. Non plura de illis revelavit discipulis, nam dicitur apud Esaiam,

Exactionem sustinuit, non tamen aperuit os Suum. Sicut agnus ad mactationem, et sicut ovis coram tonsoribus suis, obmutescit et non aperuit os Suum. 53:7.

De tentationibus Ipsius in Gethsemane, videatur apud Matthaeum 26:36-44, apud Marcum 14:32-42, et apud Lucam 22:39-46; et de tentationibus super cruce, apud Matthaeum 27:33-57, apud Marcum 15:22-38, apud Lucam 23:33-49, et apud Johannem 19:17-37. Tentationes non aliud sunt quam pugnae contra inferna. De tentationibus seu pugnis Domini, videatur in opusculo **De Nova Hierosolyma et ejus Doctrina Caelesti**, Londini edito, n.201 et 302; et de tentationibus in genere, n.187-200 ibi.

30   edito DD^3: edita DD^1, DD^2
30   187 DD^3: 189 DD^1, DD^2

The Lord came into the world to subdue the hells and to glorify His Human And His passion on the cross was the final conflict through which He completely conquered the hells and completely glorified His Human

12   The church knows that the Lord conquered death, by which hell is meant, and that after this He went up to heaven in glory; but it does not as yet know that the Lord conquered death or hell by means of conflicts, that is, temptations, or that by means of these He at the same time glorified His Human. Nor does it know that His passion on the cross was the final conflict or temptation through which He achieved that conquest and glorification. These things are very much the subject in the works of the Prophets and David but not so much in those of the Evangelists. In the latter His temptations, which He underwent right from childhood, are portrayed briefly by His temptations in the wilderness, and afterwards those by the devil[1]; and the final ones by the things He suffered in Gethsemane and on the cross. Regarding His temptations in the wilderness, and afterwards by the devil, see Matthew 4:1-11, Mark 1:12,13, and Luke 4:1-13. Yet these temptations serve to mean all, right through to the final ones. No more concerning them was revealed to the disciples, for it says in Isaiah,

He was oppressed, yet He did not open His mouth. Like a lamb to the slaughter, and like a sheep before its shearers, He was dumb and did not open His mouth. 53:7.

Regarding His temptations in Gethsemane, see Matthew 26:36-44, Mark 14:32-42, and Luke 22:39-46; and His temptations on the cross, Matthew 27:33-57, Mark 15:22-38, Luke 23:33-49, and John 19:17-37. Temptations are nothing other than conflicts with the hells. Regarding the Lord's temptations or conflicts, see the small work published in London, **The New Jerusalem and Heaven's Teaching for it**, §§201 and 302; and regarding temptations in general, §§187-200 there.

---

1   See Luke 4:13

13 Quod Dominus per passionem crucis plene vicerit inferna, docet Ipse apud Johannem,

Nunc judicium est mundi hujus, **nunc princeps mundi hujus ejicietur foras**. 12:31.

Haec loquutus est Dominus cum instabat passio crucis. Apud eundem,

Princeps hujus mundi judicatus est. 16:11.

Apud eundem,

Confidite, **Ego vici mundum**. 16:33.

Et apud Lucam,

Dixit Jesus, Vidi **Satanam sicut fulmen e caelo cadentem**. 10:18.

Per mundum, principem mundi, Satanam, et diabolum intelligitur infernum.
   Quod Dominus per passionem crucis etiam plene glorificaverit Humanum Suum, docet apud Johannem,

Postquam Judas exivit, dixit Jesus, Nunc **glorificatus est Filius Hominis, et Deus glorificatus est** in Ipso. Si Deus **glorificatus** est in Ipso, etiam Deus **glorificabit** Ipsum in Se Ipso, et statim **glorificabit** Ipsum. 13:31,32.

Apud eundem,

Pater, venit hora; **glorifica** Filium Tuum, ut etiam Filius Tuus **glorificet** Te. 17:1,5.

Apud eundem,

Nunc anima mea turbata est. Et dixit, Pater, **glorifica** nomen Tuum. Et exiit vox e caelo, Et **glorificavi** et rursus **glorificabo**. 12:27,28.

Apud Lucam,

Nonne hoc oportebat pati Christum et ingredi in **gloriam Suam**? 24:26.

13   By His passion on the cross the Lord completely conquered the hells. He Himself tells us this in John,

Now is the judgment of this world, **now will the prince of this world be cast outdoors.** 12:31.

This the Lord said when the passion on the cross was imminent. In the same gospel,

The prince of this world has been judged. 16:11.

In the same gospel,

Have confidence, **I have overcome the world.** 16:33.

And in Luke,

Jesus said, I saw **Satan falling like lightning from heaven.** 10:18.

Hell is meant by world, prince of the world, Satan, and devil.
    By His passion on the cross the Lord also completely glorified His Human. He tells us this in John,

After Judas went out Jesus said, Now **is the Son of Man glorified, and God glorified** in Him. If God is **glorified** in Him, God will also **glorify** Him in Himself, and will **glorify** Him at once. 13:31,32.

In the same gospel,

Father, the hour has come. **Glorify** Your Son, that Your Son also may **glorify** You. 17:1,5.

In the same gospel,

Now my soul is troubled. And He said, Father, **glorify** Your name. And a voice came from heaven, I have both **glorified** it and will **glorify** it again. 12:27,28.

In Luke,

Ought not the Christ to have suffered this and to enter into **His glory?** 24:26.

Haec dicta sunt de passione. Glorificatio est unitio Divini et Humani, quare dicitur, Et Deus glorificabit Ipsum in Se Ipso.

14 Quod Dominus in mundum venerit ut omnia in caelis et inde in terris in ordinem redigeret, et quod hoc factum sit per pugnas contra inferna, quae tunc infestabant omnem hominem venientem in mundum et exeuntem e mundo, et quod per id Justitia factus sit ac salvaverit homines, qui absque eo non salvari potuerunt, multis in locis apud Prophetas praedicitur, quorum modo aliqua afferentur. Apud Esaiam,

Quis Hic qui venit ex Edom, conspersus vestes ex Bozra, Hic honorabilis in vestitu Suo, incedens in multitudine roboris Sui? Ego qui loquor in justitia, magnus ad salvandum. Quare rubicundus quoad vestem Tuam, et vestes Tuae sicut calcantis in torculari? Torcular calcavi solus, et de populo non vir Mecum; propterea calcavi illos in ira Mea et conculcavi eos in excandescentia Mea, inde sparsa est victoria eorum super vestes Meas. Nam dies vindictae in corde Meo et annus redemptorum Meorum venit. Salutem praestitit Mihi brachium Meum, descendere feci in terram victoriam eorum. Dixit, Certe populus Meus illi, filii; ideo factus est illis in Salvatorem. Ob amorem Suum et ob clementiam Suam Ille redemit eos. 63:1-9.

Haec de pugnis Domini contra inferna. Per vestem, in qua honorabilis fuit et quae rubicunda, intelligitur Verbum, cui violentia a populo Judaico illata est. Ipsa pugna contra inferna et victoria super illa describitur per quod calcaverit illos in ira Sua et conculcaverit in excandescentia Sua. Quod solus et ex propria potentia pugnaverit, describitur per haec, De populo non vir Mecum, salutem praestitit Mihi brachium Meum, descendere feci in terram victoriam eorum. Quod per id salvaverit et redemerit describitur per haec, Ideo factus est illis in Salvatorem; ob amorem Suum et clementiam Suam Ille redemit eos. Quod hoc fuerit causa adventus Ipsius, describitur per haec, Dies vindictae in corde Meo et annus redemptorum Meorum venit. Apud Esaiam,

---

13 vestes Tuae: vestis tua *DD*
19 Certe: Ecce *DD*
30 *om* Suum *DD*

These things were said in reference to His passion. Glorification is the uniting of Divine and Human, and that is why it says, And God will glorify Him in Himself.

14 The Lord came into the world to restore to order everything in heaven and consequently on earth; and this was accomplished by means of conflicts with the hells, which were at that time molesting everyone coming into and going out of the world. And by accomplishing that He became Righteousness and saved people, who – unless He had accomplished it – were unable to be saved. All this is foretold in many places in the Prophets, just some of which will be mentioned. In Isaiah,

Who is This who comes from Edom, with spattered clothes from Bozra, He that is glorious in His apparel, marching in the vast numbers of His strength? It is I who speak in righteousness, mighty to save. Why is Your clothing red, and Your clothes like his who treads in the winepress? I have trodden the winepress alone, and from the people not a man was with Me; therefore I trod them in My anger and trampled them in My wrath. Consequently their blood[1] has been sprinkled on My clothes. For the day of vengeance was in My heart and the year of My redeemed had come. My own arm brought salvation to Me, I made their blood[1] go down into the ground. He said, Surely they are My people, children. Therefore He became their Saviour. Because of His love and His compassion He redeemed them. 63:1-9.

All this refers to the Lord's conflicts with the hells. The clothing in which He was glorious and which was red means the Word, which suffered violence from the Jewish people. His actual conflict with and victory over the hells is described by His having trodden them in His anger and trampled them in His wrath. His having battled with them, alone and by His own power, is described by, From the people not a man was with Me; My own arm brought salvation to Me; I made their blood go down into the ground. His having through this accomplished salvation and redemption is described by, Therefore He became their Saviour; because of His love and His compassion He redeemed them. That this was the reason for His coming is described by, The day of vengeance was in My heart and the year of My redeemed has come. In Isaiah,

---

1 In Sebastian Schmidt's Latin version of Isaiah, which Swedenborg is following here, a parenthesis containing a word meaning *blood* comes after that which generally denotes *victory* in battle

Vidit quod non quisquam et obstupuit quod non esset intercedens; ideo salutem praestitit Ipsi brachium Suum, et justitia Ipsius suscitavit Ipsum. Inde induit justitiam sicut loricam, et galeam salutis super caput Suum, et induit vestes vindictae, et texit Se sicut pallio zelo. Tunc venit Zioni Redemptor. 59:16,17,20.

Haec quoque de pugnis Domini, cum fuit in mundo, contra inferna. Quod solus ex propria potentia pugnaverit contra illa, intelligitur per haec, Vidit quod non quisquam, ideo salutem praestitit Ipsi brachium Suum. Quod inde Justitia factus sit, per haec, Justitia Ipsius suscitavit Ipsum, unde induit justitiam sicut loricam. Quod ita redemerit, per haec, Tunc venit Zioni Redemptor. Apud Jeremiam,

Illi consternati sunt, fortes eorum contusi sunt, fugam fugerunt, nec respexerunt. Dies ille Domino Jehovih Zebaoth, dies ultionis, ut vindictam sumat de hostibus Suis, comedatque gladius, et saturetur. 46:5,10.

Pugna Domini cum infernis et victoria super illa describitur per quod consternati sint, quod fortes eorum contusi fugam fugerint, et non respexerint; fortes eorum et hostes sunt inferna, quia omnes ibi odio habent Dominum. Adventus Ipsius in mundum propterea intelligitur per haec, Dies ille Domino Jehovih Zebaoth, dies ultionis, ut vindictam sumat de hostibus Suis. Apud Jeremiam,

Cadent juvenes in plateis, et omnes viri belli exscindentur in die illo. 49:26.

Apud Joelem,

Jehovah edidit vocem coram exercitu Suo. Magnus dies Jehovae, terribilis valde. Quis ergo sustinebit illum? 2:11.

Apud Zephaniam,

In die sacrificii Jehovae visitabo super principes, super filios regis, super omnes indutos indumento alienigenae. Dies hic, dies angustiae, dies buccinae et clangoris. 1:8,9,15,16.

He saw that there was not anyone, and wondered that there was no intercessor; therefore His own arm brought salvation to Him, and His righteousness lifted Him up. Consequently He put on righteousness as a breastplate, and a helmet of salvation upon His head; and He put on clothes of vengeance, and clothed Himself with zeal as if with a cloak. At that time the Redeemer came to Zion. 59:16,17,20.

This too refers to the Lord's conflicts, when He was in the world, with the hells. His having battled with them, alone, by His own power, is meant by, He saw that there was not anyone, therefore His own arm brought salvation to Him. His having as a consequence become Righteousness is described by, His righteousness lifted Him up; consequently He put on righteousness as a breastplate. His accomplishment of redemption by having done so is meant by, At that time the Redeemer came to Zion. In Jeremiah, 4

They were dismayed, their strong ones were smitten, they took to flight and did not look back. That day belongs to the Lord Jehovih Zebaoth, a day of vengeance, that He may take vengeance of His enemies, and the sword may devour and be satiated. 46:5,10.

The Lord's conflict with and victory over the hells is described by their having been dismayed, their strong ones having been smitten, taken to flight, and not looking back; their strong ones and His enemies mean the hells because everyone there hates the Lord. It is therefore His coming into the world that is meant by, That day belongs to the Lord Jehovih Zebaoth, a day of vengeance, that He may take vengeance on His enemies. In Jeremiah, 5

The young men will fall in the streets, and all the men of war will be cut down on that day. 49:26.

In Joel,

Jehovah uttered His voice before His army. The day of Jehovah is great, extremely terrifying. Who therefore will endure it? 2:11.

In Zephaniah,

On the day of Jehovah's sacrifice I will punish the princes, the king's sons, all clothed with the clothing of one who is a foreigner. This day is a day of distress, a day of trumpet and blast. 1:8,9,15,16.

Apud Sachariam,

Jehovah exibit et pugnabit contra gentes, juxta diem pugnare Ipsum in die praelii. Stabunt pedes Ipsius in die illo super Monte Olivarum, qui ante facies Hierosolymae. Tunc fugietis in vallem montium Meorum. In die illo non erit lux et splendor. Jehovah autem erit in Regem super tota terra; in die illo erit Jehovah unus, et nomen Ipsius unum. 14:3-6,9.

In his locis etiam agitur de pugnis Domini. Per diem illum intelligitur adventus Ipsius. Mons Olivarum, qui ante facies Hierosolymae, erat ubi Dominus solito commoratus est, videatur Marc.13:3; 14:26; Luc.21:37; 22:39; Joh.8:1; et alibi. Apud Davidem,

Circumdederunt Me funes mortis; funes inferni circumdederunt Me, praevenerunt Me laquei mortis. Ideo misit tela, et fulmina multa, et conturbavit illos. Persequar hostes Meos et comprehendam eos, nec revertar usque dum consumpsero; percussero eos, ut resurgere non possint. Accinges Me robore ad bellum et dabis hostes in fugam. Conteram eos sicut pulverem coram faciebus venti, sicut caenum platearum attenuabo eos. Ps.18:5,6,15,38-41,43.

Funes et laquei mortis, qui circumdederunt et praevenerunt, significant tentationes, quae quia ab inferno sunt, etiam vocantur funes inferni. Haec et reliqua in toto illo psalmo agunt de pugnis et de victoriis Domini, quare etiam dicitur,

Pones Me in caput gentium; populus non noveram, servient Mihi. vers.44,45.

Apud Davidem,

Accinge gladium super femur, Potens. Tela Tua acuta, populi cadent sub Te; e corde hostes Regis. Thronus Tuus in saeculum et in aeternum; amasti justitiam, propterea unxit Te, Deus. Ps.45:4-8.

Haec quoque de pugna cum infernis et de subjugatione illorum, nam in toto illo psalmo agitur de Domino, nempe de Ipsius pugnis, de Ipsius glorificatione, et de salvatione fidelium ab Ipso. Apud Davidem,

3   qui *DD*³: quae *DD*¹, *DD*²

In Zechariah,

Jehovah will go out and fight against the nations, as He fights on a day of battle. His feet will stand on that day upon the Mount of Olives, which faces Jerusalem. At that time you will flee to the valley of My mountains. On that day there will be no light and brightness. But Jehovah will be King over all the earth; on that day Jehovah will be one, and His name one. 14:3-6,9.

In these places as well the Lord's conflicts are the subject. That day means His coming. The Mount of Olives, which faces Jerusalem, was somewhere that the Lord was accustomed to retire to, see Mark 13:3; 14:26; Luke 21:37; 22:39; John 8:1; and elsewhere. In David, 6

The cords of death encompassed Me; the cords of hell encompassed Me, the snares of death confronted Me. Therefore He sent arrows, and many thunderbolts, and scattered them. I will pursue My enemies and overtake them, and not turn back until I have devoured them. I will thrust them through, so that they are not able to rise. You will gird Me with strength for war, and you will put enemies to flight. I will beat them fine like dust before the wind; like the mire of the streets will I diminish them. Ps.18:4,5,14,37-40,42.

The cords and snares of death which surrounded and confronted Him mean temptations, and because these spring from hell they are also called the cords of hell. These words and all the rest in the whole of that psalm relate to the Lord's conflicts and victories, which is why it also says,

You will make Me the head of the nations; a people whom I have not known will serve Me. Verses 43,44.

In David, 7

Gird your sword on your thigh, O Mighty One. Your arrows are sharp, the peoples will fall under You; from the heart they are enemies of the King. Your throne will be for ever and ever; You have loved righteousness, therefore He has anointed You. Ps.45:3-7.

These words too refer to conflicts with the hells and to subduing them, for the subject in the whole of this psalm is the Lord, that is, His conflicts, His glorification, and the saving by Him of those who are loyal and sincere. In David,

Ignis coram Ipso ibit, inflammabit circumcirca hostes Ipsius. Videbit et timebit terra. Montes sicut cera liquefient coram Domino totius terrae. Annuntiabunt caeli justitiam Ipsius et videbunt omnes populi gloriam Ipsius. Ps.97:3-6.

Pariter in hoc psalmo agitur de Domino et de similibus. Apud Davidem,

Dictum Jehovae ad Dominum meum, Sede ad dextram Meam, usque dum posuero inimicos tuos scabellum pedum tuorum. Dominare in medio inimicorum tuorum. Dominus ad dextram tuam, percussit in die irae suae reges. Implevit cadaveribus, percussit caput super terram multam. Ps.110:1,2,5,6.

Quod haec de Domino dicta sint, constat ex Ipsius Domini verbis apud Matthaeum 22:42, apud Marcum 12:36, et apud Lucam 20:42. Per sedere ad dextram significatur omnipotentia; per inimicos significantur inferna; per reges, illi ibi qui in falsis mali sunt; per ponere illos scabellum pedum, percutere in die irae, implere cadaveribus, significatur destruere potentiam illorum; et per percutere caput super terram multam significatur destruere omnem.

Quoniam Dominus solus vicit inferna, cum nulla ope alicujus angeli, ideo vocatur **Heros** et **Vir bellorum**, Esai.42:13; **Rex gloriae, Jehovah fortis, Heros belli**, Ps.24:8,10; **Fortis Jacobi**, Ps.132:2; ac multis in locis **Jehovah Zebaoth**, hoc est, Jehovah exercituum belli. Et quoque vocatur adventus Ipsius **Dies Jehovae** terribilis, crudelis, indignationis, excandescentiae, irae, vindictae, exitii, belli, buccinae et clangoris, tumultus; ut ex locis supra n.4 allatis, videri potest.

Quoniam ultimum judicium a Domino, cum fuit in mundo, factum est per pugnas cum infernis et per subjugationem illorum, ideo multis in locis agitur de **judicio** quod facturus est, ut apud Davidem,

Jehovah venit ad judicandum terram; judicabit orbem in justitia et populos in veritate. Ps.96:13.

11	1,2,5,6 *DD³*: 1 ad fin *DD¹, DD²*	
26-27	buccinae et clangoris: buccinae, clangoris *DD¹, DD²*; buccinae clangoris *DD³*	
33	Ps.96.13 *DD³*: Ps.95.13 *DD¹, DD²*	

Fire will go before Him and burn up His enemies roundabout. The earth will see and be afraid. The mountains will melt like wax before the Lord of the whole earth. The heavens will proclaim His righteousness and all the peoples see His glory. Ps.97:3-6.

Equally in this psalm the Lord and the same kinds of things are the subject. In David, 8

Jehovah said to my Lord, Sit at My right hand, till I make Your enemies Your footstool. Rule in the midst of Your enemies. The Lord at Your right hand has crushed kings on the day of His anger. He has filled it with dead bodies, He has crushed the head over much land. Ps.110:1,2,5,6.

The fact that all this refers to the Lord is clear from His own words in Matthew 22:44, Mark 12:36, and Luke 20:42. Sitting at the right hand means His almighty power; enemies mean the hells; kings, those there who are full of falsities that go with evil; making them a footstool, crushing on the day of anger, filling with dead bodies, mean destroying their power; and crushing the head over much land means destroying it all.

Because the Lord alone, without the help of any angel, overcame the hells, He is therefore called **Mighty One** and **Man of wars**, Isa.42:13; **King of glory, Jehovah strong, Mighty man in battle**, Ps.24:8,10; **Mighty One of Jacob**, Ps.132:2; and in many other places **Jehovah Zebaoth**, that is, Jehovah of armies of war. Furthermore His coming is called **the Day of Jehovah**, a day that is terrifying, cruel, one of indignation, wrath, anger, vengeance, destruction, war, trumpet and blast, uproar, as may be seen in the places quoted above in §4. 9

Since a last judgment was accomplished by the Lord, when He was in the world, by means of His conflicts with and subjecting of the hells, many places refer to that **judgment** He was going to accomplish, such as this in David, 10

Jehovah comes to judge the earth; He will judge the world in righteousness and the peoples in truth. Ps.96:13.

Sic pluries alibi.

Haec e propheticis Verbi. In historicis Verbi autem similia repraesentata sunt per bella filiorum Israelis cum variis gentibus, nam in Verbo, tam Prophetico quam Historico, omne quod scriptum est, de Domino scriptum est; inde Verbum est Divinum. In ritualibus Ecclesiae Israeliticae, ut in holocaustis et sacrificiis, tum in sabbathis et festis ejus, ac in sacerdotio Aharonis et Levitarum, multa arcana glorificationis Domini continentur. Similiter in reliquis apud Mosen, quae vocantur leges, judicia, et statuta, quod etiam intelligitur per Domini verba ad discipulos quod oporteret Ipsum implere omnia quae de Ipso scripta sunt in Lege Mosis, Luc.24:44, tum ad Judaeos quod Moses de Ipso scripserit, Joh.5:46.

Ex his nunc patet quod Dominus in mundum venerit ut subjugaret inferna et glorificaret Humanum Suum, et quod passio crucis fuerit ultima pugna, per quam plene vicit inferna et plene glorificavit Humanum. Sed plura de hac re videbuntur in sequente opusculo **De Scriptura Sacra**, ubi in unum colligentur omnia loca e Verbo Prophetico quae de pugnis Domini cum infernis et de victoriis super ea seu, quod idem, quae de ultimo judicio ab Ipso facto, cum fuit in mundo, agunt, tum quae de passione et de glorificatione Humani Ipsius, quae tot sunt ut, si adducerentur, implerent membranas.

And several other places such as this.

11

These quotations have been drawn from prophetical parts of the Word. But in the historical sections of the Word the same kinds of things concerning the Lord are represented by the children of Israel's wars against different nations, for everything written in the Word, both prophetical and historical, has been written to refer to the Lord; and that is why the Word is Divine. The ritual observances of the Israelite church – burnt offerings and sacrifices, also its sabbaths and feasts – and the priesthood of Aaron and Levites, hold within themselves many aspects of the Lord's glorification. So too do all other things written in Moses, called laws, judgments, and statutes; and so do the Lord's words addressed to the disciples, that He had to fulfil everything written about Him in the Law of Moses, Luke 24:44, and those addressed to the Jews, that Moses had written about Him, John 5:46.

From everything presented in this section it is now evident that the Lord came into the world to subdue the hells and to glorify His Human, and that His passion on the cross was the final conflict by which He completely conquered the hells and completely glorified His Human. But more on this subject will be seen in the small work concerning **Sacred Scripture** that is to follow. In this all the places will be brought together from the prophetical part of the Word which refer to the Lord's conflicts with and victories over the hells – or what amounts to the same thing, the last judgment accomplished by Him when He was in the world – as well as places referring to His passion (or suffering) and the glorification of His Human, which are so many that a large number of pages would be needed to quote them all.

12

Quod Dominus per passionem crucis non abstulerit peccata sed quod portaverit illa

15   Sunt quidam intra ecclesiam qui credunt quod Dominus per passionem crucis peccata abstulerit ac satisfecerit Patri, et sic redemerit; quidam etiam quod peccata illorum qui fidem in Ipsum habent, in Se transtulerit, portaverit, ac in profundum maris, hoc est, in infernum, conjecerit. Confirmant illa apud se per Johannis verba de Jesu,

Ecce Agnus Dei qui tollit peccatum mundi, Joh.1:29,

et per Domini verba apud Esaiam,

Ille morbos nostros tulit et dolores nostros portavit. Confossus ob praevaricationes nostras, contusus ob iniquitates nostras, castigatio pacis nostrae super Illo; vulnere Ipsius sanitas data est nobis. Jehovah incurrere fecit in Ipsum iniquitates omnium nostrum. Exactionem sustinuit, atque afflictus est, non tamen aperuit os Suum; sicut agnus ad mactationem ducitur. Excisus est e terra viventium, ob praevaricationem populi Mei, plagam illis; ut daret impios in sepulchro Suo, et divites in mortibus Suis. Ex labore animae Suae videbit, saturabitur; per scientiam Suam justificabit multos, eo quod iniquitates eorum Ipse portaverit. Exinanivit ad mortem usque animam Suam, et cum praevaricatoribus numeratus est, et peccatum multorum tulit, et pro praevaricatoribus intercessit. 53:1 ad fin.

Haec et illa dicta sunt de tentationibus Domini et de passione Ipsius; ac per tollere peccatum et morbos, perque incurrere facere in Ipsum iniquitates omnium, simile intelligitur quod

9   peccatum: peccata *DD*
24   ditto

By His passion on the cross the Lord did not take away sins but carried them

15	There are some people in the church who believe that by His passion on the cross the Lord took sins away and made satisfaction to the Father, and in doing so accomplished redemption. There are even some who believe that He has transferred to Himself, carried and cast into the depths of the sea – that is, into hell – the sins of those who believe in Him. They see a confirmation of this in John's words referring to Jesus,

Behold, the Lamb of God who takes away the sin of the world, John 1:29,

and in the Lord's words in Isaiah,

He has borne our sicknesses and carried our sorrows. He was pierced because of our transgressions, bruised because of our iniquities; the chastisement of our peace was upon Him; by His wounds we have been healed, Jehovah has imposed on Him the iniquities of us all. He was oppressed and He was afflicted, yet He did not open His mouth; like a lamb He is led to the slaughter. He was cut off out of the land of the living; on account of the transgression of My people was He stricken, that He might consign those who are wicked to their grave and those who are rich to their deaths[1]. Out of the toil of His soul He will see, He will be satisfied; by His knowledge will He make many righteous, in that He Himself has carried their iniquities. He poured out His soul to death, and was numbered with the transgressors, and bore the sin of many, and made intercession for the transgressors. Isa.53:1-end.

These words from Isaiah and those uttered by John refer to the Lord's temptations and to His passion. Taking away sin and sicknesses, making Him subject to the iniquities of all, are similar in

1	Swedenborg here is following Schmidt's literal rendering of the Hebrew, the meaning of which is most obscure – '… that he might give wicked ones in His grave, and rich ones in His deaths'

per portare dolores et iniquitates. Primum itaque dicetur quid intelligitur per portare iniquitates et postea quid per tollere illas.

Per portare iniquitates non aliud intelligitur quam graves tentationes sustinere, tum sufferre ut Judaei cum Ipso facerent quemadmodum fecerunt cum Verbo, et quod Ipsum similiter tractarent, quia Ipse fuit Verbum. Fuit enim ecclesia, quae tunc erat apud Judaeos, prorsus devastata; et devastata erat per id quod perverterint omnia Verbi, adeo ut non aliquod verum residuum esset, quare nec agnoverunt Dominum. Hoc intellectum et significatum est per omnia passionis Domini. Similiter factum est cum prophetis, quia illi repraesentabant Dominum quoad Verbum et inde quoad ecclesiam, et Dominus fuit Ipse Propheta.

Quod Dominus fuerit Ipse Propheta, constare potest ex his locis –

Jesus dixit, Non est **propheta** minus honoratus quam in patria sua et in domo sua. Matt.13:57; Marc.6:4; Luc.4:24.

Jesus dixit, Non conveniens est **prophetam** interire extra Hierosolymam. Luc.13:33.

Dixerunt de Jesu, Ille **propheta** a Nazareth. Matt.21:11,26; Joh.7:40,41.

Cepit timor omnes, laudantes Deum, dicentes quod **propheta magnus** suscitatus sit inter illos. Luc.7:16.

Quod **propheta** excitaretur e medio fratrum, cujus verbis obedirent. Deut.18:15-19.

Quod simile factum sit cum prophetis, constat ex his quae nunc sequuntur –

Mandatum est Esaiae prophetae ut ecclesiae statum repraesentaret, per quod dissolveret saccum desuper lumbis suis, et calceum exueret desuper pede suo, ac iret nudus et discalceatus tres annos, in signum et prodigium, Esai.20:2,3.

Mandatum est Jeremiae prophetae ut repraesentaret statum ecclesiae, per quod emeret sibi cingulum et poneret super lumbis suis, quod per aquam non duceret, et absconderet illud in foramine petrae juxta Euphratem; quod post dies invenit corruptum, Jer.13:1-7.

Idem etiam propheta repraesentavit statum ecclesiae per id, quod non acciperet sibi uxorem in loco illo, nec intraret in domum luctus, neque abiret ad plangendum, nec intraret domum convivii, Jer.16:2,5,8.

meaning to carrying sorrows and iniquities. What is meant by carrying iniquities will therefore be stated first and what by taking them away after that.

Nothing else is meant by carrying iniquities than enduring severe temptations. Also meant is His allowing the Jews to behave towards Him in the way they did with the Word, and to maltreat Him in a similar way, since He was the Word. For the church, which existed at that time among the Jews, was completely destroyed. It had been destroyed as a result of their having distorted everything in the Word, to such an extent that not a truth was left; and therefore they did not accept the Lord. This is what is meant and indicated by every detail of the Lord's passion. The prophets experienced similar treatment, for they represented the Lord in respect of the Word and consequently of the church, and the Lord was Himself the Prophet.

The following places make it clear that the Lord was Himself the Prophet –

Jesus said, **A prophet** is not without honour except in his own country and in his own house. Matt.13:57; Mark 6:4; Luke 4:24.
Jesus said, It is not fitting for **a prophet** to perish outside of Jerusalem. Luke 13:33.
They said about Jesus, This is **the Prophet** from Nazareth. Matt.21:11,26; John 7:40,41.
Fear seized them all, praising God, saying that **a great prophet** has been raised up among us. Luke 7:16.
A prophet would be raised up from among their brothers, whose words they were to obey. Deut.18:15-19.

And from these that follow next it is clear that the prophets experienced similar treatment –

To represent the state of the church Isaiah the prophet was commanded to loose the sackcloth from over his loins and to remove the shoes from over his feet, and to go naked and barefoot for three years, as a sign and portent. Isa.20:2,3.
To represent the state of the church Jeremiah the prophet was commanded to buy a belt for himself and put it round his waist. He was told not to take it through the water but to hide it in a cleft of a rock beside the Euphrates. Days later he found it ruined. Jer.13:1-7.
The same prophet also represented the state of the church by not taking a wife in that place, nor entering the house of mourning or going away to wail, nor entering the house of a feast. Jer.16:2,5,8.

Mandatum est Ezechieli prophetae ut repraesentaret statum ecclesiae, per quod novaculam tonsorum traduceret super caput suum et super barbam suam, et postea divideret illa. Tertiam partem combureret in medio urbis, tertiam percuteret gladio, tertiam dispergeret in ventum, et parum ex illis alligaret in alis; tandem projiceret in medium ignis et combureret, Ezech.5:1-4. Eidem prophetae mandatum est ut repraesentaret statum ecclesiae, per quod faceret vasa migrationis et migraret in locum alium in oculis filiorum Israelis, et educeret vasa interdiu, et exiret in vespera per effossum parietem, ac obtegeret facies ut non videret terram, et quod sic prodigium esset domui Israelis. Et diceret propheta, Ecce ego prodigium vestrum; quemadmodum feci, sic fiet illis. Ezech.12:3-7,11.

Mandatum est Hoscheae prophetae ut repraesentaret statum ecclesiae, per quod acciperet sibi meretricem in uxorem. Et quoque accepit, et illa peperit ei tres filios, quorum unum vocavit Jisreel, alterum Non Miseranda, et tertium Non Populum, Hos.1:2-9. Ac iterum ei mandatum est ut abiret et amaret mulierem amatam socio et adulteram, quam etiam sibi comparavit per quindecim argenti, Hos.3:1,2.

Mandatum est Ezechieli prophetae ut repraesentaret statum ecclesiae, per quod sumeret laterem et sculperet super eo Hierosolymam, et poneret obsidionem, et daret vallum et aggerem contra illam, poneret sartaginem ferri inter se et urbem, et cubaret super latere sinistro, et postea super dextro, 390 dies, et dein dies 40. Tum sumeret tritica, hordea, lentes, milium, et zeas, et ex illis sibi faceret panem, quem tunc ederet, juxta mensuram. Et quoque quod faceret sibi placentam hordeorum cum stercore fimi hominis. Et quia hoc deprecatus est, mandatum est ut faceret illam cum excrementis bovis, Ezech.4:1-15.

Praeter quod prophetae etiam alia repraesentarent, ut Zedkiah, per cornua ferri quae sibi fecit, 1 Reg.22:11. Et alius propheta, per quod percuteretur et vulneraretur, ac cinerem super oculis mitteret, 1 Reg.20:35,37,38. In genere repraesentabant prophetae Verbum in sensu ultimo, qui est sensus literae, per tunicam pili, Sach.13:4, quare Elias tali tunica indutus fuit, ac cinctus cingulo coriaceo circum lumbos, 2 Reg.1:8, similiter Johannes Baptista, qui habebat indumentum ex pilis cameli, et cingulum coriaceum circum lumbum suum, et comedit locustam et mel agreste, Matt.3:4.

16 Miseranda: Miserandum *DD*
23 390 *DD¹*, *DD²*: trecentos et nonaginta *DD³*
23 et dein dies 40: *om DD¹*, *DD²*; et dein dies quadraginta *DD³*

To represent the state of the church Ezekiel the prophet was commanded to 5
pass a barber's razor over his head and beard and then divide the shaven-
off hairs. He was to burn a third in the middle of the city, strike a third with
a sword, scatter a third to the wind, and bind a small amount of them in the
skirts of his robe, finally casting some in the middle of a fire and burning
them. Ezek.5:1-4. To represent the state of the church the same prophet was
commanded to pack his bags¹ and move away to another place, before the
eyes of the children of Israel. He was to bring the bags out during the day-
time and go away in the evening through a wall that had been breached,
and to cover his face so that he could not see the land, and in doing this
be a portent for the house of Israel. And the prophet was to say, Behold, I
am your portent; as I have done, so will it be done to them. Ezek.12:3-7,11.
To represent the state of the church Hosea the prophet was commanded 6
to take to himself a prostitute as his wife. He did so and she bore him three
children, one of whom he called Jezreel, another No Pity,² and the third
Not My People. Hos.1:2-9. Another time he was commanded to go away
and love a woman who was loved by a companion and was an adulteress,
whom he also bought for fifteen pieces of silver. Hos.3:1,2.
To represent the state of the church Ezekiel the prophet was commanded 7
to take a brick and engrave Jerusalem on it, and lay siege against it, and
supply a rampart and mound against it, place an iron griddle between
himself and the city, and lie on his left side, and after that on his right, for
390 days and then 40 days. He was also told to take wheat, barley, lentils,
millet, and spelt, and make bread for himself, which he was to eat during
that time, by weight. Also, he was told to make for himself a barley cake
with human dung. But because he begged that he should not have to do
this he was commanded to make it with ox dung. Ezek.4:1-15.

In addition prophets also performed other representations,
such as when Zedekiah made for himself horns of iron, 1 Kings 22:11,
or another prophet who, when struck and wounded, put ash over
his eyes, 1 Kings 20:35,37,38. In general prophets represented the out- 8
ermost or literal sense of the Word, by wearing a garment made of
hair, Zech.13:4. Elijah therefore was clothed with a garment like that,
and had a leather belt round the waist, 2 Kings 1:8. In a similar way
John the Baptist wore a garment of camel's hair, and a leather belt
round his waist; and he ate locust and wild honey, Matt.3:4.

1 lit. *make vessels of migration*, ie prepare baggage to go away into exile
   ('the *vessels* or *baggage* would be such necessities as exiles carry in
   bundles on their shoulders' – GA Cooke, *The International Critical
   Commentary*, 1936)
2 This second child was a daughter

Ex his patet quod prophetae repraesentaverint statum ecclesiae et Verbum. Qui enim unum, etiam alterum repraesentat, nam ecclesia est ex Verbo, et secundum receptionem ejus vita et fide. Quare etiam per prophetas, in utroque Testamento ubi nominantur, significatur doctrina ecclesiae ex Verbo; per Dominum autem ut Maximum Prophetam significatur ipsa ecclesia et ipsum Verbum.

16 Status ecclesiae ex Verbo repraesentatus in prophetis, erat quod intelligitur per portare iniquitates et peccata populi. Quod ita sit, patet ex illis quae dicuntur de Esaia propheta, quod iret nudus et discalceatus tres annos, in signum et prodigium, Esai.20:3; de Ezechiele propheta, quod educeret vasa migrationis et obtegeret facies ut non videret terram, et quod sic prodigium esset domui Israelis, et quoque diceret, Ego prodigium vestrum, Ezech.12:6,11.

Quod hoc fuerit illis portare iniquitates, manifeste constat apud Ezechielem, cum ille jussus est cubare 390 dies et 40 dies super latere sinistro et dextro contra Hierosolymam, ac edere placentam hordeorum factam cum excrementis bovis, ubi haec etiam leguntur,

Tu, cuba super latere tuo sinistro, et pone **iniquitatem domus Israelis** super illud; numerum dierum, quibus cubabis super illo, **portabis iniquitatem** eorum. Ego namque dabo tibi annos iniquitatis eorum juxta numerum dierum 390 dies, ut **portes iniquitatem domus Israelis**. Quum vero absolveris hos, jacebis super latere tuo dextro secundum, ut **portes iniquitatem domus Jehudae** 40 dies. Ezech.4:4-6.

Quod propheta, per quod sic portaverit iniquitates domus Israelis et domus Jehudae, non abstulerit illas et sic expiaverit, sed modo repraesentaverit et monstraverit, patet a sequentibus ibi,

Sic, inquit Jehovah, comedent filii Israelis panem suum immundum, inter gentes quo depulsurus sum eos. Ecce Ego frangens baculum panis in Hierosolyma, ut careant pane et aqua, et desolentur

---

17-18 390 dies et 40 dies: 390 et 40 dies DD^1, DD^2; trecentos et nonaginta dies et quadraginta dies DD^3
24 390 DD^1, DD^2: trecentos et nonaginta DD^3
26 40 DD^1, DD^2: quadraginta DD^3

From all this it is evident that prophets represented the state of the church and they represented the Word, since he who represents the one represents the other as well. For the church derives its existence from the Word, and its life and faith are determined by the way in which it receives the Word. This being so, wherever in both Testaments they are mentioned, prophets also mean the church's teaching drawn from the Word; but when the Lord as the Greatest Prophet is mentioned the church and the Word themselves are meant.

16 The condition of the church springing from the Word was represented in the prophets, and that condition was what their carrying the iniquities and sins of the people stands for. The truth of this is evident from what is said about Isaiah the prophet, that he was to go naked and barefoot for three years, as a sign and portent, Isa.20:3, and about Ezekiel the prophet, that he was to bring out the bags he had packed[1] and to cover his face so that he could not see the land, and in so doing would be a portent for the house of Israel, and was also to tell them, I am your portent, Ezek.12:6,11.

It is made perfectly clear in Ezekiel that carrying their iniquities for them was the meaning of this portent, for where he is instructed to lie for 390 days and 40 days on his left side and on his right against Jerusalem and to eat a barley cake made with ox dung we also read,

You, lie on your left side and place **the iniquity of the house of Israel** upon it; the number of the days that you lie on it **you will carry their iniquity**. For I lay on you the years of their iniquity in accordance with the number of days, 390 days, **so that you may carry the iniquity of the house of Israel**. But when you have completed these you shall lie down a second time, on your right side, **so that you may carry the iniquity of the house of Judah** 40 days. Ezek.4:4-6.

The fact that in so carrying the iniquities of the house of Israel and the house of Judah the prophet did not take them away and so made atonement for them, but only represented them and pointed them out is evident from the following verses in that chapter,

Thus, Jehovah said, shall the children of Israel eat their bread unclean, among the nations where I shall drive them. Behold, I am breaking the rod of bread in Jerusalem, so that they may be in want of bread and

---

1 See page 65 note 1

vir et frater ejus, et contabescant propter iniquitatem eorum. Ezech.4:13,16,17.

Similiter cum idem propheta ostenderet se et diceret, Ecce ego prodigium vestrum, etiam dicitur,

Quemadmodum feci, sic fiet illis. Ezech.12:6,11.

Simile itaque intelligitur de Domino, ubi dicitur,

Morbos nostros Ille tulit; dolores nostros portavit. Jehovah incurrere fecit in Illum iniquitates omnium nostrum. Per scientiam Suam justificavit multos, eo quod iniquitates eorum Ipse portaverit, Esai.53:4,6,11,

ubi in toto capite agitur de passione Domini.
    Quod Ipse sicut Maximus Propheta repraesentaverit statum ecclesiae quoad Verbum, patet a singulis passionis Illius, ut, quod a Juda proditus fuerit; quod a principibus sacerdotum et a senioribus comprehensus et condemnatus sit; quod flagellaverint, spuerint in faciem, colaphos impegerint; quod caput calamo percusserint; quod imposuerint coronam ex spinis; quod vestimenta Ipsius diviserint et super tunicam jecerint sortem; quod crucifixerint; quod dederint Ipsi acetum ad bibendum; quod transfoderint latus; quod sepultus et tertio die resurrexerit.
    Quod a Juda proditus fuerit significabat quod a gente Judaica, apud quam tunc erat Verbum, nam Judas illam repraesentabat; quod a principibus sacerdotum et a senioribus comprehensus et condemnatus sit significabat quod ab omni illa ecclesia; quod flagellaverint, spuerint in faciem, colaphos impegerint, et caput calamo percusserint significabat quod similiter fecerint cum Verbo quoad Divina Vera ejus, quae omnia agunt de Domino; quod imposuerint coronam ex spinis significabat quod illa falsificaverint et adulteraverint; quod vestimenta diviserint et super tunicam jecerint sortem significabat quod omnia vera Verbi disperserint, sed non sensum ejus spiritualem – tunica Domini hoc Verbi significabat; quod

---

2   Ezech.4:13,16,17: Vers.13,16,17, in eodem capite *DD*
10   4,6,11 *DD*³: *om DD*¹, *DD*²
16   *om* flagellaverint, spuerint in faciem *DD*

water, and will be dismayed with one another, and waste away on account of their iniquity. Ezek.4:13,16,17.

It was similar when the prophet was to present himself and say, Behold, I am your portent; there it also says, 4

As I have done, so will it be done to them. Ezek.12:6,11.

The like is therefore meant regarding the Lord, where it says,

He has borne our sicknesses, He has carried our sorrows. Jehovah has imposed on Him the iniquities of us all. By His knowledge will He make many righteous, in that He Himself has carried their iniquities. Isa.53:4,6,11.

The subject in the whole of that chapter is the Lord's passion. 5
The fact that He Himself as the Greatest Prophet represented the state of the church in respect of the Word is evident from the details of His passion, such as He was betrayed by Judas; He was arrested and condemned by the chief priests and elders; they flogged Him, spat in His face, rained blows on Him; they beat His head with a reed; they placed a crown of thorns on Him; they divided His clothes and cast lots for His inner garment; they crucified Him; they gave Him vinegar to drink; they pierced His side; He was buried and rose again on the third day.

His betrayal by Judas was a sign of its being done by the 6 Jewish nation, with whom the Word existed at that time, for Judas represented them. His arrest and condemnation by the chief priests and elders was a sign of its being done by the whole of that church. Their flogging Him, spitting in His face, raining blows on Him, and beating His head with a reed was a sign of their behaving in a similar way towards Divine Truths in the Word, all of which relate to the Lord. Their placement of a crown of thorns on Him was a sign of their falsifying and adulterating those truths. Their division of His clothes and casting lots for the inner garment was a sign of their getting rid of all truths of the Word, though not its spiritual sense, the Lord's inner garment signifying this aspect of the Word. Their

crucifixerint significabat quod totum Verbum destruxerint et prophanaverint; quod praebuerint Ipsi acetum ad bibendum significabat quod mere falsificata et falsa, quare illud non bibit, et tunc dixit, Consummatum est; quod transfoderint latus significabat quod plane exstinxerint omne verum Verbi et omne bonum ejus; quod sepultus significabat rejectionem humani residui a matre; quod tertio die resurrexerit significabat glorificationem. Similia per illa significantur apud Prophetas et apud Davidem, ubi praedicta sunt.

Quapropter, postquam flagellatus et eductus portans spinosam coronam, et vestimentum purpureum a militibus impositum, dixit, Ecce Homo, Joh.19:1,5. Hoc dictum est quia per Hominem significatur ecclesia, per Filium enim Hominis significatur verum ecclesiae, ita Verbum.

Ex his nunc patet quod per portare iniquitates intelligatur, peccata contra Divina vera Verbi in Se repraesentare et effigiare. Quod Dominus talia sustinuerit et passus sit ut Filius Hominis, et non ut Filius Dei, videbitur in sequentibus; Filius Hominis enim significat Dominum quoad Verbum.

17 Aliquid nunc dicetur quid per tollere peccata intelligitur. Per tollere peccata simile intelligitur quod per redimere hominem et salvare illum. Nam Dominus in mundum venit ut salvari posset homo; absque Ipsius adventu nemo mortalium potuit reformari et regenerari, ita salvari. Sed hoc potest fieri postquam Dominus omnem potentiam diabolo, hoc est, inferno, ademerat, et Humanum Suum glorificaverat, hoc est, univerat Divino Patris Sui. Si haec non facta fuissent, nullus hominum potuisset recipere aliquod Divinum verum manens apud illum, et adhuc minus aliquod Divinum bonum; nam diabolus, cui prius potentia superior erat, e corde illa evulsisset.

Ex his patet quod Dominus per passionem crucis non abstulerit peccata, sed quod auferat illa, hoc est, removeat, apud illos qui credunt in Ipsum, vivendo secundum praecepta Ipsius, ut quoque Dominus docet apud Matthaeum,

Nolite putare quod venerim ad solvendum Legem et Prophetas. Quisquis solverit praeceptorum horum minimum, et docuerit ita homines, minimus vocabitur in regno caelorum; qui vero facit et docet, hic magnus vocabitur in regno caelorum. 5:17,19.

crucifixion of Him was a sign of their destruction and desecration of the entire Word. Their offering Him vinegar to drink was a sign of their presentation of that which was utterly falsified and false, which He therefore did not drink and at the same time said, It is finished. Their piercing of His side was a sign of their complete annihilation of everything true in the Word and everything good there. His burial was a sign of the casting aside of what remained of the human derived from His mother. His rising again on the third day was a sign of His glorification. And these details of His passion carry the same meanings in the places where they are foretold in the works of the Prophets and David.

Such being the meanings of them He said, after He had been flogged and led out wearing the crown of thorns and the purple robe which the soldiers had put on Him, Behold the Man! John 19:1,5. He said this because the church is meant by the Man; for the truth the church possesses – that is, the Word – is meant by the Son of Man.

From all this it is now evident that carrying iniquities means representing and portraying within Himself sins that go against the Divine truths of the Word. As will be seen in what follows, the Lord underwent and suffered such experiences as the Son of Man, not as the Son of God, for Son of Man means the Lord in respect of the Word.

17   Now something will be said about what taking sins away means. Taking sins away is similar in meaning to redeeming people and saving them. For the Lord came into the world so that people might be saved; without His coming no mortal at all could have been reformed and regenerated, and so saved. But this became possible after the Lord had deprived the devil, that is, hell, of all its power, and had glorified His Human, that is, united it to the Divine being of His Father. Had these things not been done no one at all would have been able to receive any form of Divine truth remaining with them, less still any form of Divine goodness, because the devil, whose power prior to that was stronger, would have torn it away from their hearts.

From this it is evident that by His passion on the cross the Lord has not taken sins away; rather, He takes them away, that is, removes them, in the case of those who believe in Him by leading lives in keeping with His commandments, as the Lord also teaches in Matthew,

Do not think I came to destroy the Law and the Prophets. Whoever relaxes the least of these commandments and teaches people to do the same will be called least in the kingdom of heaven; but the one who does do and teach them will be called great in the kingdom of the heavens. 5:17,19.

Quisque potest videre ex sola ratione, modo in aliqua illustratione sit, quod peccata non possint auferri homini nisi quam per paenitentiam actualem, quae est, quod homo videat sua peccata, ac Domini opem imploret, et desistat ab illis.
5 Aliud videre, credere, et docere, non est ex Verbo, nec est ex sana ratione, sed ex cupiditate et prava voluntate, quae sunt proprium hominis, ex quo infatuatur intelligentia.

3 Reason alone enables everyone to see, provided they are to a degree enlightened, that sins cannot be taken away from people unless they truly repent, that is, see their sins, beg for the Lord's help, and refrain from them. Seeing, believing and teaching anything other than this does not spring from the Word, nor does it do so from sound reason but from the longings and perverse intent composing the human self, which muddles the power of understanding.

Quod imputatio meriti Domini non aliud sit quam remissio peccatorum post paenitentiam

18 In ecclesia creditur quod Dominus missus sit a Patre ut expiaret pro genere humano, et quod hoc factum sit per impletionem Legis et per passionem crucis, et quod sic sustulerit damnationem et satisfecerit, et quod absque illa expiatione, satisfactione, et propitiatione, genus humanum aeterna morte periisset; et hoc ex justitia, quae ab aliquibus etiam vocatur vindicativa. Verum est quod absque adventu Domini in mundum omnes periissent; sed quomodo intelligendum est quod Dominus impleverit omnia Legis, videatur supra in suo articulo, et cur passus est crucem, etiam supra in suo, ex quibus videri potest quod non fuerit ex aliqua justitia vindicativa, quia haec non est attributum Divinum. Attributa Divina sunt justitia, amor, misericordia, et bonum, et Deus est ipsa justitia, ipse amor, ipsa misericordia, et ipsum bonum; et ubi haec sunt, non est aliquid vindictae, ita non justitia vindicativa.

Quoniam impletio Legis et passio crucis hactenus a multis non aliter intellectae sunt quam quod Dominus per illa bina satisfecerit pro humano genere, et ei damnationem praevisam aut destinatam abstulerit, ex nexu et simul ex principio quod homo salvetur ex sola fide quod ita sit, sequutum est dogma de imputatione meriti Domini, accipiendo illa duo, quae fuerunt meriti Domini, pro satisfactione. Sed hoc cadit ex illis quae dicta sunt de impletione Legis a Domino et de passione crucis Ipsius; et simul tunc videri potest quod imputatio meriti sit vox nullius rei nisi per illam intelligatur remissio peccatorum post paenitentiam. Nam non aliquid Domini potest imputari homini, sed potest addicari salus a Domino postquam homo paenitentiam egerat, hoc est, postquam viderat et agnoverat sua peccata et dein desistat ab illis, et hoc ex Domino. Tunc

The imputation of the Lord's merit is nothing other than the forgiveness of sins following repentance

18   In the church the belief is that the Lord was sent by the Father to make expiation or atonement on behalf of the human race; that He achieved this through fulfilling the Law and suffering the cross, as a result of which He took away damnation and made satisfaction; that without His making that expiation, satisfaction, and propitiation, the human race would have perished in eternal death, and that it would have done so because of the demands of justice or righteousness, which some also term vindictive justice. It is right that without the Lord's coming into the world everyone would have perished, but from the section above about how the Lord's fulfilling everything in the Law should be understood, also the section about why He suffered the cross, it can be seen that it was not because of any kind of vindictive justice, for the latter is not a Divine attribute. Justice, love, mercy and goodness are Divine attributes, and God is justice itself, love itself, mercy itself, and goodness itself; and where these are present no vindictiveness at all exists, nor thus any vindictive justice.

Many up to now have taken fulfilling the Law and suffering the cross to mean nothing other than this, that through these two actions the Lord made satisfaction for the human race and took away from it the damnation that had been foreseen or else destined. This linking together of the two, and at the same time the assumption that a person is saved by merely believing it to be so, have led on to the doctrine of the imputation of Christ's merit, by the two actions that constituted Christ's merit being taken to be a satisfaction. But because of what has been stated about the fulfilment of the Law by the Lord and about His passion on the cross, that doctrine falls apart; and at the same time it may be seen that the imputation of merit is an expression that has no substance to it unless it is taken to mean the forgiveness of sins following repentance. For no attribute that is the Lord's can be imputed or made over to a person, but salvation from the Lord may be granted to people after they have repented, that is, have seen and acknowledged their sins and then refrain from them,

2

addicatur ei salus eo modo, quod homo non ex suo merito et ex propria justitia salvetur, sed ex Domino, qui solus pugnavit et vicit inferna, et qui postea etiam solus pugnat pro homine et vincit inferna pro illo. Haec sunt meritum et justitia Domini, et haec nusquam possunt imputari homini, nam si imputarentur, forent meritum et justitia Domini appropriata homini sicut ejus, et hoc nusquam fit nec fieri potest. Si imputatio dabilis foret, potuisset homo impaenitens et impius imputare sibi meritum Domini, et ex eo cogitare se justificatum, quod tamen foret conspurcare sanctum prophanis, et prophanare nomen Domini; nam foret tenere cogitationem in Domino et voluntatem in inferno, et tamen voluntas est omne hominis. Est fides **Dei** et est fides hominis. Fidem **Dei** habent qui paenitentiam agunt, fidem autem hominis qui non paenitentiam agunt et usque de imputatione cogitant; ac fides Dei est fides viva, at fides hominis est fides mortua.

Quod Ipse Dominus et discipuli Ipsius praedicaverint paenitentiam ac remissionem peccatorum, constat ex his sequentibus,

Jesus incepit praedicare et dicere, **Paeniteat vos**, appropinquavit enim regnum caelorum. Matt.4:17.

Johannes dixit, Facite fructus dignos **paenitentia**. Jamjam securis ad radicem arborum jacet. Omnis arbor non faciens fructus bonum exscinditur et in ignem conjicitur. Luc.3:8,9.

Jesus dixit, Nisi **paenitentiam** egeritis, omnes peribitis. Luc.13:3,5.

Jesus praedicans evangelium regni Dei, dicens, Impletum est tempus, et appropinquavit regnum Dei; **paenitentiam** agite, et credite evangelio. Marc.1:14,15.

Jesus emisit discipulos, qui exeuntes praedicarunt ut **paenitentiam** agerent. Marc.6:12.

Jesus dixit ad apostolos quod illos oporteat praedicare in nomine Ipsius **paenitentiam** et **remissionem peccatorum**, in omnibus gentibus, incipiendo a Hierosolyma. Luc.24:47.

Johannes praedicavit baptisma **paenitentiae** in **remissionem peccatorum**. Luc.3:3; Marc.1:4.

Per baptisma intelligitur lavatio spiritualis, quae est a peccatis, et vocatur regeneratio. Describitur paenitentia et remissio peccatorum a Domino ita apud Johannem,

22 Johannes DD^2 DD^3: Jesus DD^1

and doing so in reliance on the Lord. The following then are the circumstances in which that salvation is granted to them – that they are saved not by virtue of any merit or righteousness of their own but of the Lord's, who has fought and conquered the hells alone, and who subsequently, and again alone, fights and conquers the hells on their behalf. These are the Lord's merit and righteousness. They can never be imputed to people, for if they were they would be the Lord's merit and righteousness made over to them as their own, and this is never done nor can it be. Were imputation possible people who are unrepentant and ungodly would be able to impute the Lord's merit to themselves and consequently think they have been made righteous. But this would be to defile what is holy with profanities and to profane the Lord's name, for it would mean that their thought rested in the Lord and their will or intention in hell. Yet the will constitutes the all of a person. There is faith that is the faith of **God**, and there is faith that is the faith of man. Those who are repentant possess the faith of **God**, but those who are not, yet have thoughts about imputation, possess the faith of man. And the faith of God is a living faith, whereas the faith of man is a dead faith. 3

The Lord Himself and His disciples preached repentance and the forgiveness of sins, as is clear from the following – 4

Jesus began to preach and say, **Repent**, for the kingdom of heaven is at hand. Matt.4:17.
John said, Bear fruits worthy of **repentance**. Already the axe lies at the root of the trees. Every tree not bearing good fruit is cut down and thrown into the fire. Luke 3:8,9.
Jesus said, Unless you **repent** you will all perish. Luke 13:3,5.
Jesus came preaching the gospel of the kingdom of God, saying, The time is fulfilled, and the kingdom of God is at hand; **repent**, and believe the gospel. Mark 1:14,15.
Jesus sent out the disciples, who as they went preached that people should **repent**. Mark 6:12.
Jesus said to the apostles that they should preach in His name **repentance** and **the forgiveness of sins**, among all nations, beginning from Jerusalem. Luke 24:47.
John preached a baptism of **repentance** for **the forgiveness of sins**. Luke 3:3; Mark 1:4.

A spiritual washing is meant by baptism, which is a washing from sins and is termed regeneration. Repentance and the forgiveness of sins by the Lord are described in the following way in John, 5

In propria venit, sed proprii Ipsum non receperunt. Quotquot vero receperunt, dedit illis potestatem ut filii Dei essent, credentibus in nomen Ipsius, qui non ex sanguinibus, neque ex voluntate carnis, neque ex voluntate viri, sed ex Deo nati sunt. 1:11-13.

5   Per proprios intelliguntur qui tunc ab ecclesia, ubi erat Verbum; per filios Dei, et credentes in nomen Ipsius, intelliguntur qui in Dominum credunt et qui Verbo credunt; per sanguines intelliguntur falsificationes Verbi et confirmationes falsi per illud; voluntas carnis est proprium voluntarium hominis,
10 quod in se est malum; voluntas viri est proprium intellectuale hominis, quod in se est falsum; nati a Deo sunt qui a Domino regenerati sunt. Ex his patet quod illi salventur qui in bono amoris et in veris fidei sunt a Domino et non qui in proprio.

He came to His own, but His own people did not receive Him. Yet as many as received Him, to them He gave power to become children of God, to those believing in His name, who were born not of blood, nor of the will of the flesh, nor of the will of man, but of God. 1:11-13.

His own people means those who at that time belonged to the church, where the Word existed. Children of God and those believing in His name mean those who believe in the Lord and believe the Word. Blood means falsification of the Word and the use of the Word to justify what is false. The will of the flesh is a person's own willpower, which in itself is bad, and the will of man is a person's own power of understanding, which in itself is false. Born of God are those who have been regenerated by the Lord. From all this it is evident that they are saved who are governed by the goodness of love and the truths of faith which they derive from the Lord and not by what is their own.

Quod Dominus quoad Divinum Humanum dicatur Filius Dei et quoad Verbum dicatur Filius Hominis

19 In ecclesia non aliud scitur quam quod Filius Dei sit altera Persona Divinitatis, distincta a Persona Patris; inde est fides de Filio Dei nato ab aeterno. Hoc quia universaliter receptum est, et de Deo, non data est copia ac venia cogitandi de eo ex aliquo intellectu, ne quidem ita, Quid est nasci ab aeterno? Nam qui cogitat de eo ex intellectu, omnino secum dicet, Hoc transcendit, sed usque dico quia dicunt, et credo quia credunt. At sciant quod non sit Filius ab aeterno sed quod sit Dominus ab aeterno. Dum scitur quid Dominus, et quid Filius, potest etiam ex intellectu cogitare de Deo triuno, et non prius.

Quod Humanum Domini conceptum a Jehovah Patre et natum a Maria virgine sit Filius Dei, patet manifeste ex his sequentibus – Apud Lucam,

Missus est angelus Gabriel a Deo in urbem Galilaeae, cui nomen Nazareth, ad virginem desponsatam viro cui nomen Joseph, e domo Davidis; nomen autem virginis, Maria. Quum ingressus est angelus ad illam, dixit, Salve, gratiam consequuta, Dominus tecum est; benedicta inter mulieres. Illa videns conturbata est super verbo ejus, et cogitavit quanta esset salutatio illa. Sed dixit angelus illi, Ne timeto, Maria; invenisti gratiam apud Deum. Ecce concipies et paries Filium, et vocabis nomen Ipsius Jesum. Hic erit magnus et **Filius Altissimi** vocabitur. Maria vero dixit ad angelum, Quomodo fiet hoc, quoniam virum non cognosco? Cui respondens angelus dixit, **Spiritus sanctus veniet super te,** et **virtus Altissimi obumbrabit** te; unde etiam quod nascitur ex te **sanctum,** vocabitur **Filius Dei.** 1:26-35.

In respect of His Divine Humanity the Lord is called Son of God and in respect of the Word He is called Son of Man

19   Within the church people know nothing different from this, that the Son of God is the second Person of the Godhead, distinct from the Person of the Father; and this has led to a belief in a Son of God born from eternity. Because this notion has been accepted everywhere and is about God Himself no one has been given the opportunity or leave to think about it with any degree of understanding, not even to think, What does being born from eternity mean? For a person who does think with understanding about it will say, This is beyond me; nevertheless I repeat it because others do and believe it because they do. But let these people know it is not the Son who exists from eternity but the Lord. Once they know what is meant by the Lord and what by the Son, they are then also able to think with understanding about a triune God, but not before.

The Son of God is the Lord's Human, conceived from Jehovah, the Father, and born from Mary, a virgin. This is plainly evident from the following places – In Luke,   2

The angel Gabriel was sent from God to a city of Galilee named Nazareth, to a virgin betrothed to a man whose name was Joseph, of the house of David; and the virgin's name was Mary. When the angel came into her presence he said, Greetings, you who have obtained favour, the Lord is with you; blessed are you among women. Seeing him she was troubled at his saying and thought what kind of greeting this might be. But the angel said to her, Do not be afraid, Mary; you have found favour with God. Behold, you will conceive and bear a Son, and you will call His name Jesus. He will be great and will be called **the Son of the Most High**. But Mary said to the angel, How will this come about, since I do not know a man? Answering her the angel said, **The Holy Spirit will come upon you**, and **the power of the Most High will overshadow** you; therefore also **that holy thing** born from you will be called **the Son of God**. 1:26-35.

Dicitur hic, Concipies et paries Filium, Hic erit magnus et vocabitur **Filius Altissimi**, ac iterum, Quod nascetur ex te sanctum, vocabitur **Filius Dei**, ex quo patet quod Humanum conceptum a Deo et natum a Maria virgine sit quod vocatur
5 Filius Dei. Apud Esaiam,

> Dat Dominus Ipse vobis signum: Ecce virgo concipiet et pariet **Filium**, et vocabit nomen Ipsius **Deus nobiscum**. 7:14.

Quod Filius natus a virgine et conceptus a Deo sit qui vocabitur Deus nobiscum, ita qui est Filius Dei, patet. Quod
10 sit, etiam confirmatur apud Matthaeum 1:22,23. Apud Esaiam,

> **Puer** natus est nobis, **Filius** datus est nobis, super cujus humero principatus; et vocabit nomen Ipsius, Mirabilis, Consiliarius, Deus, Heros, **Pater aeternitatis**, Princeps pacis. 9:5,6.

Similiter hic, nam dicitur, Puer natus est nobis, Filius datus est
15 nobis, qui non est Filius ab aeterno sed Filius natus in mundo, quod etiam patet a Prophetae verbis, vers.6 ibi, et a Gabrielis angeli verbis ad Mariam, Luc.1:32,33, quae similia sunt. Apud Davidem,

> Annuntiabo de statuto. Jehovah dixit, **Filius Meus Tu**; Ego hodie
20 > genui Te. Osculamini **Filium**, ne irascatur et pereatis in via. Ps.2:7,12.

Hic nec intelligitur Filius ab aeterno sed Filius natus in mundo, nam est propheticum de Domino venturo, quare vocatur statutum de quo Jehovah annuntiavit Davidi. Hodie non est ab aeterno sed est in tempore. Apud Davidem,

25 > Ponam in mari manum Ipsius. Ille vocabit Me, Pater Meus Tu. Ego **Primogenitum** dabo Ipsum. Ps.89:26-28,37.

In toto hoc psalmo agitur de Domino venturo, quare intelligitur Ipse, qui vocabit Jehovam Patrem Suum et qui erit Primogenitus, ita qui est Filius Dei.
30   Pariter alibi, ubi vocatur Virga e trunco Jishaji, Esai.11:1,2,10; Germen Davidis, Jer.23:5,6; Semen Mulieris,

---

31   11:1,2,10: 11:1,2,20 *DD¹*, *DD²*; 11:1 *DD³*

Here it says, You will conceive and bear a Son; He will be great and will be called **the Son of the Most High**; and in addition it says, That holy thing born from you will be called **the Son of God**. From this it is evident that the Human conceived from God and born from Mary the virgin is what is called the Son of God. In Isaiah,

The Lord Himself gives you a sign: Behold, a virgin will conceive and bear **a Son**, and will call His name **God with us**. 7:14.

Clearly the Son born from a virgin and conceived from God is the one who was going to be called God with us, and so who is the Son of God. There is also confirmation of this in Matthew 1:22,23. In Isaiah,

To us **a Boy** is born, to us **a Son** is given, upon whose shoulder is the government; and He will call His name Wonderful, Counsellor, God, Mighty One, **Father of Eternity**, Prince of Peace. 9:6,7.

Much the same occurs here, for it says, To us a Boy is born, to us a Son is given, who is not a Son from eternity but a Son born in the world, as is evident from the prophet's words in verse 7 of that chapter, and from the angel Gabriel's words to Mary, in Luke 1:32,33, which are similar to the prophet's. In David,

I will tell of the decree: Jehovah has said, **You** are **My Son**; today I have begotten You. Kiss **the Son**, lest He be angry and you perish on the way. Ps.2:7,12.

Nor is a Son from eternity meant here but a Son born in the world, for here is a prophecy regarding the Lord who was to come, and therefore it is called a decree that Jehovah told David about. Today does not mean from eternity but in time. In David,

I will set His hand in the sea. He will cry to Me, You are My Father. I will make Him **the Firstborn**. Ps.89:25-27,36.

The Lord who is going to come is the subject in the whole of this psalm, and therefore it is He who is meant by the one who will call Jehovah His Father and will be the Firstborn, and so who is the Son of God.
    The same is so in other places, where He is called Shoot from the trunk of Jesse, Isa.11:1,2,10; Branch of David, Jer.23:5,6; Seed

Gen.3:15; Unigenitus, Gen.22:2; Joh.1:18; Sacerdos in aeternum, et Dominus, Ps.110:4,5.

    In Ecclesia Judaica per Filium Dei intellectus est Messias quem exspectaverunt, de quo sciebant quod nasceretur in Bethlechem. Quod per Filium Dei ab illis intellectus sit Messias, patet ex his locis – Apud Johannem,

Dixit Petrus, Credimus et agnoscimus quod Tu sis **Christus, Filius Dei** viventis. 6:69.

Apud eundem,

Tu es **Christus, Filius Dei**, qui in mundum venturus est. 11:27.

Apud Matthaeum,

Princeps sacerdotum interrogavit Jesum num esset **Christus, Filius Dei**. Jesus dixit, Ego sum. 26:63; Marc.14:62.

Apud Johannem,

Haec scripta sunt ut credatis quod Jesus sit **Christus, Filius Dei**. 20:31; tum Marc.1:1.

Christus est vox Graeca et significat Unctum, similiter Messias in lingua Hebraea, quare dicit Johannes,

Invenimus Messiam, quod est, si interpreteris, **Christus**. 1:42.

Et alibi,

Dixit mulier, Scio quod **Messias** veniat, qui dicitur **Christus**. 4:25.

    Quod Lex et Prophetae, seu totum Verbum Veteris Testamenti, sit de Domino, in primo articulo indicatum est, quare non alius per Filium Dei venturum potest intelligi quam Humanum quod Dominus suscepit in mundo. Ex quo

---

1   Gen.22:2; Joh.1:18: Gen.1:18 *DD*[1], *DD*[2]; Joh.1:18 *DD*[3]

of the Woman, Gen.3:15; Only begotten, Gen.22:2; John 1:18; Priest for ever, and Lord, Ps.110:4,5.

In the Jewish Church they took Son of God to mean the Messiah they waited for, whom they knew was to be born in Bethlehem. The fact that they took Son of God to mean the Messiah is evident from the following places – In John, 8

Peter said, We have believed and come to know that You are **the Christ, the Son of** the living **God**. 6:69.

In the same gospel,

You are **the Christ, the Son of God**, who is coming into the world. 11:27.

In Matthew,

The high priest asked Jesus whether He was **the Christ, the Son of God**. Jesus said, I am. 26:63; Mark 14:62.[1]

In John,

These things have been written that you may believe that Jesus is **the Christ, the Son of God**. 20:31; also Mark 1:1.

Christ is a Greek word which means Anointed, as does Messiah in the Hebrew language, and this is why John[2] says, 9

We have found the Messiah, that is, when translated, **the Christ**. 1:41.

And in another place,

The woman said, I know that **the Messiah** is coming, He who is called **Christ**. 4:25.

It was shown in the first section that the Law and the Prophets – that is, the entire Old Testament Word – has to do with the Lord, and therefore none other can be meant by the Son of God who was to come than the Human which the Lord took upon Himself in the

---

1   The words *I am* do not occur at this point in Matthew, only at Mark 14:62
2   ie John's Gospel. The words quoted were spoken by Andrew

sequitur quod hoc intellectum sit per Filium a Jehovah e caelo dictum, cum baptizabatur,

Hic est **Filius Meus dilectus**, *in quo complacuit Mihi.* Matt.3:17; Marc.1:11; Luc.3:22;

nam Humanum Ipsius baptizabatur. Et quando transformatus,

Hic est **Filius Meus dilectus**, *in quo Mihi complacuit; Ipsum audite.* Matt.17:5; Marc.9:7; Luc.9:35.

Tum etiam alibi, ut Matt.8:29; 14:33; 16:16; 27:43,54; Marc.3:11; 15:39; Joh.1:18,34,50; 3:18; 5:25; 10:36; 11:4.

20 Quoniam per Filium Dei intelligitur Dominus quoad Humanum quod in mundo suscepit, quod est Divinum Humanum, patet quid intelligitur per quod Dominus toties dixerit, quod **missus sit a Patre in mundum**, et per quod **exiverit a Patre**. Per quod missus sit a Patre in mundum intelligitur quod a Jehovah Patre conceptus sit. Quod non aliud per mitti et missum a Patre intelligatur, constat ex omnibus locis ubi etiam dicitur quod voluntatem Patris et opera Ipsius faceret, quae erant quod vinceret inferna, glorificaret Humanum, doceret Verbum, et novam ecclesiam instauraret, quae non potuerunt fieri nisi quam per Humanum conceptum a Jehovah et natum a virgine, hoc est, nisi Deus Homo factus sit. Evolve loca ubi dicitur **mitti** et **missus**, et videbis, ut Matt.10:40; 15:24; Marc.9:37; Luc.4:43; 9:48; 10:16; Joh.3:17,34; 4:34; 5:23,24,36-38; 6:29,39,40,44,57; 7:16,18,28,29; 8:16,18,29,42; 9:4; 10:36; 11:42; 12:44,45,49; 13:20; 14:24; 15:21; 16:5; 17:3,8,21,23,25; 20:21. Tum etiam loca ubi Dominus Jehovam appellat Patrem.

21 Multi hodie non aliter cogitant de Domino quam sicut de vulgari homine, sui simili, quia solum de Humano Ipsius et non simul de Divino, cum tamen Divinum et Humanum Ipsius non separari possunt,

Est enim Dominus Deus et Homo, ac Deus et Homo in Domino non sunt duo sed una Persona, ita prorsus una sicut anima et corpus sunt unus homo,

---

8   16:16; 27:43,54: 18:43,54 *DD¹, DD²*; 27:43,54 *DD³*
24 10:36; 11:42: 11:41,42 *DD*

world. From this it follows that this Human was meant, when He was baptized, by the Son in the words spoken by Jehovah from heaven,

This is **My beloved Son**, in whom I am well pleased. Matt.3:17; Mark 1:11; Luke 3:22;

for it was His Human that was baptized. And when He was transfigured,

This is **My beloved Son**, in whom I am well pleased; hear Him. Matt.17:5; Mark 9:7; Luke 9:35.

And His Human is meant in other places as well, such as Matt.8:29; 14:33; 16:16; 27:43,54; Mark3:11; 15:39; John 1:18,34,49; 3:18; 5:25; 10:36; 11:4. Since Son of God means the Human which the Lord took upon Himself in the world, that is, the Divine Human, the meaning of what the Lord said so many times – that **He was sent by the Father into the world** and that **He came forth from the Father** – is quite plain. He was sent by the Father into the world means that He was conceived from Jehovah the Father. The truth that nothing other is meant by being sent and having been sent from the Father is clear from all the places where it also says that He was doing the will of the Father and His works. These were His conquest of the hells, glorification of His Human, teaching of the Word, and establishment of a new church, none of which could have been accomplished except by a Human conceived from Jehovah and born from a virgin, that is, by God made Man. This you will recognize if you turn to the places where the expressions **being sent** and **having been sent** occur, such as Matt.10:40; 15:24; Mark 9:37; Luke 4:43; 9:48; 10:16; John 3:17,34; 4:34; 5:23,24,36-38; 6:29,39,40,44,57; 7:16,18,28,29; 8:16,18,29,42; 9:4; 10:36; 11:42; 12:44,45,49; 13:20; 14:24; 15:21; 16:5; 17:3,8,21,23,25; 20:21. And also the places where the Lord calls Jehovah, Father.

21   Many at the present day have no idea of the Lord other than that He was an ordinary human being like themselves, because they think only of His Humanity and not at the same time of His Divinity. Yet His Divinity and Humanity are inseparable, for, as accords with the teaching that exists in the whole Christian world, which is derived from the Councils of the Church and is called the Athanasian faith and teaching,

The Lord is God and Man, and God and Man in the Lord are not two but one Person, completely so, even as soul and body together are one in a human being.

secundum doctrinam in toto Christiano orbe, quae est ex Conciliis, ac Doctrina Fidei Athanasianae vocatur. Ne itaque homo posthac cogitatione separet Divinum et Humanum in Domino, legat quaeso illa quae ex Luca supra allata sunt, tum etiam haec apud Matthaeum –

Jesu Christi nativitas talis est: Desponsata matre Ipsius Josepho, antequam illi congrederentur, inventa est in utero habens, ex **Spiritu Sancto**. Et Josephus sponsus ejus, quum justus esset et non vellet illam diffamare, voluit clam dimittere illam. Verum cum ille haec cogitaret, ecce angelus Domini in somnio apparuit illi, dicens, Joseph, fili Davidis, ne timeas accipere Mariam sponsam tuam, nam quod in illa natum, ex **Spiritu Sancto** est; et pariet Filium et vocabis nomen Ipsius Jesum. Ille salvabit populum Suum a peccatis eorum. Et expergefactus Josephus a somno, fecit sicut praecepit illi angelus Domini, et accepit sponsam suam. **At non cognovit illam**, usque dum peperit Filium suum primogenitum; et vocavit nomen Ipsius Jesum. 1:18-25.

Ex his, et ex illis quae apud Lucam de nativitate Domini scripta sunt, et ex supra allatis, constat quod Filius Dei sit Jesus conceptus a Jehovah Patre et natus a virgine Maria, de quo omnes Prophetae et Lex usque ad Johannem prophetarunt.
22 Qui novit quid apud Dominum Filius Dei significat et quid apud Ipsum Filius Hominis, ille plura arcana Verbi videre potest, nam Dominus nunc Se vocat Filium, nunc Filium Dei, nunc Filium Hominis, ubivis secundum rem de qua agitur. Cum agitur de Divinitate Ipsius, de Uno cum Patre, de Divina Potestate, de Fide in Ipsum, de Vita ab Ipso, tunc vocat Se Filium et Filium Dei, ut Joh.5:17-26, et alibi. Ubi autem agitur de Passione, de Judicio, de Adventu, et in genere de Redemptione, Salvatione, Reformatione, Regeneratione, tunc vocat Se Filium Hominis, causa est quia Ipse quoad Verbum tunc intelligitur. Dominus variis nominibus insignitur in Verbo Veteris Testamenti; nominatur ibi Jehovah, Jah, Dominus, Deus, Dominus Jehovih, Jehovah Zebaoth, Deus Israelis, Sanctus Israelis, Fortis Jacobi, Schaddai, Petra, tum Creator, Formator, Salvator, Redemptor, ubivis secundum rem de qua agitur. In Verbo Novi Testamenti similiter, ubi nominatur Jesus, Christus, Dominus, Deus, Filius Dei, Filius

Therefore to prevent from now on the separation in people's minds of the Divine and the Human within the Lord, let them please read the words quoted above from Luke[1], as well as these in Matthew –

The birth of Jesus Christ is like this: When His mother had been betrothed to Joseph, before they came together, she was found to be with child from **the Holy Spirit**. And Joseph her husband, being a righteous man and not willing to put her to shame, was willing to divorce her privately. But while he was contemplating these things, behold, an angel of the Lord appeared to him in a dream, saying, Joseph, son of David, do not fear to take Mary as your wife, for that which is born in her is from **the Holy Spirit**; and she will bear a Son, and you shall call His name Jesus. He will save His people from their sins. And when Joseph woke from sleep he did as the angel of the Lord commanded him, and took his wife. **But he did not know her** until she had given birth to her firstborn Son; and he called His name Jesus. 1:18-25.

From these words and from those used in Luke regarding the Lord's birth, and those from other places quoted above, it is clear that the Son of God is Jesus, who was conceived from Jehovah the Father and born from the virgin Mary, and about whom all the Prophets and the Law until John made prophecies.

22 People who know what the term Son of God relating to the Lord means, and what Son of Man relating to Him means, are able to perceive very many arcana contained in the Word. For at one point the Lord refers to Himself as the Son, another as the Son of God, and another as the Son of Man, depending in every instance on whatever the subject may be. When the subject is His Divinity, Oneness with the Father, Divine Power, Belief in Him, or Life from Him, He refers to Himself as the Son and the Son of God, as in John 5:17-26, and other places. But when the subject is His Suffering, Judgment, and Coming, or in general Redemption, Salvation, Reformation, and Regeneration, He refers to Himself as the Son of Man, for the reason that then the Lord in respect of the Word is meant. In the Old Testament Word various titles are used in reference to the Lord. Titles used there include Jehovah, Jah, Lord, God, Lord Jehovih, Jehovah Zebaoth, God of Israel, Holy One of Israel, Mighty One of Jacob, Shaddai, Rock, as well as Creator, He who forms, Saviour, Redeemer, depending in every instance on whatever the subject may be. Titles used in a similar way in the New Testament Word are Jesus, Christ, Lord, God, Son of God,

---

1   ie Luke 1:28-35 on page 81

Hominis, Propheta, Agnus, et quoque aliter, etiam ubivis secundum rem de qua ibi agitur.

23   Ex quo Dominus vocatur Filius Dei, hactenus dictum est; nunc ex quo Dominus vocatur Filius Hominis, dicetur. Vocatur Filius Hominis ubi agitur de Passione, de Judicio, de Adventu, et in genere ubi de Redemptione, Salvatione, Reformatione, et Regeneratione. Causa est quia Filius Hominis est Dominus quoad Verbum; ac Ipse ut Verbum passus est, judicat, venit in mundum, redimit, salvat, reformat, et regenerat. Quod ita sit, ex nunc sequentibus constare potest.

24   **Quod Dominus dicatur Filius Hominis cum agitur de passione**, constat ex his –

Jesus dixit ad discipulos, Ecce ascendimus Hierosolymam, et **Filius Hominis** tradetur principibus sacerdotum et scribis, qui condemnabunt Ipsum mortis, et tradent Ipsum gentibus. Et flagellabunt Ipsum, et exspuent in Ipsum, et occident Ipsum; tertia tamen die resurget. Marc.10:33,34.

Similiter alibi, ubi praedicit passionem Suam, ut Matt.20:18,19; Marc.8:31; Luc.9:22.

Jesus dixit ad discipulos, Ecce adest hora, et **Filius Hominis** tradetur in manus peccatorum. Matt.26:45.
Angelus dixit ad mulieres venientes ad monumentum, Mementote quod loquutus est vobis, quod oporteat **Filium Hominis** prodi in manus hominum peccatorum, et crucifigi, et tertia die resurgere. Luc.24:6,7.

Quod Dominus tunc Se vocaverit Filium Hominis, est quia passus est Sibi fieri similiter, quemadmodum illi fecerunt cum Verbo, ut multis supra ostensum est.

25   **Quod Dominus dicatur Filius Hominis cum agitur de judicio**, constat ex his –

Quando venerit **Filius Hominis** in gloria Sua, tunc sedebit super throno gloriae Suae, ac statuet oves a dextris et hircos a sinistris. Matt.25:31,33.
Quando sedebit **Filius Hominis** super throno gloriae Suae, judicaturus duodecim tribus Israelis. Matt.19:28.
Venturus est **Filius Hominis** in gloria Patris Sui, et tunc reddet unicuique secundum facta ejus. Matt.16:27.

Son of Man, Prophet, Lamb, and still more, again depending in every instance on whatever the subject may be.

23 Up to this point the reasons why the Lord is called the Son of God have been presented; now the reasons why the Lord is called the Son of Man will be stated. He is called the Son of Man where the subject is His Suffering, Judgment, and Coming, and in general where it is Redemption, Salvation, Reformation, and Regeneration. The reason why He is the Son of Man is that this title denotes the Lord in respect of His being the Word; and it is He, as the Word, who has suffered, judges, comes into the world, redeems, saves, reforms, and regenerates. The truth of all this becomes clear from what follows immediately below.

24 **The Lord is called the Son of Man when His suffering is the subject.** This is clear from these places –

Jesus said to the disciples, Behold, we are going up to Jerusalem, and **the Son of Man** will be delivered to the chief priests and the scribes, who will condemn Him to death and deliver Him to the gentiles. And they will scourge Him, and spit on Him, and kill Him; but on the third day He will rise again. Mark 10:33,34.

The like occurs in other places, where He foretells His suffering, for example, Matt.20:18,19; Mark 8:31: Luke 9:22.

Jesus said to the disciples, Behold, the hour is at hand, and **the Son of Man** will be delivered into the hands of sinners. Matt.26:45.
The angel said to the women coming to the tomb, Remember what He told you, that **the Son of Man** must be betrayed into the hands of sinful men, and be crucified, and on the third day rise again. Luke 24:6,7.

The reason why at these times the Lord called Himself the Son of Man is that He allowed Himself to be treated in ways comparable to those in which they treated the Word, as shown many times above.

25 **The Lord is called the Son of Man when judgment is the subject.** This is clear from these places –

When **the Son of Man** comes in His glory, He will sit on His glorious throne, and He will place the sheep on the right and the goats on the left. Matt.25:31,33.
When **the Son of Man** sits on His glorious throne, He is going to judge the twelve tribes of Israel. Matt.19:28.
The Son of Man is going to come in the glory of His Father, and then He will repay every one according to their deeds. Matt.16:27.

Vigilate omni tempore, ut digni habeamini ad consistendum coram **Filio Hominis**. Luc.21:36.
Qua hora non putatis, **Filius Hominis** venit. Matt.24:44; Luc.12:40.
Pater non judicat quemquam, sed omne judicium dedit Filio, quia **Filius Hominis** est. Joh.5:22,27.

Causa quod Dominus, cum de judicio agitur, Se dicat Filium Hominis, est quia omne judicium fit secundum Divinum Verum, quod est in Verbo. Quod hoc judicet unumquemvis, dicit Ipse apud Johannem,

Si quis audiverit verba Mea, non tamen crediderit, Ego non judico illum, non enim veni ut judicem mundum. **Verbum quod loquutus sum**, illud judicabit illum in extrema die. 12:47,48.

Et alibi,

Non venit **Filius Hominis** ut judicet mundum sed ut salvetur per Ipsum. Qui credit in Ipsum non judicatur; qui autem non credit, jam judicatus est, quia non credidit in nomen unigeniti Filii Dei. 3:17,18.

Quod Dominus neminem ad infernum judicet seu in infernum dejiciat, sed quod ipse malus spiritus semet, videatur in opere **De Caelo et Inferno**, n.545-550,574. Per **nomen** Jehovae, Domini, Filii Dei intelligitur Divinum Verum, ita quoque Verbum, quod est ab Ipso, de Ipso, et sic Ipse.

26 **Quod Dominus dicatur Filius Hominis ubi agitur de adventu Ipsius**, constat ex his –

Discipuli dicebant ad Jesum, Quodnam signum Tui adventus et consummationis saeculi? Et tunc Dominus praedixit status ecclesiae successivos usque ad finem, et de fine ejus haec,

Tunc apparebit signum **Filii Hominis**, et videbunt **Filium Hominis** venientem in nubibus caeli cum virtute et gloria. Matt.24:3,30; Marc.13:26; Luc.21:27.

Per consummationem saeculi intelligitur ultimum tempus ecclesiae, per adventum in nubibus caeli cum gloria intelligitur

---

10 Si quis audiverit DD^3: Si quis non audiverit DD^1; Si quis [non] audiverit DD^2

Stay awake at all times, that you may be held worthy to stand firm before **the Son of Man**. Luke 21:36.
At an hour you do not expect **the Son of Man** is coming. Matt.24:44; Luke 12:40.
The Father does not judge anyone, but has granted all judging to the Son, because He is **the Son of Man**. John 5:22,27.

The reason why the Lord refers to Himself as the Son of Man when judgment is the subject is that all judgment is determined by Divine Truth, which lies in the Word. That this is what everyone is judged by, He Himself declares in John,

If anyone hears My words, yet does not believe them, I do not judge him, for I did not come to judge the world. **The word that I have spoken**, that will judge on the last day. 12:47,48.

And in another place,

The Son of Man has not come to judge the world but so that it may be saved through Him. Those who believe in Him are not judged, but those who do not believe have been judged already because they have not believed in the name of the only begotten Son of God. 3:17,18.

The Lord does not sentence anyone to hell. He does not cast anyone down into hell; but wicked spirits themselves do so to themselves. See the work **Heaven and Hell**, §§545-550,574. By **the name** of Jehovah, the Lord, the Son of God is meant Divine Truth, and so also the Word, which comes from Him, has to do with Him, and consequently is Himself.

26 **The Lord is called the Son of Man where His coming is the subject**. This is clear from these places –

The disciples were saying to Jesus – What will be the sign of Your coming and of the close of the age? – at which point He foretold the consecutive phases of the church through to the end. And referring to its end, He said,
Then the sign of **the Son of Man** will appear, and they will see **the Son of Man** coming in the clouds of heaven with power and glory. Matt.24:3,30; Mark 13:26; Luke 21:27.

The close of the age means the end-time of the church, coming or arrival in the clouds of heaven with glory means the opening of the

aperitio Verbi et manifestatio quod Verbum de Ipso solo scriptum sit. Apud Danielem,

Vidi, et ecce cum nubibus caelorum **Filius Hominis** veniens. 7:13.

In Apocalypsi,

Ecce venit cum nubibus. et videbit Ipsum omnis oculus. 1:7.

Hoc etiam de **Filio Hominis**, ut patet a vers.13, ibi. Tum alibi in Apocalypsi,

Vidi, cum ecce nubes alba, et super nube sedens similis **Filio Hominis**. 14:14.

Quod Dominus aliud apud Se intellexerit per Filium Dei et aliud per Filium Hominis, patet a responso Ipsius ad principem sacerdotum,

Sacerdos magnus dixit ad Jesum, Adjuro Te per Deum viventem, ut nobis dicas num Tu sis Christus, **Filius Dei**. Dixit illi Jesus, Tu dixisti; Ego sum. Veruntamen dico vobis, a nunc videbitis **Filium Hominis** sedentem a dextris potentiae et venientem in nubibus caeli. Matt.26:63,64.

Hic primum confessus est quod sit Filius Dei, et postea dicit quod visuri sint Filium Hominis sedentem a dextris potentiae et venientem in nubibus caeli, per quae intelligitur quod post passionem crucis in Divina Potentia esset aperiendi Verbum et instaurandi ecclesiam, quod non prius fieri potuit, quia non prius vicerat infernum et glorificaverat Humanum Suum. Quid per sedere super nubibus caeli et venire in gloria significatur, in opere **De Caelo et Inferno**, n.1, explicatum est.
27 **Quod Dominus dicatur Filius Hominis ubi agitur de redemptione, salvatione, reformatione, et regeneratione**, constat ex his –

Filius Hominis venit ut det animam redemptionem pro multis. Matt.20:28; Marc.10:45.

Word and disclosure that the Word has been written with reference to Him alone. In Daniel,

I saw, and behold, with the clouds of the heavens came **the Son of Man**. 7:13.

In the Book of Revelation,

Behold, He is coming with the clouds, and every eye will see Him. 1:7.

This too refers to **the Son of Man**, as is evident from verse 13 in the same chapter. And in another place in that book,

I saw, when behold, a white cloud, and on the cloud one was sitting like **the Son of Man**. 14:14.

The fact that the Lord meant one aspect of Himself by Son of God and another by Son of Man is evident from His reply to the chief one of the priests, 2

The high priest said to Jesus, I adjure You by the living God that You tell us if You are the Christ, **the Son of God**. *Jesus said to him, You have said so; I am.*[1] *But I say to you, Hereafter you will see* **the Son of Man** *sitting on the right hand of power and coming in the clouds of heaven.* Matt.26:63,64.

Here He first of all confesses that He is the Son of God, after which He says that they were going to see the Son of Man sitting on the right hand of power and coming in the clouds of heaven. By this He meant that after His suffering on the cross He would with Divine Power be opening the Word and establishing a church, which could not have been accomplished previously because He had not yet conquered hell and glorified His Human. As for the meaning of sitting on the clouds of heaven and coming in glory, this has been explained in the work **Heaven and Hell**, §1.

27 **The Lord is called the Son of Man where redemption, salvation, reformation, and regeneration are the subject**. This is clear from these places –

The Son of Man came to give His life as a redemption for many. Matt.20:28; Mark 10:45.

---

[1] See note 1 on page 85

Venit **Filius Hominis** ad salvandum et non ad perdendum. Matt.18:11; Luc.9:56.
Venit **Filius Hominis** ad quaerendum et salvandum id quod perierat. Luc.19:10.
5 Venit **Filius Hominis** ut mundus salvetur per Ipsum. Joh.3:17.
Qui seminat bonum semen est **Filius Hominis**. Matt.13:37.

Ibi de redemptione et salvatione agitur, quae quia a Domino fiunt per Verbum, ideo Se vocat ibi Filium Hominis. Dicit Dominus quod **Filius Hominis** potestatem habeat remittendi
10 peccata, Marc.2:10; Luc.5:24, hoc est, salvandi; tum, quod sit Dominus Sabbathi, quia est **Filius Hominis**, Matt.12:8; Marc.2:28; Luc.6:5, quia est Verbum, quod Ipse tunc docet. Praeterea dicit apud Johannem,

Operamini cibum non qui perit sed cibum qui manet in vitam
15 aeternam, quem **Filius Hominis** vobis dabit. 6:27.

Per cibum intelligitur omne verum et bonum doctrinae ex Verbo, ita a Domino. Hoc quoque ibi intelligitur per mannam et per panem qui e caelo descendit, et quoque per hoc in eodem capite,

20 Nisi comederitis carnem **Filii Hominis** et biberitis Ipsius sanguinem, non habebitis vitam in vobis. vers.53.

Caro seu panis est bonum amoris ex Verbo, sanguis seu vinum est bonum fidei ex Verbo, utrumque a Domino.
   Simile per Filium Hominis, in aliis locis ubi dicitur,
25 significatur, ut in his –

Vulpes foveas habent, et volucres nidos, **Filius** vero **Hominis** non habet ubi caput inclinet. Matt.8:20; Luc.9:58.

Per hoc intelligitur quod Verbum non haberet locum apud Judaeos, ut quoque dicit Dominus, Joh.8:37; nec esset manens
30 apud illos, quia non agnoverunt Ipsum, Joh.5:38,39. Per Filium Hominis intelligitur Dominus quoad Verbum, etiam in Apocalypsi,

The Son of Man came to save and not to destroy. Matt.18:11; Luke 9:56.
The Son of Man came to seek and save that which had become lost. Luke 19:10.
The Son of Man came so that the world might be saved through Him. John 3:17.
He who sows the good seed is **the Son of Man**. Matt.13:37.

In these places redemption and salvation are the subject, and because these are accomplished by the Lord by means of the Word He refers to Himself in those places as the Son of Man. The Lord says that **the Son of Man** has the power to forgive sins, Mark 2:10; Luke 5:24, that is, the power to save, and also that being **the Son of Man** He is Lord of the Sabbath, Matt.12:8; Mark 2:28; Luke 6:5, for He is the Word which He teaches then. In addition He says in John,

Do not labour for the food which perishes but for the food which endures to eternal life, which **the Son of Man** will give you. 6:27.

By food is meant everything true and good in teaching which is derived from the Word, and so comes from the Lord. That is also what is meant there by the manna and bread which comes down from heaven, as well as by this statement in the same chapter –

Unless you eat the flesh of **the Son of Man** and drink His blood, you will have no life in you. Verse 53.

Flesh or bread is the goodness that belongs to love and is derived from the Word, while blood or wine is the goodness that belongs to faith and is derived from the Word, both of which are provided by the Lord.

2 The like is meant by the Son of Man in other places where this title occurs, as it is in these places –

Foxes have holes, and birds have nests, but **the Son of Man** has nowhere to lay His head. Matt.8:20; Luke 9:58.

This means that the Word found no place among the Jews, as also the Lord says, in John 8:37; nor did it abide with them, because they did not accept Him, John 5:38,39. In the Book of Revelation as well the Lord in respect of the Word is meant by the Son of Man,

In medio septem candelabrorum vidi similem **Filio Hominis**, indutum talari et circumcinctum ad ubera zona aurea. 1:13,seq.

Ibi per varia repraesentatus est Dominus ut Verbum, quare etiam vocatur Filius Hominis. Apud Davidem,

Sit manus Tua pro Viro dextrae Tuae, pro **Filio Hominis** confortasti Te. Tunc non recedemus a Te. Vivifica nos. Ps.80:18-20.

Vir dextrae est quoque hic Dominus quoad Verbum; similiter Filius Hominis. Vocatur Vir dextrae, quia Domino ex Divino Vero, quod etiam est Verbum, est potentia, ac Ipsi Divina Potentia fuit quando totum Verbum implevit. Inde etiam dixerat quod visuri sint **Filium Hominis** sedentem a dextris Patris, cum potentia, Marc.14:62.

28 **Quod Filius Hominis significet Dominum quoad Verbum, erat quia Prophetae etiam dicti sunt filii hominis.** Quod prophetae filii hominis dicti sint, erat quia repraesentabant Dominum quoad Verbum, et inde significabant doctrinam ecclesiae ex Verbo. Non aliud in caelo per prophetas ubi nominantur in Verbo, intelligitur, significatio enim spiritualis prophetae, tum etiam filii hominis, est **doctrina ecclesiae ex Verbo**; et cum de Domino, est **ipsum Verbum**. Quod Propheta Daniel vocatus sit filius hominis, videatur apud illum, 8:17. Quod Propheta Ezechiel vocatus sit filius hominis, videatur apud illum, 2:1,3,6,8; 3:1,3,4,10,17,25; 4:1,16; 5:1; 6:2; 7:2; 8:5,6,8,12,15; 11:2,4,15; 12:2,3,9,18,22,27; 13:2,17; 14:3,13; 15:2; 16:2; 17:2; 20:3,4,27,46; 21:2,7,9,12,14,19,28; 22:18,24; 23:2,36; 24:2,16,25; 25:2; 26:2; 27:2; 28:2,12,21; 29:2,18; 30:2,21; 31:2; 32:2,18; 33:2,7,10,12,24,30; 34:2; 35:2; 36:1,17; 37:3,9,11,16; 38:2,14; 39:1,17; 40:4; 43:7,10,18; 44:5.

Ex his nunc patet quod Dominus quoad Divinum Humanum dicatur Filius Dei, et quoad Verbum Filius Hominis.

---

6   18-20 *DD¹, DD²*: 18,20 *DD³*
25 23:2,36 *DD¹, DD²*: 23:2,3,6 *DD³*
26 31:2 *DD³*: 31:1,2 *DD³*
27 44:5 *DD³*: 44:1,4 *DD¹, DD²*

In the midst of the seven lampstands I saw one like **the Son of Man**, clothed with a long robe and girded with a golden girdle around the breasts. 1:13, and following verses.

Here the Lord as the Word was represented by various objects, and also is therefore called the Son of Man. In David,

Let Your hand be for the Man on Your right hand, for **the Son of Man** whom You have made strong for Yourself. Then we will not turn back from You. Give us life. Ps.80:17-19.

Here Man on the right hand as well as Son of Man means the Lord in respect of the Word. The expression Man on the right hand is used, because the power the Lord possesses springs from Divine Truth, which also is the Word, and Divine Power was His when He fulfilled the whole Word. This also explains why He said that they would see **the Son of Man** sitting with power on the right hand of the Father, Mark 14:62.

28   **The reason why Son of Man means the Lord in respect of the Word is that Prophets too were called sons of man**. Prophets were called sons of man because they represented the Lord in respect of the Word and as a consequence served to mean the church's teachings derived from the Word. Nothing other is understood in heaven by prophets when these are mentioned in the Word, for the spiritual meaning of a prophet as well as of a son of man is **the church's teachings derived from the Word**; and when the two titles relate to the Lord **the Word itself** is meant. For Daniel's being called son of man, see Dan.8:17; and for Ezekiel's being called so, see Ezek.2:1,3,6,8; 3:1,3,4,10,17,25; 4:1,16; 5:1; 6:2; 7:2; 8:5,6,8,12,15; 11:2,4,15; 12:2,3,9,18,22,27; 13:2,17; 14:3,13; 15:2; 16:2; 17:2; 20:3,4,27,46; 21:2,6,9,12,14,19,28; 22:18,24; 23:2,36; 24:2,16,25; 25:2; 26:2; 27:2; 28:2,12,21; 29:2,18; 30:2,21; 31:2; 32:2,18; 33:2,7,10,12,24,30; 34:2; 35:2; 36:1,17; 37:3,9,11,16; 38:2,14; 39:1,17; 40:4; 43:7,10,18; 44:5.

From all this it is now evident that in respect of His Divine Human the Lord is called Son of God, and in respect of the Word Son of Man.

Quod Dominus Humanum Suum fecerit Divinum ex Divino in Ipso, et quod sic unum factus sit cum Patre

29   Ex doctrina Ecclesiae recepta in universo Christiano orbe est,

Quod noster Dominus Jesus Christus, Filius Dei, sit et Deus et Homo; et quamvis est Deus et Homo, usque non sunt duo, sed est unus Christus. Est unus, quia Divinum suscepit ad Se Humanum; imo est prorsus unus, est enim una Persona. Quoniam sicut anima et corpus faciunt unum hominem, ita Deus et Homo est unus Christus.

Haec verba ex doctrina fidei Athanasianae, quae in universo Christiano orbe recepta est, desumpta sunt. Haec ibi sunt essentialia de unitione Divini et Humani in Domino; reliqua quae in eadem doctrina de Domino dicuntur, in suo articulo explicabuntur. Ex illis clare patet quod ex fide Ecclesiae Christianae sit, quod Divinum et Humanum in Domino non sint duo sed unum, sicut anima et corpus est unus homo, et quod Divinum in Ipso susceperit Humanum.

Ex hoc sequitur quod non Divinum ab Humano, nec Humanum a Divino, possint separari, nam illa separare foret sicut separare animam et corpus. Quod ita sit, etiam omnis agnoscet qui legit illa quae supra, n.19 et 21, ex binis Evangelistis, nempe ex Luca 1:26-35, et ex Matthaeo 1:18-25, de nativitate Domini, allata sunt, ex quibus manifestum est quod Jesus conceptus sit a Jehovah Deo et natus a Maria virgine, ita quod in Ipso fuerit Divinum, et illud anima Ipsius. Nunc quia anima Ipsius fuit Ipsum Divinum Patris, sequitur quod corpus seu Humanum Ipsius etiam factum sit Divinum, nam ubi unum

The Lord made His Human Divine from the Divine within Him and in so doing became one with the Father

29   According to the teaching of the church accepted in the entire Christian world,

Our Lord Jesus Christ, the Son of God, is both God and man.
And although He is God and man, yet He is not two, but one Christ.
He is one because the Divine took to itself the Human.
Or rather, He is totally one, for He is one Person.
Because, just as soul and body make one human being, so God and Man is one Christ.

These words are taken from the teaching in the Athanasian Creed, which is accepted in the entire Christian world.[1] They are the essential statements in it regarding the union of the Divine and the Human within the Lord; the rest of the statements in that teaching regarding the Lord will be explained in a section on their own.[2] From all this it is plainly evident that according to the creed of the Christian church the Divine and the Human in the Lord are not two but one, just as soul and body make one human being, and that the Divine in Him took on the Human.

From this it follows that the Divine is inseparable from the Human, and the Human from the Divine, for separating them would be like separating soul and body. The truth of this will be recognized by everyone who reads what is quoted above, in §19 and §21, from the two gospels – from Luke 1:26-35 and Matthew 1:18-25 – regarding the Lord's birth. These show plainly that Jesus was conceived from Jehovah God and born from Mary the virgin, thus that the Divine was within Him, and was His soul. Now because His soul was the actual Divine of the Father it follows that His body, that is, His Human, was made Divine, for where the one is, so also

---

1 See pages x-xi above
2 See pages 183-197 below

est, etiam erit alterum. Ita et non aliter Pater et Filius unum sunt, Pater in Filio et Filius in Patre, tum omnia Filii Patris sunt et omnia Patris Filii, ut Ipse Dominus in Verbo suo docet.

Sed quomodo unitio facta est, dicetur hoc ordine –

i Quod Dominus ab aeterno sit Jehovah
ii Quod Dominus ab aeterno seu Jehovah susceperit Humanum ad salvandum homines
iii Quod Humanum Divinum fecerit ex Divino in Se
iv Quod Humanum Divinum fecerit per tentationes in Se admissas, et per continuas tunc victorias
v Quod plena unitio Divini et Humani in Ipso facta sit per passionem crucis, quae fuit tentationum ultima
vi Quod Humanum ex matre susceptum successive exuerit, et Humanum ex Divino in Ipso induerit, quod est Divinum Humanum et Filius Dei
vii Quod ita Deus factus sit Homo, ut in primis, etiam in ultimis

30 **Quod Dominus ab aeterno sit Jehovah**, notum est ex Verbo, nam Dominus dixit Judaeis,

Amen dico vobis, Priusquam Abrahamus fuit, Ego sum. Joh.8:58.

Et alibi,

Glorifica Me Tu, Pater, gloria quam habui, antequam mundus esset, apud Te. Joh.17:5,

per quae intelligitur Dominus ab aeterno et non Filius ab aeterno, nam Filius est Humanum Ipsius conceptum a Jehovah Patre et natum a Maria virgine in tempore, ut supra ostensum est.

Quod Dominus ab aeterno sit Ipse Jehovah, constat a multis locis in Verbo, ex quibus haec pauca in praesenti adducentur –

Dicetur in die illo, **Deus noster Hic**, quem exspectavimus ut liberet nos, **Jehovah**, quem exspectavimus. Exultemus et laetemur in salute Ipsius, Esai.25:9,

10 *om* et per continuas tunc victorias *DD*
32 25:9 *DD³*: 16:10,14 *DD¹, DD²*

must the other be. In this and no other way are Father and Son one, the Father in the Son and the Son in the Father; and also all that is the Son's is the Father's, and all the Father's is the Son's, as the Lord Himself teaches in His Word.

But how the union was accomplished will be presented in the following sequence of ideas – 3

i   The Lord from eternity is Jehovah
ii   The Lord from eternity, or Jehovah, took upon Himself the Human in order to save people
iii   He made His Human Divine from the Divine within Him
iv   He made the Human Divine by means of the temptations He underwent and by His unbroken chain of victories in them
v   The full union of the Divine and the Human within Him was accomplished by the passion on the cross, which was the final temptation
vi   He cast off in consecutive stages the Human taken on from the mother and put on the Human from the Divine within Him, which is the Divine Human and the Son of God
vii   In this way God became Man in last things as well as in first

30   **The Lord from eternity is Jehovah.** This is known from the Word, for the Lord told the Jews,

Truly I say to you, Before Abraham was, I am. John 8:58.

And in another place,

Father, glorify Me with the glory I had with You before the world was. John 17:5.

The Lord from eternity is meant in these two places, not a Son from eternity, because the Son is His Human conceived in time from Jehovah the Father and born from Mary the virgin, as has been shown above.

From many places in the Word it is clear that Lord from eternity means Jehovah Himself. For now just a few of those places will be quoted – 2

It will be said on that day, **This is our God**, whom we have waited for to deliver us, **Jehovah**, whom we have waited for. Let us be glad and rejoice in His salvation. Isa.25:9.

ex quibus patet quod Ipse Deus Jehovah exspectatus sit.

Vox clamantis in deserto, Parate viam **Jehovae**, complanate in solitudine semitam **Deo nostro**. Revelabitur gloria **Jehovae**, et videbit omnis caro simul. Ecce, **Dominus Jehovih** in forti venit. Esai.40:3,5,10; Matt.3:3; Marc.1:3; Luc.3:4.

Hic etiam Dominus dicitur Jehovah, qui venturus est.

Ego Jehovah dabo Te in faedus populo, in lucem gentium. **Ego Jehovah, hoc nomen Meum; et gloriam Meam non alteri dabo**. Esai.42:6-8.

Faedus populo, et lux gentium, est Dominus quoad Humanum. Quia hoc est a Jehovah, ac factum unum cum Jehovah, dicitur, Ego Jehovah, hoc nomen Meum, et gloriam Meam non alteri dabo, hoc est, non alteri quam Sibi Ipsi. Gloriam dare est glorificare seu unire Sibi.

Subito veniet ad templum Suum **Dominus** quem vos quaeritis. Mal.3:1.

Per templum intelligitur templum corporis Ipsius, ut Joh.2:19,21.

Visitavit nos **ortus ab alto**. Luc.1:78.

Ortus ab alto etiam est Jehovah, seu Dominus ab aeterno.
Ex his patet quod per Dominum ab aeterno intelligatur Divinum Ipsius a quo, quod in Verbo est Jehovah. Ex locis autem infra afferendis patebit quod per Dominum et quoque per Jehovam, postquam glorificatum est Humanum Ipsius, intelligatur Divinum et Humanum simul, ut unum, et quod per Filium solum intelligatur Divinum Humanum.

31 **Quod Dominus ab aeterno seu Jehovah susceperit Humanum ad salvandum homines**, confirmatum est ex Verbo in antecedentibus articulis; quod homo non aliter salvari potuerit, alibi dicetur. Quod susceperit Humanum, constat etiam ex locis in Verbo ubi dicitur quod exiverit ex Deo, descenderit e caelo, et quod missus sit in mundum, ut ex his –

27 Verbo: verbo *DD*

From these words it is evident that God Himself, Jehovah, was being waited for.

The voice of one crying in the wilderness, Prepare the way of **Jehovah**; make level in the lonely place a path for **our God**. The glory of **Jehovah** will be revealed, and all flesh will see it together. Behold, **the Lord Jehovih** will come with might. Isa.40:3,5,10; Matt.3:3; Mark 1:3; Luke 3:4.

Here also the Lord is said to be Jehovah, who was going to come.

I Jehovah will give You to be a covenant for the people, a light of the nations. **I am Jehovah, this is My name; and My glory I will not give to another**. Isa.42:6-8.

A covenant for the people and a light of the nations is the Lord in respect of His Human. And since this is from Jehovah and was made one with Jehovah it says, I am Jehovah, this is My name, and My glory I will not give to another, that is, to no other than Himself. Giving glory means glorifying or making one with Himself.

Suddenly there will come to His temple **the Lord** whom you are seeking. Mal.3:1.

By temple is meant the temple of His body, as in John 2:19,21.

The risen sun from on high has visited us. Luke 1:78.

The risen sun from on high too means Jehovah, that is, the Lord from eternity.
    These few quotations show that by Lord from eternity is meant the Divine from which He sprang, which in the Word is Jehovah. However, after the glorification of His Human, as the places quoted below will show, Lord and also Jehovah means Divine and Human together as one, while Son on its own means the Divine Human.

31   **The Lord from eternity, or Jehovah, took upon Himself the Human in order to save people**. This has been verified from the Word in previous sections; and the truth that there was no other way in which people could be saved will be discussed elsewhere. The taking of the Human upon Himself is also evident from those places in the Word where it says that He came out from God, came down from heaven, and that He was sent into the world, such as these –

Exivi a Patre, et **veni** in mundum. Joh.16:28.
Ego a **Deo exivi et venio**; neque a Me Ipso veni, sed Ille Me **misit**. Joh.8:42.
Pater vos amat, quia credidistis quod **Ego a Deo exiverim**. Joh.16:26,27.
Nemo ascendit in caelum nisi qui **e caelo descendit**. Joh.3:13.
Panis Dei est qui **descendit e caelo**, et vitam dat mundo. Joh.6:33,35,41,50,51.
Qui **desuper venit**, supra omnes est; qui **e caelo venit**, supra omnes est. Joh.3:31.
Ego novi Patrem, quia **ab Illo sum,** et **Ille misit Me**. Joh.7:29.

Quod per mitti a Patre in mundum intelligatur suscipere Humanum, videatur supra, n.20.

32 **Quod Dominus Humanum Suum Divinum fecerit ex Divino in Se**, constare potest ex multis locis e Verbo, ex quo nunc illa loca adducentur, quae confirmant –

i **Quod hoc successive factum sit**, quae sunt,

Jesus crevit et corroboratus est spiritu et sapientia, et gratia Dei erat super Ipsum. Luc.2:40.
Jesus profecit sapientia, aetate, et gratia apud Deum et homines. Luc.2:52.

ii **Quod Divinum operatum sit per Humanum, sicut anima per corpus**, ex his –

Non potest Filius facere a Se Ipso quicquam, nisi quid viderit Patrem facientem. Joh.5:19.
A Me Ipso facio nihil, sed sicut docuit Me Pater Meus, haec loquor. Qui misit Me, Mecum est; non reliquit Me solum. Joh.8:28,29; 5:30.
Ego non ex Me Ipso loquutus sum; sed qui misit Me Pater, Mihi praeceptum dedit, quid dicere et quid loqui debeam. Joh.12:49,50.
Verba quae Ego loquor vobis, a Me Ipso non loquor. Pater, qui in Me manet, Ille facit opera. Joh.14:10.
Non sum solus, quia Pater Mecum. Joh.16:32.

---

6 in caelum *DD*³: e caelo *DD*¹, *DD*²
21 Luc.2:52 *DD*³: om *DD*¹, *DD*²
24 quid *DD*³: om *DD*¹, *DD*²

I came out from the Father and have come into the world. John 16:28.
From God I came out and now come; nor have I come of Myself, but He sent Me. John 8:42.
The Father loves you because you have believed that **I came out from God**. John 16:26,27.
No one has gone up into heaven except Him who **came down from heaven**. John 3:13.
The bread of God is He who **comes down from heaven** and gives life to the world. John 6:33,35,41,50,51.
He who **comes from above** is above all; He who **comes from heaven** is above all. John 3:31.
I know the Father, because **I am from Him** and **He sent Me**. John 7:29.

Being sent from the Father into the world means taking on the Human, see §20 above.

32 **The Lord made His Human Divine from the Divine within Him**. This becomes clear from many places derived from the Word, from which those substantiating the following points will now be quoted –

i **It was made so in consecutive stages**

Jesus grew and became strong in spirit and wisdom, and the grace of God was upon Him. Luke 2:40.
Jesus advanced in wisdom, in years, and in grace with God and people. Luke 2:52.

ii **The Divine acted through the Human, as the soul does through the body**

The Son cannot do anything of Himself, only what He sees the Father doing. John 5:19.
I do nothing from Myself, but speak just as My Father has taught Me. He who sent Me is with Me; He has not left Me alone. John 8:28,29; 5:30.
I have not spoken from Myself; but He, the Father, who sent Me has given Me a command, what I ought to say and what to speak. John 12:49,50.
The words that I speak to you I do not speak from Myself. The Father who dwells in Me does the works. John 14:10.
I am not alone, for the Father is with Me. John 16:32.

iii Quod Divinum et Humanum unanimiter operatum sit, ex his –

Quae Pater facit, haec etiam Filius similiter facit. Joh.5:19.
Quemadmodum Pater suscitat mortuos et vivificat, ita etiam Filius, quos vult, vivificat. Joh.5:21.
Quemadmodum Pater habet vitam in Se Ipso, ita dedit etiam Filio vitam habere in Se Ipso. Joh.5:26.
Nunc cognoverunt quod omnia quae dedisti Mihi, a Te sint. Joh.17:7.

iv Quod unitum sit Divinum Humano et Humanum Divino, ex his –

Si cognovistis Me, etiam Patrem Meum cognovistis, et vidistis Ipsum. Dixit ad Philippum volentem videre Patrem, Tantum tempus vobiscum sum et non nosti Me, Philippe? Qui vidit Me, vidit Patrem. Nonne credis quod Ego in Patre et Pater in Me sit? Credite Mihi, quod Ego in Patre et Pater in Me sit. Joh.14:6-11.
Si non facio opera Patris Mei, ne credite Mihi; si facio, operibus credite, ut cognoscatis et credatis quod Pater in Me et Ego in Patre. Joh.10:37,38.
Ut omnes unum sint, sicut Tu, Pater, in Me et Ego in Te. Joh.17:21.
In illo die cognoscetis quod Ego in Patre Meo. Joh.14:20.
Non rapiet quis oves e manu Patris Mei. Ego et Pater unum sumus. Joh.10:30.
Pater amat Filium et omnia dedit in manum Ipsius. Joh.3:35.
Omnia quaecunque Pater habet, Mea sunt. Joh.16:15.
Omnia Mea Tua sunt, et Tua Mea. Joh.17:10.
Dedisti Filio potestatem omnis carnis. Joh.17:2.
Data est Mihi omnis potestas in caelo et in terra. Matt.28:18.

v Quod Divinum Humanum adeundum sit, patet ex his –

Ut omnes honorent Filium, quemadmodum honorant Patrem. Joh.5:23.
Si Me nossetis, etiam Patrem Meum nossetis. Joh.8:19.
Qui videt Me, videt Ipsum qui misit Me. Joh.12:45.
Si cognovistis Me, etiam Patrem meum cognovistis, et abhinc cognovistis Ipsum et vidistis Ipsum. Joh.14:7.
Qui Me suscipit, suscipit Ipsum qui misit Me. Joh.13:20.

iii   **The Divine and the Human acted with one and the same mind**   3

What the Father does, this also the Son in like manner does. John 5:19.
As the Father raises up the dead and bestows life on them, so also the Son bestows life on whom He will. John 5:21.
As the Father has life in Himself, so He has also granted the Son to have life in Himself. John 5:26.
Now they know that everything which You have given Me is from You. John 17:7.

iv   **The Divine was united to the Human, and the Human to the Divine**   4

If you know Me you know My Father also, and have seen Him. He said to Philip who wished to see the Father, Have I been with you so long and you do not know Me, Philip? Whoever has seen Me has seen the Father. Do you not believe that I am in the Father and the Father is in Me? Believe Me, that I am in the Father and the Father is in Me. John 14:6-11.
If I am not doing the works of My Father, do not believe Me; if I am doing, believe the works, that you may know and believe that the Father is in Me and I am in the Father. John 10:37,38.
That they may all be one, as You, Father, are in Me and I am in You. John 17:21.
On that day you will know that I am in My Father. John 14:20.
No one will snatch the sheep out of My Father's hand. I and the Father are one. John 10:30.
The Father loves the Son and has given all things into His hand. John 3:35.
All that the Father has is Mine. John 16:15.
All Mine are Yours, and Yours are Mine. John 17:10.
You have given the Son power over all flesh. John 17:2.
All power in heaven and on earth has been given to Me. Matt.28:18.

v   **It is the Divine Human that people should approach**   5

That all may honour the Son, just as they honour the Father. John 5:23.
If you knew Me you would know My Father also. John 8:19.
He who sees Me sees Him who sent Me. John 12:45.
If you know Me you know My Father also, and from now on you know Him and have seen Him. John 14:7.
Whoever receives Me receives Him who sent Me. John 13:20.

Causa est quia nemo potest Ipsum Divinum, quod Pater vocatur, videre, sed Divinum Humanum, dicit enim Dominus,

Deum nemo vidit unquam; unigenitus Filius, qui in sinu Patris est, Ille exposuit. Joh.1:18.
Non Patrem vidit quis, nisi qui est apud Patrem; Hic vidit Patrem. Joh.6:46.
Non vocem Patris audivistis unquam, neque speciem Ipsius vidistis. Joh.5:37.

vi **Quia Dominus Humanum Suum fecit Divinum ex Divino in Se, et quia illud adeundum est, et hoc est Filius Dei, ideo in Dominum, qui et Pater et Filius est, credendum est.** Hoc patet ex his,

Jesus dixit, Quotquot receperunt Ipsum, dedit illis potestatem ut filii Dei essent, **credentibus in nomen Ipsius.** Joh.1:12.
Ut omnis qui **credit in Ipsum** non pereat sed vitam aeternam habeat. Joh.3:15.
Adeo dilexit Deus mundum ut Filium Suum unigenitum dederit, ut omnis qui **credit in Ipsum**, vitam aeternam habeat. Joh.3:16.
Qui **credit in Filium**, non judicatur; qui autem **non credit** jam judicatus est, quia **non credidit in nomen unigeniti Filii Dei.** Joh.3:18.
Qui **credit in Filium** habet vitam aeternam; qui vero **non credit Filio**, non videbit vitam, sed ira Dei manet super illo. Joh.3:36.
Panis Dei est qui descendit e caelo et vitam dat mundo. Qui venit ad Me, non esuriet, et qui **credit in Me**, non sitiet unquam. Joh.6:33,35.
Haec est voluntas Ipsius qui misit Me, ut omnis qui videt Filium, et **credit in Ipsum**, habeat vitam aeternam, et resuscitem illum Ego in extremo die. Joh.6:40.
Dixerunt ad Jesum, Quid faciemus ut operemur opera Dei? Respondit Jesus, Hoc est opus Dei, ut credatis in Eum quem misit Ille. Joh.6:28,29.
Amen dico vobis, Qui **credit in Me** habet vitam aeternam. Joh.6:47.
Jesus clamavit, dicens, Si quis sitiverit, venito ad Me et bibito. Quisquis **credit in Me**, sicut dixit Scriptura, Flumina e ventre illius fluent aquae viventis. Joh.7:37,38.

The reason why is that no one can see the actual Divine, called the Father, only the Divine Human, for the Lord says,

No one has ever seen God; the only begotten Son, who is in the bosom of the Father, He has made Him known. John 1:18.
No one has seen the Father except Him who is with the Father[1]; He has seen the Father. John 6:46.
You have never heard the Father's voice nor seen His shape. John 5:37.

vi **Because the Lord made His Human Divine from the Divine within Him, and because it is this Human made Divine, which is the Son of God, that people should approach, they should believe in the Lord, who is both Father and Son**

Jesus said, As many as received Him, to them He gave power to be sons of God, **to those believing in His name.** John 1:12.
That everyone who **believes in Him** may not perish but have eternal life. John 3:15.
God so loved the world that He gave His only begotten Son, that everyone who **believes in Him** may have eternal life. John 3:16.
Whoever **believes in the Son** is not judged; but whoever **does not believe** is judged already, because **they do not believe in the name of the only begotten Son of God.** John 3:18.
Whoever **believes in the Son** has eternal life; but whoever **does not believe in the Son** will not see life, but the wrath of God rests on them. John 3:36.
The bread of God is He who comes down out of heaven and gives life to the world. Whoever comes to Me will not hunger, and whoever **believes in Me** will never thirst. John 6:33,35.
This is the will of Him who sent Me, that everyone who sees the Son and **believes in Him** may have eternal life, and I will raise them up on the last day. John 6:40.
They said to Jesus, What shall we do, that we may do the works of God? Jesus answered, This is the work of God, that you believe in Him whom He has sent. John 6:28,29.
Truly I say to you, whoever **believes in Me** has eternal life. John 6:47.
Jesus cried out, saying, If anyone thirsts let them come to Me and drink. Whoever **believes in Me**, as the Scripture has said, Out of his belly will flow rivers of living water. John 7:37,38.

1 Swedenborg is following Sebastian Schmidt, but the original Greek means *who is from God*

Nisi credideritis quod Ego sim, moriemini in peccatis vestris. Joh.8:24.
Jesus dixit, Ego sum resurrectio et vita. Qui **credit in Me**, etsi moriatur, vivet. Omnis vero qui vivit, et **credit in Me**, non morietur in aeternum. Joh.11:25,26.
Jesus dixit, Ego lux in mundum veni, ut omnis **qui credit in Me**, in tenebris non maneat. Joh.12:46; 8:12.
Quousque lucem habetis, **credite in lucem**, ut filii lucis sitis. Joh.12:36.
Amen dico vobis, quod mortui audient vocem Filii Dei, et qui audient vivent. Joh.5:25.
Manete in Me, etiam Ego in vobis. Ego sum vitis, vos palmites. Qui manet in Me, et Ego in illo, hic fert fructum multum, quia sine Me non potestis facere quicquam. Joh.15:4,5.
Quod mansuri sint in Domino, et Dominus in illis. Joh.14:20; 17:23.
Ego sum via, veritas, et vita; nemo venit ad Patrem nisi per Me. Joh.14:6.

In his locis, et in omnibus aliis ubi nominatur Pater, intelligitur Divinum quod ex conceptione fuit in Domino, quod, secundum doctrinam fidei Christiani orbis, fuit sicut anima in corpore apud hominem. Ipsum Humanum ex hoc Divino est Filius Dei. Nunc quia hoc quoque Divinum factum est, ne homo adeat Patrem solum et per id in cogitatione, fide, et inde in cultu separet Patrem a Domino in quo est, ideo – postquam Dominus docuit quod Pater et Ipse unum sint, et quod Pater in Ipso et Ipse in Patre sit, et quod mansuri sint in Ipso, et quod nemo veniat ad Patrem nisi per Ipsum – etiam docet quod in Ipsum credendum sit, et quod homo ex fide directa in Ipsum salvetur.

Quod Humanum in Domino Divinum factum sit, in Christianismo apud plures non potest aliqua idea capi, ex causa imprimis quia de homine cogitant ex materiali ejus corpore et non ex spirituali, cum tamen omnes angeli, qui spirituales sunt, etiam in plena forma homines sunt, et omne Divinum quod procedit a Jehovah Deo, a primis ejus in caelo ad ultimum ejus in mundo, in formam humanam tendit. Quod angeli sint formae humanae, et quod omne Divinum tendat in formam humanam, videatur in opere **De Caelo et Inferno**, n.73-77 et n.453-460; ac plenius videbitur in sequentibus operibus quae erunt ex sapientia angelica de Domino.

13 15:4,5: 15:1-5 *DD*

Unless you believe that I am, you will die in your sins. John 8:24.
Jesus said, I am the resurrection and the life. Those who **believe in Me**, though they die, yet they will live. And everyone who lives and **believes in Me** will never die. John 11:25,26.
Jesus said, I have come as light into the world, so that everyone who **believes in Me** may not remain in darkness. John 12:46; 8:12.
As long as you have the light, **believe in the light**, that you may be sons of light. John 12:36.
Truly I say to you, that the dead will hear the voice of the Son of God, and those who hear will live. John 5:25.
Abide in Me, and I in you. I am the vine, you are the branches. Those who abide in Me, and I in them, bear much fruit, for apart from Me you cannot do anything. John 15:4,5.
They will be abiding in the Lord, and the Lord in them. John 14:20; 17:23.
I am the way, the truth, and the life; no one comes to the Father except through Me. John 14:6.

In these and all other places where the Father is mentioned the Divine is meant, which was present in the Lord from conception, which – according to the teaching in the creed of the Christian world – was like the soul present in a person's body. The actual Human conceived from that Divine is the Son of God. Now since this became Divine as well, the Lord also said certain things to prevent people from approaching the Father alone, and to prevent their separating – in their thought, belief and resulting worship – the Father from the Lord in whom He is present. To this end, after declaring that the Father and He are one, that the Father is in Him and He is in the Father, that they should abide in Him, and that no one comes to the Father except through Him, He added that people should believe in Him, and that a person is saved by believing directly in Him. 7

Very many in Christendom are incapable of gaining any idea at all that the Human in the Lord was made Divine, mainly because when they think about the human being they start from the material, not the spiritual, body. They do so even though all angels, who are spiritual beings, are in their outward form human, completely so, and everything Divine emanating from Jehovah God, from the first aspects of it in heaven to the last in the world, inclines towards the human form. That angels are human forms and that everything Divine inclines towards the human form may be seen in the work **Heaven and Hell**, §§73-77 and §§453-460, and will be seen in greater detail in the works to follow which will draw on angelic wisdom concerning the Lord. 8

33   Quod Dominus Humanum Suum Divinum fecerit per tentationes in Se admissas, et per continuas tunc victorias, actum est supra, n.12-14, quibus hoc solum addendum est. Tentationes non aliud sunt quam pugnae contra mala et falsa; et quia mala et falsa ab inferno sunt, sunt quoque pugnae contra infernum. Etiam apud homines qui tentationes spirituales subeunt, sunt mali spiritus ab inferno qui illas inducunt. Quod mali spiritus inducant tentationes, homo nescit; quod tamen sint, ex multa experientia datum est scire.

Ex eo est quod homo, dum ex Domino vincit in tentationibus, ab inferno extrahatur ac in caelum elevetur; inde est quod homo per tentationes seu pugnas contra mala fiat spiritualis, ita angelus. Dominus autem ex propria potentia pugnavit contra omnia inferna, et illa prorsus domavit et subjugavit; et per id, quod simul glorificaverit Humanum Suum, illa in aeternum domata et subjugata tenet.

Inferna enim ante Domini adventum usque ad illam altitudinem succreverunt ut ipsos angelos caeli inciperent infestare, et similiter omnem hominem venientem in mundum et exeuntem e mundo. Quod inferna in talem altitudinem succreverint, erat causa quia ecclesia prorsus devastata fuit et homines mundi ex idololatriis in meris falsis et malis fuerunt; et ex hominibus sunt inferna. Inde fuit quod nisi Dominus in mundum venisset, nemo hominum potuisset salvari. De his Domini pugnis, multis agitur in Psalmis Davidis et in Prophetis, at parum in Evangelistis. Pugnae illae sunt quae intelliguntur per tentationes quas Dominus sustinuit, quarum ultima fuit passio crucis. Ex illis est quod Dominus dicatur Salvator et Redemptor.

Hoc in ecclesia in tantum notum est ut dicant quod Dominus vicerit mortem seu diabolum, hoc est, infernum, et quod cum victoria resurrexerit; tum etiam quod absque Domino nulla salus. Quod etiam glorificaverit Humanum Suum et quod per id Salvator, Redemptor, Reformator, et Regenerator in aeternum factus sit, in sequentibus videbitur. Quod Dominus per pugnas seu tentationes Salvator factus sit, ex locis supra, n.12-14, in copia allatis, patet, et ex hoc apud Esaiam,

33 **The Lord made His Human Divine by means of the temptations He underwent and and by His unbroken chain of victories of victories in them**. This was dealt with above, in §§12-14, to which only this needs to be added. Temptations are nothing other than conflicts with evils and falsities; and since evils and falsities come from hell they are also conflicts with hell. Furthermore, in the case of people who undergo spiritual temptations they are evil spirits from hell who bring them on. People do not know that temptations are brought on by evil spirits, but from much experience I have been led to know it is so.

2 It follows on from this that when with the Lord's aid people are winning in temptations they are being pulled out of hell and raised into heaven, and therefore that by means of temptations or conflicts with evils people are made spiritual, that is, angels. But the Lord fought against all the hells with His own power, and completely tamed and brought them under control; and, having at the same time glorified His Human, He keeps them tamed and under control.

3 For before the Lord's coming the hells had swelled up so high that they were beginning to molest the very angels of heaven, and in like manner every person coming into and going out of the world. The reason why the hells had swelled up to such a height was that the church had been utterly destroyed and as a result of forms of idolatry people in the world were immersed in nothing but falsity and evil; and the hells are made up of people. So unless the Lord had come into the world no one at all would have been able to be saved. These conflicts that were the Lord's are very much the subject in the Psalms of David and in the Prophets, but only to a small extent in the Gospels. Those conflicts are what are meant by the temptations He suffered, the last of which was His passion on the cross. It is on account of those conflicts that the Lord is called Saviour and Redeemer.

4 This is something so well known in the church that people say that the Lord overcame death or the devil – that is, hell – and rose again victorious, and also that without the Lord there would be no salvation. The truth that He also glorified His Human and in doing so became the Saviour, Redeemer, Reformer and Regenerator for ever will be seen in what is to follow. That the Lord became the Saviour by means of His conflicts or temptations is evident from the large number of places quoted above in §§12-14, and also from this in Isaiah,

Dies vindictae in corde Meo, et **annus redemptorum** Meorum venerat. Conculcavi illos in ira Mea; descendere feci in terram victoriam illorum; **ideo factus est illis in Salvatorem**. 63:4,6,8.

Agitur in eo capite de pugnis Domini. Et apud Davidem,

Attollite, portae, capita vestra, extollimini, ostia mundi, ut ingrediatur **Rex gloriae**. Quis hic **Rex gloriae**? **Jehovah fortis et Heros, Jehovah Heros belli**. Ps.24:7,8.

Haec etiam de Domino.

34 **Quod plena unitio Divini et Humani in Ipso facta sit per passionem crucis, quae fuit tentationum ultima**, confirmatum est in suo articulo supra, in quo ostensum est quod Dominus in mundum venerit ut subjugaret inferna et glorificaret Humanum Suum, et quod passio crucis fuerit ultima pugna, per quam plene vicit inferna et plene glorificavit Humanum Suum. Nunc quia Dominus per passionem crucis plene glorificavit Humanum Suum, hoc est, univit illud Divino Suo, et sic Humanum Suum etiam fecit Divinum, sequitur quod Ipse sit Jehovah et Deus quoad utrumque. Quare in Verbo multis in locis vocatur Jehovah, Deus, et Sanctus Israelis, Redemptor, Salvator, et Formator, ut in sequentibus his –

Maria dixit, Magnificat anima mea **Dominum**, et exultavit spiritus meus super **Deo Salvatore meo**. Luc.1:46,47.
Angelus dixit ad pastores, Ecce, evangelizo vobis gaudium magnum quod fiet omni populo, quod natus sit hodie **Salvator**, qui est **Christus Dominus**, in urbe Davidis. Luc.2:10,11.
Dixerunt, Hic est vere **Salvator mundi Christus**. Joh.4:42.
Ego Jehovah Deus adjuvo te, et **Redemptor Sanctus Israelis** Esai.41:14.
Dixit **Jehovah**, Creator tuus, Jacob, et **Formator tuus**, Israel, nam redemi te. Ego **Jehovah Deus tuus, Sanctus Israelis Salvator tuus**. Esai.43:1,3.
Dixit **Jehovah Redemptor** vester **Sanctus Israelis**, Ego **Jehovah Sanctus vester**, Creator Israelis **Rex vester**. Esai.43:14,15.
Sic dixit **Jehovah Sanctus Israelis**, et Formator ejus, **Deus Israelis Salvator**. Esai.45:11,15.

34-35   **Deus Israelis Salvator**: *om DD¹, DD²*; **Salvator** *DD³*

The day of vengeance was in My heart, and **the year of My redeemed** had come. I trod them down in My anger; I made their blood[1] go down into the ground. **Therefore He became their Saviour.** Isa.63:4,6,8.

The Lord's conflicts are the subject in this chapter. And in David,

Lift up your heads, O gates, be lifted up, O ancient doors[2], so that the **King of glory** may come in. Who is this **King of glory**? **Jehovah strong and mighty, Jehovah mighty in battle.** Ps.24:7,8.

These words as well are referring to the Lord.

34 **The full union of the Divine and the Human within Him was accomplished by the passion on the cross, which was the final temptation.** This was firmly established above in a section on its own, in which it was shown that the Lord came into the world to subdue the hells and to glorify His Human, and that His passion on the cross was the final conflict, by which He completely conquered the hells and completely glorified His Human. Now because by the passion on the cross the Lord completely glorified His Human, that is, united it to His Divine and in so doing made His Human Divine as well, it follows that He is Jehovah and God in respect of them both. This is why in many places in the Word He is called Jehovah, God, and Holy One of Israel, Redeemer, Saviour, and He who forms, as in the following places – 2

Mary said, My soul magnifies **the Lord**, and my spirit has rejoiced in **God my Saviour.** Luke 1:46,47.
The angel said to the shepherds, Behold, I bring you good news of a great joy which will be for all people, that there is born today, in the city of David, **a Saviour**, who is **Christ the Lord.** Luke 2:10,11.
They said, This is indeed **the Saviour of the world the Christ.** John 4:42.
I Jehovah God am helping you, and your **Redeemer, the Holy One of Israel.** Isa.41:14.
Jehovah said, I am your Creator, O Jacob, and **He who formed you**, O Israel, for I **have redeemed you. I am Jehovah your God, the Holy One of Israel, your Saviour.** Isa.43:1,3.
Jehovah your **Redeemer the Holy One of Israel** said, I am **Jehovah your Holy One**, the Creator of Israel **your King.** Isa.43:14,15.
Thus said **Jehovah the Holy One of Israel**, and He who formed him, **the God of Israel the Saviour.** Isa.45:11,15.

---

1 See note 1 on page 51
2 The Hebrew idiom here means literally *doors of the world*

Sic dixit **Jehovah Redemptor** tuus **Sanctus Israelis**. Esai.48:17.
Ut sciat omnis caro, quod Ego **Jehovah Salvator** tuus, et **Redemptor tuus Fortis Jacobi**. Esai.49:26.
Tunc veniet Zioni **Redemptor**. Esai.59:20.
5 Ut scias quod Ego **Jehovah Salvator** tuus, et **Redemptor** tuus, **Potens Jacobi**. Esai.60:16.
Jehovah Formator meus ab utero. Esai.49:5.
Jehovah Petra mea, et **Redemptor meus**. Ps.19:15.
Recordati sunt quod Deus esset Petra eorum, et **Deus excelsus**
10 **Redemptor eorum**. Ps.78:35.
Dixit **Jehovah Redemptor tuus**, et **Formator tuus** ab utero. Esai.44:24.
Quod ad **Redemptorem nostrum**, **Jehovah Zebaoth** nomen Ipsius, Sanctus Israelis. Esai.47:4.
Cum misericordia aeternitatis miserebor tui; sic dixit **Redemptor**
15 **tuus Jehovah**. Esai.54:8.
Redemptor eorum fortis; **Jehovah Zebaoth** nomen Ipsius. Jer.50:34.
Speret Israel in **Jehovah**, quia **cum Jehovah** misericordia, plurima cum Ipso **redemptio**. **Ille redimet** Israelem ab omnibus iniquitatibus ejus. Ps.130:7,8.
20 **Jehovah Deus** Petra mea, propugnaculum meum, cornu salutis meae, **Salvator meus**. 2 Sam.22:2,3.
Sic dixit **Jehovah Redemptor** Israelis, **Sanctus ipsius**, Reges videbunt et subsistent propter Jehovam, qui fidelis, Sanctum Israelis, qui elegit te. Esai.49:7.
25 Tantummodo inter te Deus, et **praeterea non alius Deus**. Profecto Tu Deus occultus, **Deus Israelis Salvator**. Esai.45:14,15.
Dixit Jehovah Rex Israelis, et **Redemptor ejus Jehovah Zebaoth**, **Praeter Me non Deus**. Esai.44:6.
Ego Jehovah, et praeter Me non Salvator. Esai.43:11.
30 **Nonne Ego Jehovah, et non amplius Deus praeter Me? et Salvator non est praeter Me**. Esai.45:21.
Ego **Jehovah Deus tuus**, et Deum praeter Me non agnosces, et **Salvator non est praeter Me**. Hos.13:4.
Nonne **Ego Jehovah**, et non amplius Deus praeter Me? Deus justus
35 et **Salvator non est praeter Me**. Respicite ad Me ut **salvemini**, omnes fines terrae; quia **Ego Deus, et non praeterea**. Esai.45:21,22.
Jehovah Zebaoth nomen Ipsius, et Redemptor tuus Sanctus Israelis; Deus totius terrae vocabitur. Esai.54:5.

7 meus: tuus *DD*
16 **Zebaoth** *DD³: om DD¹, DD²*
30 *om* **Deus** *DD*

Thus said **Jehovah** your **Redeemer the Holy One of Israel**. Isa.48:17.
That all flesh may know that I am **Jehovah** your **Saviour**, and **your Redeemer, the Mighty One of Jacob**. Isa.49:26.
Then **the Redeemer** will come to Zion. Isa.59:20.
That you may know that I **Jehovah** am your **Saviour**, and your **Redeemer, the Powerful One of Jacob**. Isa.60:16.
Jehovah who formed me from the womb. Isa.49:5.
Jehovah my Rock and **my Redeemer**. Ps.19:14.
They remembered that God was their Rock, and **the most high God their Redeemer**. Ps.78:35.
Jehovah your Redeemer said, and **He who formed you** from the womb. Isa.44:24.
As for **our Redeemer, Jehovah Zebaoth** is His name, the Holy One of Israel. Isa.47:4.
With everlasting mercy will I have compassion on you; so said **your Redeemer Jehovah**. Isa.54:8.
Their Redeemer is strong; Jehovah Zebaoth is His name. Jer.50:34.
Let Israel hope in **Jehovah**, for **with Jehovah** there is mercy, and with Him very much **Redemption**. **He will redeem** Israel from all his iniquities. Ps.130:7,8.
Jehovah God is my Rock, my fortress, the horn of my salvation, **my Saviour**. 2 Sam.22:2,3.
Thus said **Jehovah the Redeemer** of Israel, his **Holy One**, Kings will see and sink down because of Jehovah, who is faithful, the Holy One of Israel, who has chosen you. Isa.49:7.
God is with you only, and **there is no other besides God**. Truly You are a hidden God, **O God of Israel the Saviour**. Isa.45:14,15.
Jehovah the King of Israel said, and his **Redeemer Jehovah Zebaoth, Besides Me there is no God**. Isa.44:6.
I am Jehovah, and besides Me there is no Saviour. Isa.43:11.
Is it not I Jehovah, and there is no God else besides Me? And there is no Saviour besides Me. Isa.45:21.
I am **Jehovah your God**, and you are not to acknowledge any God besides Me, and **there is no Saviour besides Me**. Hos.13:4.
Is it not **I Jehovah**, and there is no God else besides Me? A just God and **a Saviour, there is none besides Me**. Look to Me and **be saved**, all ends of the earth; for **I am God, and there is no other**. Isa.45:21,22.
Jehovah Zebaoth is His name, and your Redeemer, the Holy One of Israel; the God of the whole earth He will be called. Isa.54:5.

Ex his videri potest quod Divinum Domini, quod Pater vocatur et hic Jehovah et Deus, ac Divinum Humanum – quod Filius vocatur et hic Redemptor et Salvator, tum Formator, hoc est, Reformator et Regenerator – non duo sint sed unum. Nam non solum dicitur Jehovah Deus et Sanctus Israelis Redemptor et Salvator, sed etiam dicitur Jehovah Redemptor et Salvator, imo etiam dicitur Jehovah Salvator et non praeter Me, ex quibus manifeste patet quod Divinum et Humanum in Domino sint una Persona, et quod Humanum etiam Divinum sit, nam Redemptor et Salvator mundi non alius est quam Dominus quoad Divinum Humanum, quod Filius vocatur. Redemptio et salvatio enim est attributum proprium Humani Ipsius, quod vocatur meritum et justitia, nam Humanum Ipsius sustinuit tentationes et passionem crucis; ita per Humanum redemit et salvavit.

Nunc quia post unitionem Humani cum Divino in Se, quae fuit sicut animae et corporis apud hominem, non amplius erant duo sed una Persona, secundum Doctrinam Christiani orbis, ideo Dominus quoad utrumque est Jehovah et Deus, quare dicitur nunc Jehovah et Sanctus Israelis Redemptor et Salvator, nunc Jehovah Redemptor et Salvator, ut ex adductis locis videri potest quod ibi dicatur, **Salvator Christus**, Luc.2:10,11; Joh.4:42; **Deus, et Deus Israelis Salvator et Redemptor**, Luc.1:47; Esai.45:15; 54:5; Ps.78:35; **Jehovah Sanctus Israelis Salvator et Redemptor**, Esai.41:14; 43:3,11,14,15; 48:17; 49:7; 54:5; **Jehovah Salvator, Redemptor, et Formator**, Esai.44:6; 47:4; 49:26; 54:8; 63:16; Jer.50:34; Ps.19:15; Ps.130:7,8; 2 Sam.22:2,3; **Jehovah Deus Redemptor, et Salvator, et praeter Me non alius**, Esai.43:11; 44:6; 45:14,15,21,22; Hos.13:4.

35 **Quod Dominus Humanum ex matre susceptum successive exuerit, et Humanum ex Divino in Ipso induerit, quod est Divinum Humanum et Filius Dei.** Quod Domino fuerit Divinum et Humanum, Divinum ex Jehovah patre et Humanum ex Maria virgine, notum est; inde est quod fuerit Deus et Homo, et sic Ipsi Essentia Divina et Natura Humana – Essentia Divina ex Patre, Natura Humana ex matre – et inde aequalis Patri quoad Divinum et minor Patre quoad Humanum; tum quod Humanam hanc ex matre Naturam non transmutaverit in Essentiam Divinam nec ei commiscuerit

From all this it can be seen that the Lord's Divine (which 3 is called the Father, and in these places Jehovah and God) and His Divine Human (which is called the Son, and in these places Redeemer and Saviour, and also He who forms, that is, reforms and regenerates) are not two but one. For these places include references not only to Jehovah God and to the Holy One of Israel the Redeemer and Saviour, but also to Jehovah the Redeemer and Saviour, and even to Jehovah the Saviour and none besides Me. All this plainly shows that the Divine and the Human in the Lord are one Person, and that His Human as well is Divine, for the Redeemer and Saviour of the world is none other than the Lord's Divine Human, called the Son. Furthermore, redemption and salvation are an attribute which belongs properly to His Human and is called His merit and righteousness, because it was His Human that underwent temptations and the passion on the cross, and so it was through the Human that He accomplished redemption and salvation.

Now because the Human and the Divine in Him – after the 4 uniting of the former to the latter, which made them like soul and body in an ordinary human being – were no longer two but one Person, as is the teaching in the Christian world, both the Lord's Human and His Divine are Jehovah and God. This explains why reference is made sometimes to Jehovah and the Holy One of Israel the Redeemer and Saviour, and sometimes to Jehovah the Redeemer and Saviour, as may be seen in the places which have been quoted. These speak of **the Saviour, the Christ**, Luke 2:10,11; John 4:42; **God, and the God of Israel the Redeemer and Saviour**, Luke 1:47; Isa.45:15; 54:5; Ps.78:35; **Jehovah the Holy One of Israel the Saviour and Redeemer**, Isa.41:14; 43:3,11,14,15; 48:17; 49:7; 54:5; **Jehovah the Saviour, Redeemer, and He who forms**, Isa.44:6; 47:4; 49:26; 54:8; 63:16; Jer.50:34; Ps.19:14; Ps.130:7,8; 2 Sam.22:2,3; **Jehovah God the Redeemer, the Saviour, and no other besides Me**, Isa.43:11; 44:6; 45:14,15,21,22; Hos.13:4.

35 **The Lord cast off in consecutive stages the Human taken on from the mother and put on the Human from the Divine within Him, which is the Divine Human and the Son of God.** It is well known that the Lord had a Divine and a Human, a Divine from Jehovah the Father and a Human from Mary a virgin; that He was therefore God and Man, and so had a Divine Essence and a Human Nature – the Divine Essence derived from the Father and the Human Nature from the mother – and was therefore equal to the Father in respect of the Divine but less than the Father in respect of the Human; and also that He did not convert this Human Nature from the mother into the Divine Essence, nor mingle it with that Essence, as the teaching in the

illam, ut docet **Doctrina Fidei**, quae **Athanasiana** vocatur, nam Natura Humana in Essentiam Divinam non potest transmutari nec potest ei commisceri.

Et tamen ex eadem nostra doctrina est quod Divinum susceperit Humanum, hoc est, univerit se illi, sicut anima suo corpori, usque ut non duo essent sed una Persona. Ex eo sequitur quod Humanum ex matre, quod in se erat simile humano alterius hominis et sic materiale, exuerit, ac Humanum ex Patre, quod in se simile Divino Suo et sic substantiale, induerit, ex quo Humanum etiam factum est Divinum. Inde est quod Dominus in Verbo Prophetarum etiam quoad Humanum dicatur Jehovah et Deus, ac in Verbo Evangelistarum Dominus, Deus, Messias seu Christus, et Filius Dei, in quem credendum est et a quo salvandi sunt.

Nunc quia Domino fuit ab initio Humanum ex matre, et hoc successive exuit, ideo, dum in mundo erat, fuerunt Ipsi duo status, qui vocantur status humiliationis seu exinanitionis, et status glorificationis seu unitionis cum Divino quod Pater vocatur – status humiliationis quantum et quando fuit in Humano ex matre, et status glorificationis quantum et quando fuit in Humano ex Patre. In statu humiliationis oravit Patrem sicut alium a Se, in statu glorificationis autem loquutus est cum Patre ut cum Se. In hoc statu dixit quod Pater esset in Se et Ipse in Patre, et quod Pater et Ipse unum essent; in statu autem humiliationis subiit tentationes, et passus est crucem, et oravit ne Pater Ipsum desereret, nam Divinum non potuit tentari et minus adhuc crucem pati. Ex his nunc patet quod per tentationes et continuas tunc victorias, ac per passionem crucis, quae fuit ultima tentationum, plene vicerit inferna et plene glorificaverit Humanum, ut prius ostensum est.

Quod Dominus exuerit Humanum ex matre et induerit Humanum ex Divino in Ipso, quod Pater vocatur, patet etiam ex eo quod Dominus quoties Ipse ex Suo ore loquutus est ad matrem, non vocaverit illam Matrem sed Mulierem. Apud Evangelistas legitur modo ter quod ex Suo ore loquutus sit ad matrem et de illa, et tunc bis quod appellaverit illam Mulierem, et semel quod non agnoverit illam pro matre. Bis quod appellaverit illam Mulierem, legitur apud Johannem,

Dixit mater Jesu ad Ipsum, Vinum non habent. Dicit illi Jesus, Quid Mihi et tibi, **Mulier**? Nondum venit hora Mea. 2:3,4.

creed called **the Athanasian** declares, for the Human Nature cannot be converted into the Divine Essence, nor can it be mingled with it.

Yet this same teaching of ours declares that the Divine took on the Human, that is, made it one with itself, like soul with body, so that they were not two but one Person. It follows from this that He cast off the Human from the mother, which in itself was like that of anyone else and so was made of matter, and put on the Human from the Father, which in itself was like His Divine and so consisted of substance, as a result of which the Human was made Divine as well. This explains why in the Word, in the Prophets, the Lord even in respect of His Human is called Jehovah and God, and in the Gospels Lord, God, Messiah or Christ, and Son of God, in whom there must be belief, and by whom people must be saved. 2

Now because the Lord had the Human from the mother initially and then cast it off in consecutive stages, He experienced two states while He was in the world. These are called a state of humility or exinanition and a state of glorification or oneness with the Divine called the Father. It was a state of humility insofar as and whenever He was functioning in the Human from the mother, and a state of glorification insofar as and whenever He was doing so within the Human from the Father. In a state of humility He prayed to the Father as if to another apart from Himself, but in a state of glorification He talked with the Father as if together with Himself. In this latter state He said that the Father was in Him and He in the Father, and that the Father and He were one; but in a state of humility He underwent temptations, suffered the cross, and prayed to the Father not to abandon Him, for the Divine could not be tempted, let alone suffer the cross. From all this it is now evident that by means of temptations and the unbroken chain of victories in them, and by means of the passion on the cross, which was the final temptation, the hells were fully conquered by Him and the Human fully glorified, as shown previously. 3

The truth that the Lord cast off the Human received from the mother and put on the Human from the Divine within Him, called the Father, is also evident from the fact that as often as the Lord spoke with words out of His own mouth to His mother He did not address her as Mother but Woman. We read in the Gospels of only three occasions when He spoke to her or about her with words out of His own mouth. Twice He called her Woman, and once He did not acknowledge her. The two times He called her Woman occur in John, 4

The mother of Jesus said to Him, They have no wine. Jesus said to her, **Woman**, what have you to do with Me? My hour has not yet come. 2:3,4.

Et apud eundem,

Jesus e cruce videt matrem, et discipulum adstantem quem amabat. Dicit matri Suae, **Mulier**, ecce filius tuus! Deinde dicit discipulo, Ecce mater tua! 19:26,27.

Semel quod non agnoverit illam, apud Lucam,

Nuntiatum est Jesu a dicentibus, Mater Tua et fratres Tui foris stant, et volunt te videre. Jesus respondens dixit ad illos, Mater Mea et fratres Mei hi sunt qui audiunt verbum Dei et faciunt illud. 8:20,21; Matt.12:46-49; Marc.3:31-35.

In aliis locis vocatur Maria Ipsius mater sed non ab Ipsius ore.

Hoc etiam confirmatur per id quod non agnoverit Se esse filium Davidis, legitur enim apud Evangelistas,

Interrogavit Jesus Pharisaeos, dicens, Quid vobis videtur de Christo? Cujus filius est? Dicunt Ipsi, Davidis. Dixit illis, Quomodo ergo David Ipsum in spiritu Dominum suum vocat, dicens, Dixit Dominus Domino meo, Sede a dextris Meis, donec posuero inimicos Tuos scabellum pedum Tuorum. Si ergo David vocat Ipsum Dominum, quomodo filius ejus est? Et nemo poterat Ipsi respondere verbum. Matt.22:39-44; Marc.12:35-37; Luc.20:41-44; Ps.110:1.

Ex his patet quod Dominus quoad Humanum glorificatum non fuerit Mariae nec Davidis filius.

Quale fuit Humanum Ipsius glorificatum, ostendit Petro, Jacobo, et Johanni, cum transformatus est coram illis, Quod splenduerit facies Ipsius sicut sol, et vestimenta Ipsius fuerint sicut lux. Et tunc vox e nube dixit, Hic est Filius Meus dilectus, in quo Mihi complacuit; Ipsum audite. Matt.17:1-8; Marc.9:2-8; Luc.9:28-36.

Dominus etiam est visus Johanni,

Sicut sol lucens in virtute sua. Apoc.1:16.

Quod Humanum Domini glorificatum sit, constat ex illis quae de glorificatione Ipsius apud Evangelistas dicuntur, ut ex his
– Apud Johannem,

And in the same gospel,

From the cross Jesus saw His mother, and the disciple whom He loved standing by. He said to His mother, **Woman**, behold your son! Then He said to the disciple, Behold your mother! 19:26,27.

Of the one occasion He did not acknowledge her we read in Luke,

It was reported to Jesus from people saying, Your mother and Your brothers are standing outside and wish to see You. Jesus answered and said to them, My mother and My brothers are these who hear the word of God and do it. 8:20,21; Matt.12:46-49; Mark 3:31-35.

In other places she is called Mary His mother but not in the words that come from the Lord's own mouth.

In addition and in support of this there is His refusal to acknowledge that He was the son of David, for we read in the Gospels,

Jesus questioned the Pharisees, saying, What do you think about the Christ? Whose son is He? They said to Him, David's. He said to them, How is it then that David in the spirit calls Him his Lord, saying, The Lord said to my Lord, Sit at My right hand until I make Your enemies Your footstool. If therefore David calls Him Lord, how is He his son? And no one was able to answer Him a word. Matt.22:41-46; Mark 12:35-37; Luke 20:41-44; Ps.110:1.

From all this it is evident that with respect to His glorified Human the Lord was neither Mary's nor David's son.

As for what His glorified Human was like, He showed Peter, James and John, when He was transfigured in front of them,
His face shone like the sun, and His garments were like the light. And at this time a voice from the cloud said, This is My beloved Son, in whom I am well pleased; listen to Him. Matt.17:1-8; Mark 9:2-8; Luke 9:28-36.

And when the Lord was seen by John He was,

Like the sun shining in full strength. Rev.1:16.

As for the Lord's Human, that it was glorified, this is clear from the things said in the Gospels about His glorification, such as these – In John,

DOCTRINA DE DOMINO

Venit hora ut glorificetur Filius Hominis. Dixit, Pater, glorifica Tuum nomen. Exiit vox e caelo, Et glorificavi et rursus glorificabo. 12:23,28.

Quia Dominus successive glorificatus est, ideo dicitur, Et glorificavi et rursus glorificabo. Apud eundem,

Postquam Judas exivit, dixit Jesus, Nunc glorificatus est Filius Hominis, et Deus glorificatus est in Ipso; etiam Deus glorificabit Ipsum in Se Ipso, et statim glorificabit Ipsum. 13:31,32.

Apud eundem,

Jesus dixit, Pater, venit hora. Glorifica Filium Tuum, ut etiam Filius glorificet Te. 17:1,5.

Et apud Lucam,

Nonne hoc oportebat pati Christum et ingredi in gloriam Suam? 24:26.

Haec dicta sunt de Humano Ipsius. Dixit Dominus, Deus glorificatus est in Ipso, etiam, Deus glorificabit Ipsum in Se Ipso, tum, Glorifica Filium Tuum, ut etiam Filius Tuus glorificet Te. Haec Dominus dixit quia unitio fuit reciproca, Divini cum Humano ac Humani cum Divino, quare etiam dixerat,

Ego in Patre et Pater in Me. Joh.14:10,11.

Tum,

Omnia Mea Tua sunt et omnia Tua Mea. Joh.17:10.

Inde fuit unitio plenaria. Simile est cum omni unitione, quae nisi sit reciproca, non est plena. Qualis etiam erit Domini cum homine et hominis cum Domino, ut docet apud Johannem,

In illa die cognoscetis quod vos in Me et Ego in vobis. 14:20.

Et alibi,

The hour has come that the Son of Man should be glorified. He said, Father, glorify Your name. A voice came from heaven, I have both glorified it and will glorify it again. 12:23,28.

It was because the Lord was glorified in consecutive stages that the declaration came, I have both glorified it and will glorify it again. In the same gospel,

After Judas went out Jesus said, Now has the Son of Man been glorified, and God has been glorified in Him. God will also glorify Him in Himself, and will glorify Him at once. 13:31,32.

In the same gospel,

Jesus said, Father, the hour has come. Glorify Your Son, that the Son may also glorify You. 17:1,5.

And in Luke,

Ought not the Christ to have suffered this and to enter into His glory? 24:26.

These things were said with reference to His Human. The Lord said, God has been glorified in Him, also, God will glorify Him in Himself, and then, Glorify Your Son, that Your Son may also glorify You. The Lord said these things because the union was reciprocal, Divine with Human and Human with Divine, which is why He also said,

I am in the Father and the Father is in Me. John 14:10,11.

And also,

All Mine are Yours and all Yours are Mine. John 17:10.

It was therefore a complete union. It is similarly so with any other union, which is not a full one if it is not reciprocal. That of the Lord with a person and of a person with the Lord is also going to be such, as He declares in John,

On that day you will know that you are in Me and I in you. 14:20.

And in another place,

DOCTRINA DE DOMINO

Manete in Me, etiam Ego in vobis. Qui manet in Me et Ego in illo, hic fert fructum multum. 15:4,5.

Quoniam Humanum Domini glorificatum est, hoc est, Divinum factum est, ideo post mortem tertia die cum toto corpore resurrexit, quod non fit alicui homini, nam homo solum quoad spiritum, non autem quoad corpus resurgit. Ut homo sciret et nemo dubitaret quin Dominus cum toto corpore resurrexerit, non modo dixit id per angelos qui erant in sepulchro sed etiam ostendit Se in humano Suo corpore coram discipulis, dicens illis, cum crediderunt se videre spiritum,

Videte manus Meas et pedes Meos, quod Ipse Ego sim; palpate Me et videte, nam spiritus carnem et ossa non habet, sicut Me videtis habere. Hocque cum dixisset, ostendit illis manus et pedes. Luc.24:39,40; Joh.20:20.

Et porro,

Jesus dixit Thomae, Mitte digitum tuum huc, et vide manus Meas, et mitte manum tuam, ac immitte in latus Meum; et non esto incredulus sed credulus. Tunc dixit Thomas, Domine mi et Deus mi. Joh.20:27,28.

Ut Dominus adhuc confirmaret quod non spiritus sed Homo esset, dixit discipulis,

Habetis ne aliquid edulii hic? Illi dederunt Ipsi piscis assi partem, et de favo apiario, quae accipiens coram illis comedit. Luc.24:41-43.

Quoniam corpus Ipsius nunc non materiale sed substantiale Divinum fuit, ideo venit ad discipulos januis clausis, Joh.20:19,26, et postquam visus est, invisibilis factus est, Luc.24:31. Talis nunc Dominus sublatus est et consedit a dextris Dei, nam dicitur apud Lucam,

Factum est, cum benediceret Jesus discipulis, secessit ab illis et sublatus est in caelum. 24:51.

Et apud Marcum,

Postquam loquutus est illis, sublatus est in caelum et consedit a dextris Dei. 16:19.

Abide in Me, and I in you. Those who abide in Me, and I in them, they it is that bear much fruit. 15:4,5.

Because the Lord's Human was glorified, that is, made Divine, He therefore rose again on the third day after death with His entire body, which does not happen to anyone else, for a person's spirit rises again, but not the body. To enable people to know, and none be in doubt, that the Lord rose again with His entire body He not only declared this through the angels who were in the tomb but also revealed Himself in His human body to the disciples, and said to them when they thought they were seeing a spirit, 9

See My hands and My feet, that it is I Myself; handle Me and see, for a spirit does not have flesh and bones as you see Me to have. And when He had said this He showed them His hands and feet. Luke 24:39,40; John 20:20.

And in addition to this,

Jesus said to Thomas, Put your finger here, and see My hands, and put out your hand and put it into My side; and do not be unbelieving but believing. Then Thomas said, My Lord and my God. John 20:27,28.

To provide further proof that He was not a spirit but a Man the Lord said to the disciples, 10

Do you have any food at all here? They gave Him part of a broiled fish and some honeycomb, which He took and ate in their presence. Luke 24:41-43.

Since His body now consisted not of matter but of Divine substance He therefore came to the disciples when the doors were shut, John 20:19,26; and after He had been recognized vanished from sight, Luke 24:31. This being what the Lord was now like He was carried up and sat down at the right hand of God, for it says in Luke,

It happened that while He was blessing them He parted from them and was carried up into heaven. 24:51.

And in Mark,

After He had spoken to them He was carried up into heaven and sat down at the right hand of God, 16:19.

Sedere a dextris Dei significat Divinam Omnipotentiam.

Quoniam Dominus cum Divino et Humano unito in unum ascendit in caelum et consedit a dextris Dei, per quod significatur Divina Omnipotentia, sequitur quod Humana Ipsius Substantia seu Essentia sit sicut Ipsius Divina. Si homo aliter cogitaret, foret sicut cogitaret quod Divinum Ipsius sublatum esset in caelum ac sederet a dextris Dei, et non simul Humanum, quod contra Scripturam est et quoque contra doctrinam Christianam, quae est quod Deus et Homo in Christo sint sicut anima et corpus, quae separare foret contra sanam rationem. Haec unitio Patris cum Filio seu Divini cum Humano intelligitur etiam in his sequentibus,

Exivi a Patre et veni in mundum; iterum relinquo mundum et vado ad Patrem. Joh.16:28.
Abeo et venio ad Illum qui misit Me. Joh.7:33; 16:5,16; 17:11,13.
Si ergo videritis Filium Hominis ascendentem ubi erat prius? Joh.6:62.
Nemo ascendit in caelum nisi qui e caelo descendit. Joh.3:13.

Quisque homo qui salvatur ascendit in caelum, sed non a se, verum a Domino. Solus Dominus ascendit a Se.

36 **Quod ita Deus factus sit Homo, ut in primis, etiam in ultimis.** Quod Deus sit Homo, et quod ex Deo omnis angelus et spiritus sit homo, in opere **De Caelo et Inferno** aliquibus ostensum est, et ulterius in opusculis de **Sapientia Angelica** ostendetur. Sed Deus ab initio fuit Homo in primis, non autem in ultimis; at postquam suscepit Humanum in mundo, etiam factus est Homo in ultimis. Hoc sequitur ex supra confirmatis quod Dominus univerit Humanum Suum Divino Suo, et sic Humanum Suum etiam Divinum fecerit. Ex eo est quod Dominus dicatur Principium et Finis, Primus et Ultimus, atque Alpha et Omega. Hoc in Apocalypsi,

Ego sum Alpha et Omega, Principium et Finis, inquit Dominus, Ille qui est, et qui fuit, et qui venturus est, omnipotens. 1:8,11.

---

15   17:11,13 *DD*³: 17:11,13; 19:27 *DD*¹, *DD*²

Sitting at the right hand of God means the Almighty Power of God.

Because the Lord went up to heaven with His Human and Divine joined into one and sat down at the right hand of God, by which is meant the Almighty Power of God, it follows that His Human Substance or Essence is as His Divine Substance. To entertain any other idea than this would be like imagining that His Divine were carried up into heaven and became seated at the right hand of God, but not His Human at the same time, which is contrary to Scripture. Such an idea is also contrary to Christian teaching, which declares that God and Man in Christ are like soul and body, to separate which would be contrary to sound reason. This union of the Father with the Son or the Divine with the Human is also what is meant in the following places,

I came out from the Father and have come into the world; again I am leaving the world and going to the Father. John 16:28.
I am going away and coming to Him who sent Me. John 7:33; 16:5,16; 17:11,13.
What if you were to see the Son of Man going up to where He was before? John 6:62.
No one has gone up to heaven except Him who came down from heaven. John 3:13.

Everyone who is saved goes up to heaven, yet not in their own strength but the Lord's. The Lord alone has gone up in His own.

36 **In this way God became Man in last things as well as in first.** It has been shown several times in the work **Heaven and Hell** that God is Man, and that because of God every angel and spirit is someone human; and more that shows this to be so will appear in the small works regarding **Angelic Wisdom**.[1] Initially, however, God was Man in first things but not in last; only after He had taken on the Human in the world did He become Man in last things as well. This follows on from what was presented above to prove that the Lord united His Human to His Divine and consequently made His Human Divine as well. This is why the Lord is called the Beginning and the End, the First and the Last, also the Alpha and the Omega. He is called this in the Book of Revelation,

I am the Alpha and the Omega, the Beginning and the End, says the Lord, He who is and who was and who is to come, the Almighty. 1:8,11.

---

1 See author's preface, page 3 above

Johannes cum vidit Filium Hominis in medio septem candelabrorum, cecidit ad pedes Ipsius sicut mortuus. Sed imposuit dextram Suam super illum, dicens, Ego sum Primus et Ultimus. 1:13,17; 2:8; 21:6.
Ecce venio cito, ut dem unicuique secundum opus ejus. Ego sum Alpha et Omega, Principium et Finis, Primus et Ultimus. 22:12,13.

Et apud Esaiam,

Sic dixit Jehovah Rex Israelis, et Redemptor ejus Jehovah Zebaoth, Ego sum Primus et Ultimus. 44:6; 48:12.

When John saw the Son of Man in the midst of the seven lampstands, he fell at His feet as if he were dead. But He laid His right hand on him, saying, I am the First and the Last. 1:13,17; 2:8; 21:6.
Behold, I am coming quickly, to give to everyone according to their work. I am the Alpha and the Omega, the Beginning and the End, the First and the Last. 22:12,13.

And in Isaiah,

Thus said Jehovah the King of Israel, and his Redeemer Jehovah Zebaoth, I am the First and the Last. 44:6; 48:12.

Quod Dominus sit Ipse Deus,
a quo et de quo Verbum

37   In primo articulo caeptum est demonstrare quod universa Scriptura Sacra sit de Domino et quod Dominus sit Verbum. Hic ulterius demonstrabitur ex locis e Verbo ubi Dominus vocatur Jehovah, Deus Israelis et Jacobi, Sanctus Israelis, Dominus et Deus, ut et Rex, Unctus Jehovae, David. In antecessum memorare licet quod mihi datum sit omnes Prophetas et Davidis Psalmos percurrere, ac singulos versus lustrare et videre de quo ibi agitur, et visum est quod non de aliis rebus agatur quam de ecclesia a Domino instaurata et instauranda, de Domini adventu, pugnis, glorificatione, redemptione, et salvatione, et de caelo ab Ipso, et simul de oppositis. Quia omnia illa sunt Domini opera, patuit quod universa Scriptura Sacra sit de Domino et inde quod Dominus sit Verbum.

Verum hoc non videri potest nisi quam ab illis qui in illustratione sunt a Domino, et qui sensum spiritualem Verbi etiam norunt. Omnes angeli caeli in hoc sensu sunt, quare illi, cum legitur Verbum ab homine, non aliud comprehendunt. Sunt enim spiritus et angeli apud hominem jugiter, et illi, quia spirituales sunt, spiritualiter omnia intelligunt quae homo naturaliter. Quod tota Scriptura Sacra sit de Domino, solum in obscuro et sicut per transennam videri potest ex illis quae supra in articulo primo, a n.1 ad 6, ex Verbo adducta sunt, et nunc ex his quae adducentur de Domino, quod toties dicatur Dominus et Deus, ex quo potest elucere quod Ipse sit qui loquutus est per Prophetas, apud quos ubivis dicitur, **Loquutus est Jehovah, Dixit Jehovah**, et **Dictum Jehovae**.

Quod Dominus ante adventum Suum in mundum fuerit, patet ab his –

The Lord is God Himself, from whom the Word comes and has to do with

37 The first section began to show that the whole of Sacred Scripture has to do with the Lord and that the Lord is the Word. The present section will go further, showing this to be so from places in the Word where the Lord is called Jehovah, the God of Israel and Jacob, the Holy One of Israel, Lord and God, as well as King, Jehovah's Anointed, David. But in advance of this let me mention that I have been allowed to go through all the Prophets and the Psalms of David, examine individual verses and see what it is they have to do with. And I have seen that the only subjects in them are the church that has been or is to be established by the Lord; the Lord's coming, conflicts, glorification, redemption and salvation; heaven's origin in Him; and as well the things standing opposed to Him. Since all these are works of the Lord it has become plain to me that the whole of Sacred Scripture has to do with the Lord and consequently that the Lord is the Word.

But none of this can be seen except by those who receive enlightenment from the Lord and who are also aware of the spiritual level of meaning in the Word. All angels in heaven think on that level, and therefore when the Word is being read by a person in our world they understand it on no other level. For present with a person constantly there are spirits and angels, and because these are spiritual beings they understand in a spiritual way everything understood by people in a natural way. As regards the truth that the whole of Sacred Scripture has to do with the Lord, only a faint perception of it, as if seen through latticework, can be gained from the places which have been quoted from the Word in §§1-6 in the section above. The same goes for those that are going to be quoted now regarding the Lord, in which He is frequently called Lord and God, and from which it becomes clear that He it is who spoke through the Prophets, wherever in the books attributed to them the expressions **Jehovah spoke, Jehovah said**, and **Said by Jehovah** occur.

The Lord was, before His coming into the world. This is evident from the following places –

Johannes Baptista dixit de Domino,

Ille est qui post me venturus est, qui ante me fuit, cujus ego non sum dignus ut solvam Ipsius corrigiam calcei. Hic est de quo ego dixi, Qui post me venit, qui ante me fuit, quia prior me fuit. Joh.1:27,30.

In Apocalypsi,

Ceciderunt coram throno, super quo erat Dominus, dicentes, Gratias agimus Tibi, Domine Deus, Omnipotens, qui es, et qui eras, et qui venturus es. 11:16,17.

Tum apud Micham,

Tu, Bethlechem Ephrathaea, parum est ut sis inter millenas Jehudae; ex te Mihi exibit qui erit Dominator in Israele, et cujus exitus ab antiquo, a diebus aeternitatis. 5:1.

Praeter a Domini verbis apud Evangelistas, quod ante Abrahamum fuerit; quod gloriam apud Patrem habuerit ante mundi fundationem; quod exiverit ex Patre; et quod a principio fuerit Verbum apud Deum, et quod Deus esset Verbum, et quod hoc caro factum sit.

Quod Dominus dicatur Jehovah, Deus Israelis et Jacobi, Sanctus Israelis, Dominus et Deus, tum Rex, Unctus Jehovae, David, constare potest ex his sequentibus.

38   **Quod Dominus dicatur Jehovah,** patet ex his –

Dixit **Jehovah** Creator tuus, Jacob, et Formator tuus, Israel; nam **redemi** te. Ego **Jehovah** Deus tuus, Sanctus Israelis **Salvator** tuus. Esai.43:1,3.
Ego **Jehovah**, Sanctus vester, Creator Israelis, Rex vester. Esai.43:15.
Sic dixit **Jehovah,** Sanctus Israelis, et **Formator** ejus. Esai.45:11,15.
Ut sciat omnis caro quod **Ego Jehovah Salvator** tuus, et **Redemptor** tuus, Fortis Jacobi. Esai.49:26.

4	quia: et qui *DD*	
19	Dominus et Deus: Deus et Dominus *DD*	
25-26	Ego **Jehovah**, Sanctus vester, Creator Israelis, Rex vester. Esai.43:15. Sic dixit **Jehovah**, Sanctus Israelis, et **Formator** ejus. Esai.45:11,15 *DD*[3]: Ego **Jehovah** Sanctus, Creator Israelis Sanctus vester, et **Formator** ejus. Esai.45:11,15 *DD*[1], *DD*[2]	

John the Baptist said in reference to the Lord,

> He it is who is going to come after me, who was, before me, whose shoestrap I am not worthy to unloose. This is He of whom I said, There is one coming after me who was before me, for He was, before me. John 1:27,30.

In the Book of Revelation,

> They[1] fell down before the throne, on which the Lord was, saying, We give thanks to You, Lord God, the Almighty, who is, and who was, and who is to come. 11:16,17.

Also in Micah,

> You, Bethlehem Ephrathah, though you are little among the thousands of Judah, from you will come forth for Me one who will be Ruler in Israel, whose origins are from of old, from eternal days. 5:2.

And in addition to these statements there are the Lord's that appear in the Gospels – that before Abraham, He was; that He had glory with the Father before the foundation of the world; that He had come forth from the Father; and that from the beginning the Word was with God, that the Word was God, and that this became flesh.

As for His being called Jehovah, the God of Israel and Jacob, the Holy One of Israel, Lord and God, as well as King, Jehovah's Anointed, David, this becomes clear from the places that follow in the present section.

38 **The Lord is called Jehovah.** This is evident from the following places –

> Thus said **Jehovah**, your Creator, O Jacob, and He who formed you, O Israel; for **I have redeemed** you. I am **Jehovah** your God, the Holy One of Israel your **Saviour**. Isa.43:1,3.
> I am **Jehovah**, your Holy One, the Creator of Israel, your King. Isa.43:15.
> Thus said **Jehovah**, the Holy One of Israel and **He who formed** him. Isa.45:11,15.
> That all flesh may know that **I Jehovah am** your **Saviour**, and your **Redeemer**, the Mighty One of Jacob. Isa.49:26.

---

1   ie the twenty-four elders

Ut scias quod Ego **Jehovah Salvator** tuus, et **Redemptor** tuus, Potens Jacobi. Esai.60:16.
Jehovah Formator meus ab utero. Esai.49:5.
Jehovah Petra mea et **Redemptor** meus. Ps.19:15.
Dixit **Jehovah**, Factor tuus, et **Formator** ab utero, ... Sic dixit **Jehovah** Rex Israelis, et **Redemptor** ejus **Jehovah Zebaoth**. Esai.44:2,6.
Quod ad **Redemptorem** nostrum, **Jehovah Zebaoth nomen Ipsius**, Sanctus Israelis. Esai.47:4.
Cum misericordia aeternitatis miserebor; sic dixit **Redemptor** tuus **Jehovah**. Esai.54:8.
Redemptor eorum fortis; Jehovah Zebaoth nomen Ipsius. Jer.50:34.
Jehovah, Petra mea, propugnaculum meum, cornu salutis meae, **Salvator** meus. 2 Sam.22:2,3.
Dixit **Jehovah Redemptor** vester, Sanctus Israelis. Esai.43:14; 48:17.
Sic dixit **Jehovah, Redemptor** Israelis, Sanctus ipsius, Reges videbunt. Esai.49:7.
Ego **Jehovah**, et praeter Me non **Salvator**. Esai.43:11.
Nonne Ego **Jehovah**, et non amplius Deus praeter Me? et **Salvator** non est praeter Me. Respicite ad Me, ut **salvemini**, omnes fines terrae. Esai.45:21,22.
Ego **Jehovah** Deus tuus, et **Salvator** non praeter Me. Hos.13:4.
Redemeras me, **Jehovah** Deus veritatis. Ps.31:6.
Speret Israel in **Jehovah**, quia cum **Jehovah** misericordia, plurima cum Ipso **redemptio**. Ille **redimet** Israelem ab omnibus iniquitatibus ejus. Ps.130:7,8.
Jehovah Zebaoth nomen Ipsius, et **Redemptor** tuus, Sanctus Israelis; Deus totius terrae vocabitur. Esai.54:5.

In his locis vocatur Jehovah Redemptor et Salvator; et quia solus Dominus est Redemptor et Salvator, est Ipse qui per Jehovam intelligitur.

Quod Dominus sit Jehovah, hoc est, quod Jehovah sit Dominus, etiam patet ex his –

Virga de trunco Jishaji, et surculus e radicibus ejus fructum feret. Quiescet super Illo **Spiritus Jehovae**. Esai.11:1,2.

3   meus: tuus *DD*
11 **Zebaoth** *DD*³: *om DD*¹, *DD*²
12 **Jehovah**, : **Jehovah**, Deus *DD*
18 *om* Deus *DD*
22 Deus *DD*³: *om DD*¹, *DD*²

That you may know that I **Jehovah** am your **Saviour**, and your **Redeemer**, the Powerful One of Jacob. Isa.60:16.
Jehovah who formed me from the womb. Isa.49:5.
Jehovah my Rock and my **Redeemer**. Ps.19:14.
Jehovah, your Maker and **One who formed** you from the womb has said, ... Thus said **Jehovah** the King of Israel, and his **Redeemer Jehovah Zebaoth**. Isa.44:2,6.
As for our **Redeemer, Jehovah Zebaoth is His name**, the Holy One of Israel. Isa.47:4.
With everlasting mercy will I have compassion; so said your **Redeemer** Jehovah. Isa.54:8.
Their Redeemer is strong; Jehovah Zebaoth is His name. Jer.50:34.
Jehovah is my Rock, my fortress, the horn of my salvation, my **Saviour**. 2 Sam.22:2,3.
Thus said **Jehovah** your **Redeemer**, the Holy One of Israel. Isa.43:14; 48:17.
Thus said **Jehovah** the **Redeemer** of Israel, his Holy One, Kings will see. Isa.49:7.
I am **Jehovah**, and besides Me there is no **Saviour**. Isa.43:11.
Is it not I **Jehovah**, and there is no God else besides Me? And there is no **Saviour** besides Me. Look to Me so that **you may be saved**, all ends of the earth. Isa.45:21,22.
I am **Jehovah** your God, and there is no **Saviour** besides Me. Hos.13:4.
You have redeemed me, O **Jehovah** God of truth. Ps.31:5.
Let Israel hope in **Jehovah**, for with **Jehovah** there is mercy, and with Him very much **redemption**. He will **redeem** Israel from all his iniquities. Ps.130:7,8.
Jehovah Zebaoth is His name, and your **Redeemer**, the Holy One of Israel; the God of the whole earth He will be called. Isa.54:5.

In these places Jehovah is called Redeemer and Saviour, and because the Lord alone is the Redeemer and Saviour it is He who is meant by Jehovah.
    That the Lord is Jehovah, that is, Jehovah is the Lord, is also evident from the following places –

A shoot from the trunk of Jesse, and a branch out of his roots will bear fruit. **The Spirit of Jehovah** will rest upon Him. Isa.11:1,2.

Dicetur in die illo, Ecce Deus noster Hic, quem exspectavimus ut liberet nos, **Jehovah**, quem exspectavimus; exultemus et laetemur in salute Ipsius. Esai.25:9.
Vox clamantis in deserto, Parate viam **Jehovae**, complanate in solitudine semitam Deo nostro. Revelabitur enim **gloria Jehovae**, et videbunt omnis caro. Ecce **Dominus Jehovih** in forti venit, et brachium Ipsius dominabitur Ipsi. Esai.40:3,5,10.
Ego **Jehovah**, dabo Te in faedus populo, in lucem gentium. Ego **Jehovah**, hoc nomen Meum; et **gloriam Meam alteri non dabo**. Esai.42:6-8.
Ecce dies, quum suscitabo Davidi germen justum qui regnabit Rex, et prosperabitur, et faciet judicium et justitiam in terra; et hoc nomen Ipsius quod vocabunt Ipsum, **Jehovah Justitia nostra**. Jer.23:5,6; 33:15,16.
Tu Bethlechem Ephrataea, ex te Mihi exibit qui sit Dominator in Israele. Stabit et pascet in **robore Jehovae**. Mic.5:1,3.
Puer natus est nobis, Filius datus est nobis, super cujus humero principatus, et vocabitur nomen Ipsius, Deus, Heros, **Pater Aeternitatis**, super throno Davidis, ad stabiliendum et fundandum illud in judicio et justitia, a nunc et usque in aeternum. Esai.9:5,6.
Jehovah exibit et pugnabit contra gentes; et stabunt pedes Ipsius super Monte Olivarum ante facies Hierosolymae. Sach.14:3,4.
Attollite, portae, capita vestra, et extollimini, ostia mundi, ut ingrediatur Rex gloriae. Quis hic Rex gloriae? **Jehovah** fortis et heros, **Jehovah** heros belli. Ps.24:7-10.
In die illo erit **Jehovah Zebaoth** in coronam ornatus et in cidarim decoris reliquiis populi Sui. Esai.28:5.
Ego mittam vobis Eliam Prophetam, antequam venit **dies Jehovae** magnus. Mal.3:23.

Praeter alibi, ubi dicitur **dies Jehovae** magnus et propinquus, ut Ezech.30:3; 34:12; Joel 2:11; Amos 5:18,20; Zeph.1:7,14,15,18.
39   **Quod Dominus dicatur Deus Israelis et Deus Jacobi**, patet ex his –

Sumsit Moses sanguinem et sparsit super populum, et dixit, Ecce sanguis faederis quod pepigit Jehovah vobiscum. Et viderunt **Deum Israelis**, sub cujus pedibus erat quasi opus lapidis sapphiri et quasi substantia caeli. Exod.24:8-10.

---

31   30:3; 34:12: 30:12 *DD*¹, *DD*²; 30:3 *DD*³

It will be said on that day, Behold, This is our God, whom we have waited for to deliver us, **Jehovah**, whom we have waited for; let us rejoice and be glad in His salvation. Isa.25:9.

The voice of one crying in the wilderness, Prepare the way of **Jehovah**, make level in the desert a highway for our God. For **the glory of Jehovah** will be revealed, and all flesh will see it. Behold, **the Lord Jehovih** comes with might, and His arm exercises dominion for Him. Isa.40:3,5,10.

I **Jehovah** will give you to be a covenant for the people, a light of the nations. I am **Jehovah**, this is My name; and **My glory I will not give to another**. Isa.42:6-8.

Behold the day, when I shall raise up for David a righteous branch who is going to reign as King, and to prosper, and to execute judgment and righteousness in the land; and this is His name which they will call Him, **Jehovah our Righteousness**. Jer.23:5,6; 33:15,16.

You Bethlehem Ephrath, from you will come forth for Me one who is Ruler in Israel. He will stand and feed [His flock] in **the strength of Jehovah**. Mic.5:2,4.

To us a Boy is born, to us a Son is given, on whose shoulder will be the government, and His name will be called, God, Mighty One, **Father of Eternity**, upon the throne of David, to establish and uphold it in judgment and righteousness, from now and even for evermore. Isa.9:6,7.

Jehovah will go out and fight against the nations; and His feet will stand upon the Mount of Olives, which faces Jerusalem. Zech.14:3,4.

Lift up your heads, O gates, and be lifted up, O ancient doors[1], so that the King of glory may come in. Who is this King of glory? **Jehovah** strong and mighty, **Jehovah** mighty in battle. Ps.24:7-10.

On that day **Jehovah Zebaoth** will be a crown of adornment and a turban of beauty for the remnant of His people. Isa.28:5.

I am sending you Elijah the Prophet before the great **day of Jehovah** comes. Mal.4:5.

And in addition there are the places which refer to **the day of Jehovah**, to its being great and near, such as Ezek.30:3; 34:12; Joel 2:11; Amos 5:18,20; Zeph.1:7,14,15,18.

39 **The Lord is called the God of Israel and the God of Jacob**. This is evident from the following places –

Moses took the blood and sprinkled it over the people, and said, Behold, the blood of the covenant which Jehovah has made with you. And they saw **the God of Israel**, under whose feet there was that which was like a work of sapphire stone, and like the substance of the sky. Exod.24:8-10.

1 See note 2 on page 117

Turbae miratae sunt cum viderunt mutos loquentes, mutilos sanos, claudos ambulantes, caecos videntes, et glorificabant **Deum Israelis**. Matt.15:31.

Benedictus **Dominus Deus Israelis**, quia visitavit, et fecit libera-
5 tionem populo Suo Israeli, cum erexit cornu salutis nostrae in domo Davidis. Luc.1:68,69.

Dabo tibi thesauros tenebrarum, et occultas opes latibulorum, ut cognoscas quod Ego Jehovah, qui vocavi nomine tuo, **Deus Israelis**. Esai.45:3.

10 Domus Jacobi, qui jurant in nomen Jehovae et Dei Israelis. Nam ab urbe sanctitatis vocantur et super **Deo Israelis** nituntur; Jehovah Zebaoth nomen Ipsius. Esai.48:1,2.

Jacob videbit natos suos; in medio ejus sanctificabunt nomen Meum, et sanctificabunt Sanctum Jacobi, **Deumque Israelis** timebunt.
15 Esai.29:23.

In extremitate dierum ibunt populi multi et dicent, Ite et ascendamus ad montem Jehovae, ad domum **Dei Jacobi**, qui docebit nos de viis Suis ut eamus in semitis Ipsius. Esai.2:3; Mic.4:2.

Ut sciat omnis caro quod Ego Jehovah Salvator tuus, et **Redemtor**
20 tuus **Fortis Jacobi**. Esai.49:26.

Ego Jehovah Salvator tuus, et Redemptor tuus **Potens Jacobi**. Esai.60:16.

A coram Domino parturis, terra, a coram **Deo Jacobi**. Ps.114:7.

David juravit Jehovae, vovit **Forti Jacobi**, Si intravero intra tentorium
25 domus meae, usque dum invenero locum Jehovae, habitacula **Forti Jacobi**. Audivimus de Eo in Ephrata (Bethlechem) . Ps.132:2,3,5,6.

Benedictus **Deus Israelis**; implebitur gloria Ipsius omnis terra. Ps.72:18,19.

Praeter alibi, ubi Dominus vocatur Deus Israelis, Redemptor et
30 Salvator, ut Luc.1:47; Esai.45:15; 54:5; Ps.78:35; ac multis aliis in locis, ubi solum Deus Israelis, ut Esai.17:6; 21:10,17; 24:15; 29:23; Jer.7:3; 9:14; 11:3; 13:12; 16:9; 19:3,15; 23:2; 24:5; 25:15,27; 29:4,8,21,25; 30:2; 31:23; 32:14,15,36; 33:4; 34:2,13; 35:13,17-19; 37:7; 38:17; 39:16; 42:9,15,18; 43:10; 44:2,7,11,25; 48:1; 50:18; 51:33; Ezechiel 8:4; 9:3;
35 10:19,20; 11:22; 43:2; 44:2; Zeph. 2:9; Pss.41:14; 59:6; 68:9.

40 **Quod Dominus dicatur Sanctus Israelis**, patet ab his –

Angelus dixit ad Mariam, **Sanctum** quod nascetur ex te, vocabitur Filius Dei. Luc.1:35.

1 *om* mutilos sanos DD

The crowds marvelled when they saw the mute speaking, the crippled made whole, the lame walking, the blind seeing, and they glorified **the God of Israel**. Matt.15:31.

Blessed be **the Lord God of Israel**, for He has visited and brought deliverance to His people Israel, when He raised up the horn of our salvation in the house of David. Luke 1:68,69.

I will give you the treasures of darkness, and the secret wealth of concealed places, that you may know that it is I, Jehovah, who called you by your name, **the God of Israel**. Isa.45:3.

O house of Jacob, who swear by the name of Jehovah and the God of Israel. For they are called after the city of holiness and on **the God of Israel** they place their reliance; Jehovah Zebaoth is His name. Isa.48:1,2.

Jacob will see his children; in his midst they will sanctify My name, and they will sanctify the Holy One of Jacob, and will fear **the God of Israel**. Isa.29:23.

In the latter days many peoples will come and say, Come and let us go up to the mountain of Jehovah, to the house of **the God of Jacob**, who will teach us about His ways so that we may go in His paths. Isa.2:3; Mic.4:2.

That all flesh may know that I am Jehovah your Saviour, and your **Redeemer the Mighty One of Jacob**. Isa.49:26.

I, Jehovah, am your Saviour, and your Redeemer, **the Powerful One of Jacob**. Isa.60:16.

At the presence of the Lord you are in labour, O earth, at the presence of **the God of Jacob**. Ps.114:7.

David swore to Jehovah, made a vow to **the Mighty One of Jacob**, Surely I will not enter the tent of my house, until I find a place for Jehovah, dwelling places for **the Mighty One of Jacob**. We heard of Him in Ephrathah (Bethlehem). Ps.132:2,3,5,6.

Blessed be **the God of Israel**; the whole earth will be filled with His glory. Ps.72:18,19.

And in addition there are the places where the Lord is called the God of Israel, the Redeemer and Saviour, such as Luke 1:47; Isa.45:15; 54:5; Ps.78:35; and many other places where He is called simply the God of Israel, such as Isa.17:6; 21:10,17; 24:15; 29:23; Jer.7:3; 9:15; 11:3; 13:12; 16:9; 19:3,15; 23:2; 24:5; 25:15,27; 29:4,8,21,25; 30:2; 31:23; 32:14,15,36; 33:4; 34:2,13; 35:13,17-19; 37:7; 38:17; 39:16; 42:9,15,18; 43:10; 44:2,7,11,25; 48:1; 50:18; 51:33; Ezek.8:4; 9:3; 10:19,20; 11:22; 43:2; 44:2; Zeph.2:9; Pss.41:13; 59:5; 68:8.

40 **The Lord is called the Holy One of Israel**. This is evident from the following places –

The angel said to Mary, **The holy thing** that will be born from you will be called the Son of God. Luke 1:35.

Videns fui in visionibus, ecce, Vigil et **Sanctus** e caelo descendens. Dan.4:10,20.
Deus a Themane veniet, et **Sanctus** a monte Paran. Hab.3:3.
Ego Jehovah, **Sanctus** vester, Creator Israelis, Rex vester. Esai.43:15.
5 Sic dixit Jehovah **Sanctus Israelis**, et Formator ejus. Esai.45:11.
Sic dixit Jehovah, Redemptor Israelis, **Sanctus** ipsius. Esai.49:7.
Ego Jehovah Deus tuus, **Sanctus Israelis**, Salvator tuus. Esai.43:1,3.
Quod ad Redemptorem nostrum, Jehovah Zebaoth nomen Ipsius, **Sanctus Israelis**. Esai.47:4.
10 Dixit Jehovah Redemptor vester, **Sanctus Israelis**. Esai.43:14; 48:17.
Jehovah Zebaoth nomen Ipsius, et Redemptor tuus, **Sanctus Israelis**. Esai.54:5.
Tentarunt Deum et **Sanctum Israelis**. Ps.78:41.
Dereliquerunt Jehovam et provocarunt **Sanctum Israelis**. Esai.1:4.
15 Dixerunt, Cessare facite a faciebus nostris **Sanctum Israelis;** propterea sic dixit **Sanctus Israelis**. Esai.30:11,12.
Qui dicunt, Properet opus Ipsius ut videamus, et appropinquet et veniat consilium **Sancti Israelis**. Esai.5:19.
In die illo innitentur Jehovae, **Sancto Israelis**, in veritate. Esai.10:20.
20 Exclama et jubila, habitatrix Sionis, quia magnus in medio tui **Sanctus Israelis**. Esai.12:6.
Dictum Dei Israelis, In die illo respiciet homo ad Factorem suum, et oculi ejus ad **Sanctum Israelis** spectabunt. Esai.17:6,7.
Addent mansueti in Jehovah gaudium, et egeni hominum in **Sancto**
25 **Israelis** exultabunt. Esai.29:19; 41:16.
Gentes ad te current propter Jehovam Deum tuum, et propter **Sanctum Israelis**. Esai.55:5.
Mihi insulae confident, ad adducendum filios tuos e longinquo nomini Jehovae Dei tui, et **Sancto Israelis**. Esai.60:9.
30 Terra plena est reatu a **Sancto Israelis**. Jer.51.5.
Contra Jehovam insolenter egit, contra **Sanctum Israelis**. Jer.50:29.

Et pluries alibi.

4-5 Ego Jehovah **Sanctus** vester, Creator Israelis Rex vester. Esai.43:15. Sic dixit Jehovah **Sanctus Israelis**, et Formator ejus. Esai.45:11 *DD³*: Ego Jehovah **Sanctus**, Creator Israelis **Sanctus vester** et Formator ejus. Esai.44:11,15. *DD¹,DD²*
20 habitatrix: filia *DD*
24 Jehovah *DD¹, DD²*: Jehovam *DD³*
29 Dei tui: Zebaoth *DD*
30-31 Terra plena est reatu a **Sancto Israelis**. Jer.51:5. Contra Jehovam insolenter egit, contra **Sanctum Israelis**. Jer.50:29. *DD³*: Terra plena est reatu contra **Sanctum Israelis**. Jer.50:29 *DD¹, DD²*

I was looking in the visions, and behold, a Watcher and **Holy One** coming down from heaven. Dan.4:13,23.
God will come from Teman, and **the Holy One** from Mount Paran. Hab.3:3.
I am Jehovah, your **Holy One**, the Creator of Israel, your King. Isa.43:15.
Thus said Jehovah **the Holy One of Israel**, and He who formed him. Isa.45:11.
Thus said Jehovah the Redeemer of Israel, his **Holy One**. Isa.49:7.
I am Jehovah your God, **the Holy One of Israel**, your Saviour. Isa.43:1,3.
As for our Redeemer, Jehovah Zebaoth is His name, **the Holy One of Israel**. Isa.47:4
Thus said Jehovah your Redeemer, **the Holy One of Israel**. Isa.43:14; 48:17.
Jehovah Zebaoth is His name, and your Redeemer, **the Holy One of Israel**. Isa.54:5.
They tested God and **the Holy One of Israel**. Ps.78:41.
They have forsaken Jehovah and provoked **the Holy One of Israel**. Isa.1:4.
They said, Cause **the Holy One of Israel** to cease from being before our faces; therefore thus spoke **the Holy One of Israel**. Isa.30:11,12.
Those who say, Let Him speed His work that we may see it, and let the counsel of **the Holy One of Israel** draw near and come. Isa.5:19.
On that day they will lean on Jehovah, **the Holy One of Israel**, in truth. Isa.10:20.
Cry out and shout for joy, O inhabitant[1] of Zion, for great in your midst is **the Holy One of Israel**. Isa.12:6.
The God of Israel said, On that day people will look to their Maker, and their eyes will regard **the Holy One of Israel**. Isa.17:6,7.
The meek will increase their joy in Jehovah, and the needy will exult in **the Holy One of Israel**. Isa.29:19; 41:16.
Nations will run to you because of Jehovah your God, and because of **the Holy One of Israel**. Isa.55:5.
The islands will put their trust in Me, to bring your sons from afar to the name of Jehovah your God, and to **the Holy One of Israel**. Isa.60:9.
The land is full of guilt against **the Holy One of Israel**. Jer.51:5.
Against Jehovah she has behaved insolently, against **the Holy One of Israel**. Jer.50:29.

And many more places.

 1 The first and both later Latin editions have the word meaning *daughter*; but Schmidt, following the original Hebrew, has a noun that means *female inhabitant*

Per Sanctum Israelis intelligitur Dominus quoad Divinum Humanum, nam angelus Gabriel ad Mariam dixit,

Sanctum quod nascetur ex te, vocabitur Filius Dei. Luc.1:35.

Quod Jehovah et Sanctus Israelis unum sint, tametsi distincte nominantur, constare potest a locis etiam hic allatis in quibus dicitur quod Jehovah sit Ille Sanctus Israelis.

41 **Quod Dominus dicatur Dominus et Deus**, patet a tam multis locis ut, si afferentur, paginas implerent. Haec pauca sufficient –

Apud Johannem, quando Thomas ex mandato Domini vidit manus Ipsius, et tetigit latus Ipsius, dixit,

Domine mi et Deus mi. 20:27,28.

Apud Davidem,

Recordati sunt quod Deus esset Petra eorum, et **Deus excelsus Redemptor** eorum. Ps.78:35.

Et apud Esaiam,

Jehovah Zebaoth nomen Ipsius, et **Redemptor** tuus Sanctus Israelis; **Deus totius terrae vocabitur.** 54:5.

Hoc quoque patet ex eo quod adoraverint Ipsum et ceciderint super facies suas coram Ipso, Matt.9:18,19; 14:33; 15:25; 28:9; Marc.1:40; 5:22; 7:25; 10:17: Luc.17:15,16; Joh.9:38. Et apud Davidem,

Audivimus de Illo in Ephrata. Intremus in habitacula Illius, et **incurvemus nos scabello pedum Illius.** Ps.132:6,7.

Similiter in caelo, de quo in Apocalypsi,

Fui in spiritu, et ecce thronus positus in caelo, et super throno sedens, similis lapidi jaspidi et sardino; et iris circa thronum similis aspectu smaragdino. Et **ciderunt** viginti et quatuor seniores ante Sedentem super throno, et **adorabant Viventem in saecula saeculorum**, et **projecerunt coronas suas ante thronum.** 4:2,3,10.

21 9:38 DD^3: 10:17 DD^1, DD^2

By the Holy One of Israel the Lord in respect of His Divine Human is meant, for the angel Gabriel told Mary,

The Holy Thing that will be born from you will be called the Son of God. Luke 1:35.

That Jehovah and the Holy One of Israel are one, even though they are mentioned separately, becomes clear from those places quoted above in which Jehovah is spoken of as being the Holy One of Israel.

41 **The Lord is called Lord and God.** This is evident from so many places that if all were quoted they would fill page after page. These few will be enough –

In John, when Thomas at the Lord's command beheld His hands and touched His side he said,

My Lord and my God. 20:27,28.

In David,

They remembered that God was their Rock, and **the most high God** their **Redeemer**. Ps.78:35.

And in Isaiah,

Jehovah Zebaoth is His name, and your **Redeemer**, the Holy One of Israel; **the God of the whole earth He will be called.** 54:5.

It is also evident from people's worshipping Him and falling down on their faces before Him, Matt.9:18,19; 14:33; 15:25; 28:9; Mark 1:40; 5:22; 7:25; 10:17; Luke 17:15,16; John 9:38. And in David,

We heard of Him in Ephrathah. Let us enter His dwelling places, and **let us bow down at His footstool.** Ps.132:6,7.

The Book of Revelation refers to those in heaven acting in a similar way,

I was in the spirit, and behold, a throne set in heaven, and One seated on the throne, in appearance like a jasper stone and a sardius; and there was a rainbow around the throne, in appearance like an emerald. And the twenty-four elders **fell down** before the One seated on the throne, and **worshipped the One who lives for ever and ever**, and **cast their crowns before the throne.** 4:2,3,10.

Et alibi,

Vidi in dextra Sedentis super throno librum scriptum intus et a tergo, obsignatum septem sigillis; et nemo potuit illum aperire. Tunc dixit unus ex senioribus, Ecce vicit Leo, qui est ex tribu Jehudae, radix Davidis, ut aperiat librum et solvat septem sigilla ejus. Et vidi in medio throni, Agnus stans. Hic venit et sumsit librum. Et **ceciderunt coram Agno et adorarunt Viventem in saecula saeculorum**. 5:1,5-7,14.

42   **Quod Dominus dicatur Rex et Unctus**, est quia erat Messias seu Christus; ac Messias seu Christus significat Regem et Unctum. Inde est quod Dominus etiam per Regem in Verbo intelligatur; similiter per Davidem, qui erat rex super Jehudam et super Israelem. Quod Dominus Rex et Unctus Jehovae dicatur, patet a multis locis in Verbo. Ideo dicitur in Apocalypsi,

Agnus vincet eos, quia est **Dominus dominorum et Rex regum**. 17:14.

Et alibi,

Sedens super equo albo habebat super vestimento Suo nomen scriptum, **Rex regum et Dominus dominorum**. 19:16.

Ex eo quod Dominus dicatur Rex, est quod caelum et Ecclesia dicantur **Regnum Ipsius**; et quod adventus Ipsius in mundum dicatur **Evangelium Regni**.
 Quod caelum et Ecclesia dicantur **Regnum Ipsius**, videatur, Matt.12:28; 16:28; Marc.1:14,15; 9:1; 15:43; Luc.1:33; 4:43; 8:1,10; 9:2,11,60; 10:11; 16:16; 19:11; 21:31; 22:18; 23:51. Et apud Danielem,

Surgere faciet Deus **regnum**, quod in saecula non peribit. Conteret et consumet omnia alia regna, illud autem stabit in saecula. 2:44.

Apud eundem,

Videns fui in visionibus noctis, et ecce cum nubibus caelorum sicut Filius Hominis veniens fuit. Et Huic datum est **dominium**, et gloria, et **regnum**, ut omnes populi, gentes, et linguae Ipsum colerent.

30 colerent: colent *DD*

And in another place,

I saw on the right hand of the One seated on the throne a book written within and on the back, sealed with seven seals; and no one was able to open it. Then one of the elders said, Behold, the Lion, which is from the tribe of Judah, the root of David, has prevailed to open the book and to loose its seals. And I saw in the midst of the throne the Lamb standing. He came and took the book. And **they fell down before the Lamb and worshipped the One who lives for ever and ever.** 5:1,5-7,14.

42   **The Lord is called King and Anointed One.** This is because He was the Messiah or Christ, and Messiah or Christ means King and Anointed One. And it is for this reason that in the Word the Lord is also meant by King, and in a similar way by David, who was king over Judah and over Israel. That **the Lord is called King and Jehovah's Anointed** is evident from many places in the Word. It is why it says in the Book of Revelation,

The Lamb will overcome them, for He is **Lord of lords and King of kings.** 17:14.

And in another place,

The One seated on the white horse had on His robe a name written, **King of kings and Lord of lords.** 19:16.

And it is because the Lord is called King that heaven and the church are called **His Kingdom,** and His coming into the world is called **the Gospel of the Kingdom.**

    Heaven and the Church are called His Kingdom. This may be seen in Matt.12:28; 16:28; Mark 1:14,15; 9:1; 15:43; Luke 1:33; 4:43; 8:1,10; 9:2,11,60; 10:11; 16:16; 19:11; 21:31; 22:18; 23:51. And in Daniel,

God will cause **a kingdom** to arise that will never be destroyed. It will crush and consume all other kingdoms, but will itself stand for ever. 2:44.

In the same book,

I was looking in my night visions, and behold, with the clouds of heaven One like the Son of Man was coming. And to Him was given **dominion** and glory and **kingdom,** so that all peoples, nations, and tongues might

Dominium Ipsius **dominium** saeculi, et **regnum** Ipsius quod non peribit. 7:13,14,27.

Quod adventus Ipsius dicatur Evangelium Regni, videtur Matt.4:23; 9:35; 24:14.

43   **Quod Dominus dicatur David**, patet ex his –

In die illo servient Jehovae Deo suo et Davidi Regi suo quem excitabo eis. Jer.30:9.
Dein revertentur filii Israelis et quaerent Jehovam Deum suum, et Davidem Regem suum, et cum timore venient ad Jehovam, et ad bonum Ipsius, in extremitate dierum. Hos.3:5.
Excitabo super illos Pastorem unum qui pascet eos, servum Meum Davidem; hic pascet eos et Hic erit illis in Pastorem. Et Ego Jehovah ero illis in Deum, et David Princeps in medio eorum. Ezech.34:23-25.
Ut sint Mihi in populum et Ego sim illis in Deum. Servus Meus David Rex super illos, ut Pastor unus sit omnibus illis. Tunc habitabunt super terra, illi et filii illorum ac filii filiorum illorum, usque in aeternum. Et David Princeps illis in aeternum. Et pangam faedus pacis, et faedus aeternitatis erit cum illis. Ezech.37:23-26.
Pangam vobis faedus aeternitatis, misericordias Davidis firmas. En Testem populis dedi Ipsum, Principem et Legislatorem populis. Esai.55:3,4.
In die illo erigam tentorium Davidis collapsum, et obsepiam rupturas ejus, destructa ejus restituam, et aedificabo eam juxta dies aeternitatis. Amos 9:11.
Domus Davidis sicut Deus, sicut Angelus Jehovae coram illis. Sach.12:8.
In die illo erit fons apertus domui Davidis. Sach.13:1.

44   Qui novit quod Dominus per Davidem intelligatur, ille scire potest cur David in suis psalmis toties de Domino scripsit, cum de semet, ut in Psalmo 89, ubi haec –

Pepigi faedus electo Meo, juravi Davidi servo Meo; in aeternum usque firmabo semen tuum, et aedificabo in generationem et generationem thronum tuum. Et confitebuntur caeli mirabile Tuum, etiam veritatem in congregatione sanctorum. Tunc loquutus es in

---

11   illos: illis *DD*
20   et Legislatorem populis: et Legislatorem gentibus *DD*

worship Him. His **dominion** is an everlasting **dominion**, and His **kingdom** one that will not perish. 7:13,14,27.

His coming is called the Gospel of the Kingdom. This may be seen in Matt.4:23; 9:35; 24:14.

43   **The Lord is called David.** This is evident from the following places –

On that day they will serve Jehovah their God and David their King whom I will raise up for them. Jer.30:9.
Afterwards the children of Israel will return, and they will seek Jehovah their God and David their King, and they will come in fear to Jehovah, and to His goodness, in the latter days. Hos.3:5.
I will raise up over them one Shepherd who will feed them – My servant David. He will feed them and He will be their Shepherd. And I Jehovah will be their God, and David will be Prince in the midst of them. Ezek.34:23-25.
That they may be My people and I may be their God. My servant David will be King over them, that they may all have one Shepherd. Then they will dwell in the land, they and their children and their children's children, even for ever. And David will be their Prince for ever. And I will make a covenant of peace, and it will be an eternal covenant with them. Ezek.37:23-26.
I will make with you an eternal covenant, the sure mercies of David. Behold, I have given Him as a Witness to the peoples, a Prince and Lawgiver to the peoples. Isa.55:3,4.
On that day I will raise up the tent of David that is fallen down, and I will close up its breeches, restore its destroyed places, and build it as in the days of old. Amos 9:11.
The house of David will be like God, like the Angel of Jehovah before them. Zech.12:8.
On that day there will be a fountain opened for the house of David. Zech.13:1.

44   Anyone who knows that the Lord is meant by David can see why in his psalms David wrote so often about the Lord while doing so about himself, as in Psalm 89, where these words are found –

I have made a covenant with My chosen one, I have sworn to David My servant, For ever I will establish your seed, and build your throne from generation to generation. And the heavens will praise Your wonders, Your faithfulness also in the congregation of the saints. Then You

visione Sancto Tuo, et dixisti, Posui auxilium super potentem; exaltavi electum e populo. Inveni Davidem servum Meum, oleo sanctitatis Meae unxi Eum. Cum quo manus Mea firma erit, etiam brachium Meum corroborabit Eum. Veritas Mea et misericordia Mea
5 cum Eo, et in nomine Meo exaltabitur cornu Ejus. Et ponam in mari manum Ejus, et in fluviis dextram Ejus. Ille vocabit Me, Pater Meus Tu, Deus Meus et Petra salutis Meae; etiam Ego Primogenitum dabo Eum, altum regibus terrae. In aeternum servabo illi misericordiam Meam; faedus Meum stabile Illi. Ponam in aeternum semen Ejus,
10 et thronum Ejus sicut dies caelorum. Semel juravi per sanctitatem Meam, si Davidi mentiar. Semen Ejus in aeternum erit, et thronus Ejus sicut sol coram Me. Sicut luna firmus erit in aeternum, et testis in nubibus fidelis. vers.4-6,20-22,25-30,36-38.

Similiter in aliis psalmis, ut Pss.45:2-18; 122:4,5; 132:8-18.

8-9 *om* In aeternum servabo illi misericordiam Meam *DD*

spoke in a vision to Your Holy One, and said, I have laid help on One who is mighty, I have exalted One chosen from the people. I have found David My servant; with the oil of My holiness I have anointed Him, with whom My hand will be established; also My arm will strengthen Him. My truth and My mercy will be with Him, and in My name His horn will be exalted. And I will set His hand on the sea, and His right hand on the rivers. He will cry to Me, You are My Father, My God and the Rock of My salvation; I will also make Him as the Firstborn, supreme over the kings of the earth. My mercy I will keep for Him for ever, My covenant will stand firm for Him. I will make His seed endure for ever, and His throne as the days of the heavens. Once and for all I have sworn by My holiness, I will not lie to David. His seed will be for ever, and His throne as the sun before Me. Like the moon it will be established for ever, and as a faithful witness in the clouds. Verses 3-5,19-21,24-29,35-37.

Words like these are found in other psalms, such as Pss.45:1-17; 122:4,5; 132:8-18.

Quod Deus unus sit et quod Dominus sit ille Deus

45   Ex illis quae in mox praecedente articulo in aliqua copia ex Verbo allata sunt, constare potest quod Dominus dicatur Jehovah, Deus Israelis et Jacobi, Sanctus Israelis, Dominus et Deus, tum Rex, Unctus, et David, ex quibus videri potest, sed adhuc sicut per transennam, quod Dominus sit Ipse Deus, a quo et de quo Verbum. Verumtamen notum est in universo terrarum orbe quod Deus unus sit; nec ullus homo, cui sana ratio est, id negat. Superest itaque nunc ut id ex Verbo confirmetur, et insuper, quod Dominus sit ille Deus.

i   **Quod Deus unus sit, confirmatur ex his Verbi –**

Jesus dixit, Primarium omnium praeceptorum est, Audi Israel, **Dominus Deus noster Dominus unus est**. Ideo amabis Dominum Deum tuum ex toto corde et ex tota anima. Marc.12:29,30.
Audi Israel, **Jehovah Deus noster Jehovah unus**. Amabis Jehovam Deum tuum ex toto corde tuo et ex tota anima tua. Deut.6:4,5.
Unus accedens ad Jesum dixit, Magister bone, quid boni facere debeo ut habeam vitam aeternam? Jesus dixit ei, Cur Me dicis bonum? **Nemo bonus est nisi unus, Deus**. Matt.19:16,17.
Ut cognoscant omnia regna terrae quod **Tu Jehovah solus**. Esai.37:20.
Ego Jehovah et non praeterea; praeter Me non Deus. Ut cognoscant ab ortu solis et ab occasu quod **non Deus praeter Me; Ego Jehovah et non praeterea**. Esai.45:5,6.
Jehovah Zebaoth, Deus Israelis habitans cherubis, **Tu Deus es solus** super omnia regna terrae. Esai.37:16.
Num est Deus praeter Me, et Petra? Non novi. Esai.44:8.
Quis Deus praeter Jehovam? et quae Petra nisi Deus noster? Ps.18:32.

God is one, and the Lord is that God

45   The numerous places which have been quoted from the Word in the previous section demonstrate that the Lord is called Jehovah, the God of Israel and Jacob, the Holy One of Israel, Lord and God, and also King, Anointed One, and David, from all of which it may be seen, though still as if only through latticework, that the Lord is God Himself, from whom the Word comes and has to do with. But apart from all this it is recognized throughout the whole world that God is one; nor does anyone of sound reason deny it. All that is necessary now therefore is to verify it from the Word, above all that the Lord is that God.

i   **That God is one is verified by the following places in the Word –**   2

Jesus said, The first of all the commandments is, Hear, O Israel, **the Lord our God is one Lord**. Therefore you shall love the Lord your God with all your heart and with all your soul. Mark 12:29,30.

Hear, O Israel, **Jehovah our God is one Jehovah**. You shall love Jehovah your God with all your heart and with all your soul. Deut.6:4,5.

One came to Jesus and said, Good Master, what good thing must I do to have eternal life? Jesus said to him, Why do you call Me good? **No one is good except one, God**. Matt.19:16,17.

That all kingdoms of the earth may know that **You alone are Jehovah**. Isa.37:20.

I am Jehovah and there is no other; besides Me there is no God. That from the rising of the sun and from its setting they may know that there is **no God besides Me; I am Jehovah and there is no other**. Isa.45:5,6.

O Jehovah Zebaoth, the God of Israel dwelling above the cherubim, **You are God alone** over all the kingdoms of the earth. Isa.37:16.

Is there a God besides Me, or a Rock? I do not know any. Isa.44:8.

Who is God besides Jehovah? And what Rock is there except our God? Ps.18:31.

ii   **Quod Dominus sit ille Deus, confirmatur ex his Verbi** –

Tantummodo inter te Deus, **et non praeterea, non Deus**. Profecto, Tu Deus occultus, Deus Israelis **Salvator**. Esai.45:14,15.
Nonne Ego Jehovah, et **non amplius Deus praeter Me**? Deus justus et **Salvator, non praeter Me**. Respicite ad Me, ut **salvemini**, omnes fines terrae, quia **Ego Deus et non praeterea**. Esai.45:21,22.
Ego Jehovah, et **praeter Me non Salvator**. Esai.43:11.
Ego Jehovah Deus tuus, et Deum praeter Me non agnosces, et **Salvator non praeter Me**. Hos.13:4.
Sic dixit Jehovah Rex Israelis, et **Redemptor** ejus Jehovah Zebaoth, Ego Primus et Ultimus, et **praeter Me non Deus**. Esai.44:6.
Jehovah Zebaoth nomen Ipsius, et **Redemptor** Sanctus Israelis; Deus totius terrae vocabitur. Esai. 54:5.
Erit Jehovah in Regem super totam terram; in die illo erit Jehovah unus, et Nomen Ipsius unum. Sach.14:9.

Quia solus Dominus est Salvator et Redemptor, et quia dicitur quod Jehovah sit Ille et non praeter Ipsum, sequitur quod Deus unus non alius sit quam Dominus.

---

15   Erit Jehovah in: In die illo erit Jehovah in *DD*

ii   **That the Lord is that God is verified by the following**   3
       places in the Word –

God is with you alone, **and there is no other besides God**. Truly You are a hidden God, O God of Israel **the Saviour**. Isa.45:14,15.
Is it not I Jehovah, and **there is no God else besides Me**? A just God and **a Saviour, there is none besides Me**. Look to Me so that **you may be saved**, all ends of the earth, for **I am God, and there is no other**. Isa.45:21,22.
I am Jehovah, and **besides Me there is no Saviour**. Isa.43:11.
I am Jehovah your God, and you are not to acknowledge any God besides Me, and **there is no Saviour besides Me**. Hos.13:4.
Thus said Jehovah the King of Israel, and his **Redeemer** Jehovah Zebaoth, I am the First and the Last, and **besides Me there is no God**. Isa.44:6.
Jehovah Zebaoth is His name, and **the Redeemer** the Holy One of Israel; the God of the whole earth He will be called. Isa.54:5.
Jehovah will be King over all the earth; on that day Jehovah will be one, and His Name one. Zech.14:9.

Because the Lord alone is the Saviour and Redeemer, and because it is said that Jehovah is He and none besides Him, it follows that the one God is none other than the Lord.

Quod Spiritus Sanctus sit Divinum Procedens a Domino, et quod illud sit Ipse Dominus

46   Dixit Jesus apud Matthaeum,

Data est Mihi omnis potestas in caelo et in terra. Euntes ergo discipulos facite omnes gentes, baptizantes eos in nomen Patris et Filii et Spiritus Sancti, docentes eos servare omnia quaecunque mandavi vobis. Et ecce Ego vobiscum sum omnibus diebus, usque ad consummationem saeculi. 28:18-20.

Antehac ostensum est quod Divinum quod Pater vocatur, et Divinum quod Filius, in Domino sint unum. Ostendetur itaque nunc quod Spiritus Sanctus sit idem cum Domino.

Quod Dominus dixerit quod baptizarent in nomen Patris, Filii, et Spiritus Sancti, est quia trinum seu trinitas est in Domino; est enim Divinum, quod Pater vocatur, est Divinum Humanum, quod Filius, et Divinum Procedens, quod Spiritus Sanctus. Divinum quod Pater et Divinum quod Filius, est Divinum ex Quo; ac Divinum Procedens, quod Spiritus Sanctus, est Divinum per Quod. Quod non aliud Divinum sit quod procedit a Domino quam Divinum quod Est Ipse, in opusculis **De Divina Providentia**, **Omnipotentia, Omnipraesentia, et Omniscientia**, videbitur, est enim altioris indaginis.

Quod trinum sit in Domino, illustrari potest per comparationem cum angelo. Huic est anima et corpus, et quoque procedens; quod procedit ex illo, est ipse extra illum. De hoc procedente datum est scire multa, sed non hujus loci est illa adducere.

The Holy Spirit is the Divine Proceeding from the Lord, and this is the Lord Himself

46   Jesus said in Matthew,

All power in heaven and on earth has been given to Me. Go therefore and make disciples of all nations, baptizing them in the name of the Father and of the Son and of the Holy Spirit, teaching them to observe all things whatever I have commanded you. And behold, I am with you at all times, even to the close of the age. 28:18-20.

It has already been shown that the Divine which is called the Father, and the Divine called the Son, within the Lord are one. It will now be shown therefore that the Holy Spirit is the same as the Lord.

The reason why the Lord told them to baptize in the name of the Father, Son and Holy Spirit is that there are in the Lord three essentials[1], that is, a trinity; for there is the Divine, called the Father, there is the Divine Human, called the Son, and there is the Divine Proceeding, called the Holy Spirit. The Divine that is the Father and the Divine that is the Son are the from-which, and the Divine Proceeding or Holy Spirit is the through-which. There is no other Divine which proceeds from the Lord than the Divine which is His own Self, as will be seen in the small works dealing with **Divine Providence**, and **Omnipotence, Omnipresence, and Omniscience**[2], for it is a subject that needs to be gone into more deeply.   2

A clearer idea of the three essentials in the Lord may be gained by comparison with angels. These have a soul and a body, and also a proceeding; what proceeds from them is their own self outside themselves. I have been allowed to know much about this proceeding, but this is not the place to reproduce it.   3

---

1   The Latin word *trinum* may of course be translated as *trine*. However, it seems more helpful to render it as *three essentials*, an expression found at §166 of *VR*, which Swedenborg published eight years after *DD* – 'Those three, Father, Son, and Holy Spirit, are the three essentials of a single God, which make one as soul, body, and activity do with a person'

2   See pages 2-3 and note 2 on page 3

Quisque homo qui spectat ad Deum, post mortem ab angelis primum docetur quod Spiritus Sanctus non alius sit a Domino, et quod Exire et Procedere non aliud sit quam illustrare et docere per Praesentiam, quae est secundum receptionem Domini. Unde plerique post mortem exuunt ideam in mundo conceptam de Spiritu Sancto et recipiunt ideam quod sit Domini praesentia apud hominem per angelos et spiritus, ex qua et secundum quam homo illustratur et docetur. Praeterea solenne est in Verbo nominare duo Divina, et quandoque tria, quae tamen unum sunt, ut Jehovah et Deus, Jehovah et Sanctus Israelis, Jehovah et Potens Jacobi, tum Deus et Agnus, quae quia unum sunt, etiam in aliis locis dicitur, Jehovah solus est Deus, Jehovah solus est Sanctus, et Ille Sanctus Israelis et non praeter Ipsum; tum quod pro Deo nunc dicatur Agnus, et pro Agno Deus. Hoc in Apocalypsi, illud in Prophetis.

Quod sit Dominus solus qui intelligitur per Patrem, Filium, et Spiritum Sanctum, Matt.28:19, patet a praecedentibus et sequentibus ibi. In praecedente versu dicit Dominus, Data est Mihi omnis potestas in caelo et in terra; et in sequente versu dicit Dominus, Ecce Ego vobiscum sum omnibus diebus, usque ad consummationem saeculi. Ita de Se solo, quare illud dixit ut scirent quod in Ipso sit Trinitas.

Ut sciatur quod Spiritus Sanctus non sit aliud Divinum quam Ipse Dominus, ostendetur quid in Verbo intelligitur per spiritum. Per spiritum intelligitur –
i   Vita hominis in communi
ii   Quia vita hominis est varia secundum status ejus, ideo per spiritum intelligitur varia affectio vitae apud hominem
iii Tum vita regenerati, quae vocatur vita spiritualis
iv   Ubi autem dicitur Spiritus de Domino, intelligitur Divina Ipsius Vita, ita Ipse Dominus
v   In specie Vita sapientiae Ipsius, quae vocatur Divina Veritas
vi   Quod Ipse Jehovah, hoc est, Dominus, loquutus sit Verbum per Prophetas.

47 **Quod per spiritum intelligatur vita hominis**, constare potest ex communi loquela, quod homo dicatur emittere spiritum cum moritur, quare per spiritum in hoc

After they have died, all who look to God are at first told 4
by angels that the Holy Spirit is none other than the Lord, and that
the terms To Go Out and To Proceed imply nothing other than To
Enlighten and To Teach through the Lord's Presence, which all depends on their acceptance of Him. As a result of hearing this the
majority after death cast aside the idea of the Holy Spirit which they
had gained in the world and accept the idea that it is the Lord's
Presence with a person by means of angels and spirits, by which and
according to which a person is enlightened and taught.

Furthermore in the Word it is quite common to mention 5
a pair of, sometimes three, Divine names, which are nevertheless
one, such as Jehovah and God, Jehovah and the Holy One of Israel,
Jehovah and the Powerful One of Jacob, and also God and the Lamb.
But because they are one, other places in the Word say that Jehovah
alone is God, Jehovah alone is Holy, and He is the Holy One of Israel
and none besides Him; also the Lamb is sometimes used in place
of God, or God in place of the Lamb. The latter usage occurs in the
Book of Revelation, the former ones in the Prophets.

The truth that it is the Lord alone who is meant by Father, 6
Son and Holy Spirit in Matt.28:19 is evident from what comes before
and after this verse. In the verse before the Lord says, All power in
heaven and on earth has been given to Me; and in the one after the
Lord says, Behold, I am with you at all times, even to the close of
the age. These statements show that He alone is meant, and that He
therefore made them so that the disciples would know that within
Him the Trinity exists.

To enable it to be known that the Holy Spirit is not another 7
Divine separate from the Lord Himself, what the word Spirit is used
to mean in the Word will be presented. It is used to mean –

i The life in general that dwells in a person

ii Since the life in people is varied, depending on whatever states
they are passing through, spirit is therefore used to mean varying affection in the life residing with people

iii It is also used to mean the life of one who is regenerate, which is
called spiritual life

iv But where Spirit is used in reference to the Lord, His Divine Life,
and so the Lord Himself, is meant

v In particular the Life of His Wisdom, which is called Divine Truth

vi Jehovah Himself, that is, the Lord, spoke the Word through the
Prophets

47 **Spirit is used to mean the life that dwells in a person.** This
is clear from what is generally said when people die, that they give

sensu intelligitur vita respirationis. Trahit etiam vox *spiritus* derivationem suam a *respiratione*; inde est quod in lingua Hebraea una vox sit spiritus et venti. Sunt bini fontes vitae apud hominem, unus est motus cordis et alter est respiratio pulmonis. Vita ex respiratione pulmonis est quae proprie intelligitur per spiritum et quoque per animam, quae quod unum agat cum cogitatione hominis ex intellectu, at quod vita ex motu cordis unum agat cum amore voluntatis hominis, in suo loco videbitur. Quod vita hominis per spiritum in Verbo intelligatur, constat ex his –

Colligis **spiritum** eorum, exspirant et in pulverem revertuntur. Ps.104:29.
Recordatus quod caro illi, **spiritus** qui abiret non reverteretur. Ps.78:39.
Cum exiverit **spiritus** ejus, redibit in terram. Ps.146:4.
Hiskias lamentatus est quod exiret **vita spiritus** ejus. Esai.38:16.
Revixit **spiritus Jacobi**. Gen.45:27.
Fusile mendacium est, nec **spiritus** in eo. Jer.51:17.
Dixit Dominus Jehovih ossibus aridis, Ego adducam **spiritum** in vos ut vivatis. A quatuor **ventis veni, spiritus, et inspira in occisos hos** ut vivant. Et venit in eos **spiritus**, et revixerunt. Ezech.37:5,6,9,10.
Jesus apprehendens manum filiae, et reversus est **spiritus** ejus, et surrexit extemplo. Luc.8:54,55.

48 **Quia vita hominis est varia secundum status ejus, quod ideo per spiritum intelligatur varia affectio vitae apud hominem,** ut –

i **Vita sapientiae**

Bezaleel impletus **spiritu sapientiae**, intelligentiae, et scientiae. Exod.31:3.
Tu loqueris ad omnes sapientes corde, quemcunque implevi **spiritu sapientiae**. Exod.28:3.
Impletus est Joschua **spiritu sapientiae**. Deut.34:9.
Nebuchadnezar de Daniele dixit, In quo **spiritus** deorum sanctorum est. Regina dixit, quod **spiritus excellens**, scientiae, intelligentiae, et **sapientiae** esset in eo. Dan.4:5; 5:11,12.
Scient errantes **spiritu** intelligentiam. Esai.29:24.

19   ut: et *DD*
31-32   dixit, In quo **spiritus** deorum sanctorum est. Regina dixit, *DD*[3]: om *DD*[1], *DD*[2]
33   Dan.4:5; 5:11,12: Dan.4:5 *DD*[1], *DD*[2]; Dan.4:5; 5:12 *DD*[3]

up the ghost or spirit. Spirit in this sense is therefore used to mean the life that belongs to respiration. The very word *spirit* also has its origin in *respiration*, which is why in the Hebrew language the same word is used for spirit and puff of wind. Two fonts of life exist in a person, one being the motion of the heart, the other the respiration of the lungs. The life springing from the respiration of the lungs is what is meant properly by spirit and also by soul, which acts in unison with a person's thought flowing from the understanding; but the life springing from the motion of the heart acts in unison with the love in the person's will or intent, as will be seen in the proper place to present it.[1] That the life in a person is meant in the Word by spirit is clear from the following places –

You gather up their **spirit**, they breathe their last and return to dust. Ps.104:29.
He remembered that they were flesh, **a spirit** which would pass away and not return. Ps.78:39.
When his **spirit** departs he goes back to the earth. Ps.146:4.
Hezekiah grieved that **the life of his spirit** would go out. Isa.38:16.
The spirit of Jacob revived. Gen.45:27.
For the moulded image is sham, and there is no **spirit** in it. Jer.51:17.
The Lord Jehovih said to the dry bones, I will put **spirit** within you, that you may live. From the four **winds come, O spirit, and breathe on these slain**, that they may live. And **the spirit** came into them, and they lived again. Ezek.37:5,6,9,10.
Jesus took the girl's hand, and her **spirit** returned, and she arose at once. Luke 8:54,55.

48   **Since the life in people is varied, depending on whatever states they are passing through, spirit is therefore used to mean the varying affection in the life residing with people.** For instance, these –

i   **Life of wisdom**

Bezalel was filled with **the spirit of wisdom**, understanding, and knowledge. Exod.31:3.
You shall speak to all the wise in heart, whomever I have filled with **the spirit of wisdom**. Exod.28:3.
Joshua was filled with **the spirit of wisdom**. Deut.34:9.
Nebuchadnezzar said of Daniel that **the spirit** of the holy gods was in him. The queen said that an **excellent spirit**, of knowledge, understanding, and **wisdom**, was in him. Dan.4:8; 5:11,12.
Those who err **in spirit** will know understanding. Isa.29:24.

1   See **Divine Love and Wisdom**, §§371-393

ii   **Vitae excitatio**

Excitavit Jehovah **spiritum** regum Mediae. Jer.51:11.
Excitavit Jehovah **spiritum** Serubabelis et **spiritum** omnium reliquiarum populi. Hag.1:14.
5 **Do in regem Aschuris spiritum**, ut audiat famam et revertatur in terram suam. Esai.37:7.
Aggravavit Jehovah **spiritum** Sichonis regis. Deut.2:30.
Quod **ascendit super spiritum** vestrum, non fiet unquam. Ezech.20:32.

10 iii   **Vitae libertas**

Quatuor animalia, quae erant cherubi, visa prophetae, quorsum erat **spiritus** ad eundum, ibant. Ezech.1:12,20.

iv   **Vita in timore, dolore, et ira**

Ut liquescat omne cor, et remittantur omnes manus, et **contrahatur**
15 **omnis spiritus**. Ezech.21:12.
Deficit super me **spiritus** meus; in medio mei obstupescit cor meum. Pss.142:4; 143:4.
Consumtus est spiritus meus. Ps.143:7.
Indoluit spiritus meus, quod me Danielem attinet. Dan.7:15.
20 **Spiritus** Pharaonis **turbatus est**. Gen.41:8.
Nebuchadnezar dixit, **Turbatus est spiritus meus**. Dan.2:3.
Ivi tristis **in excandescentia spiritus** mei. Ezech.3:14.

v   **Vita variarum affectionum malarum**

Modo non **in spiritu ejus dolus**. Ps.32:2.
25 Jehovah commiscuit in medio ejus **spiritum perversitatum**. Esai.19:14.
Dixit prophetis **stultis** qui abeunt post **spiritum** suum. Ezech.13:3.
Stultus propheta, **insanus vir spiritus**. Hos.9:7.
Observate vos per **spiritum vestrum**, nec agite perfide. Mal.2:16.
30 **Spiritus scortationum** seduxit. Hos.4:12.
Spiritus scortationum in medio illorum. Hos.5:4.
Cum transivit super illum **spiritus zelotypiae**. Num.5:14.
Vir qui **vagabundus spiritu** et mendacium effutit. Mic.2:11.

16   Deficit: Defecit *DD*
30   Hos. *DD*³: Sach. *DD*¹, *DD*²

ii   Stirring up of Life   2

Jehovah **stirred up the spirit** of the kings of Media. Jer.51:11.
Jehovah **stirred up the spirit** of Zerubbabel and **the spirit** of all the remnant of the people. Hag.1:14.
I will put a spirit into the king of Assyria, so that he will hear a rumour and return to his own land. Isa.37:7.
Jehovah **hardened the spirit** of Sihon the king. Deut.2:30.
What **comes up onto** your **spirit**[1] will not ever be brought about. Ezek.20:32.

iii   Freedom of Life   3

The four living creatures, which were cherubs, seen by the prophet, went wherever **the spirit** was to go. Ezek.1:12,20.

iv   Life in fear, grief and anger   4

That every heart may melt, and all hands hang down, and **every spirit shrink**. Ezek.21:7.
My **spirit faints** within me; in the midst of me my heart is stunned. Pss.142:3; 143:4.
My **spirit is consumed**. Ps.143:7.
As for me Daniel, my **spirit was grieved**. Dan.7:15.
Pharaoh's **spirit was troubled**. Gen.41:8.
Nebuchadnezzar said, **My spirit is troubled**. Dan.2:3.
I went in bitterness, in **the hot anger of** my spirit. Ezek.3:14.

v   Life of various evil feelings and desires   5

Only let there be no **guile in his spirit**. Ps.32:2.
Jehovah has mingled in the midst of her **a spirit of perversity**. Isa.19:14.
He spoke to the **foolish** prophets, who go away after their own **spirit**. Ezek.13:3.
The prophet is foolish, **the man of the spirit is insane**. Hos.9:7.
Take heed through **your spirit**, and do not behave treacherously. Mal.2:16.
The spirit of whoredom has led them astray. Hos.4:12.
The spirit of whoredom is in their midst. Hos.5:4.
When **the spirit of jealousy** came upon him. Num.5:14.
A man who **wanders in spirit** and utters a lie. Mic.2:11.

---

1   ie *What you have in mind*

Generatio, cujus **non constans cum Deo spiritus**. Ps.78:8.
Effusus super illos **spiritus somnolentiae**. Esai.29:10.
Concipite quisquilias, parite stipulam; **quod ad spiritum vestrum**, ignis comedet vos. Esai.33:11.

vi   **Vita infernalis**

Spiritum immundum transire faciam e terra. Sach.13:2.
Quando **spiritus immundus** exit ab homine, perambulat loca arentia, et postea adjungit sibi septem **spiritus pejores** se, et ingressi habitant ibi. Matt.12:43-45.
Babylon facta est custodia **spiritus immundi**. Apoc.18:2.

vii   Praeter ipsos spiritus infernales, a quibus homines vexati sunt, Matt.8:16; 10:1; 12:43-45; Marc.1:23-27; 9:17-29: Luc.4:33-36; 6:17,18; 7:21; 8:2,29; 9:39,42,55; 11:24-26; 13:11; Apoc.13:15; 16:13,14.

49   **Quod per spiritum intelligatur vita regenerati, quae vocatur vita spiritualis,**

Jesus dixit, Nisi quis generatus fuerit ex aqua et **spiritu**, non potest ingredi in regnum Dei. Joh.3:5.
Dabo vobis cor novum et **spiritum novum**. **Spiritum Meum** dabo in medio vestri, et faciam ut in statutis Meis ambuletis. Ezech.36:26,27.
Dare novum cor et **novum spiritum**. Ezech.11:19.
Cor mundum crea in me, Deus, et **spiritum firmum** innova in medio mei. Reduc mihi gaudium salutis Tuae, et **spiritus spontaneus** sustentet me. Ps.51:12-14.
Facite vobis cor novum et **spiritum** novum. Quare moriemini, domus Israelis? Ezech.18:31.
Emittis **spiritum** Tuum, creantur, et renovas facies terrae. Ps.104:30.
Venit hora, et nunc est, quando veri adoratores adorabunt Patrem in **spiritu** et veritate. Joh.4:23.
Deus, Jehovah, dat animam populo, et **spiritum** ambulantibus in ea. Esai.42:5.
Jehovah format **spiritum hominis** in medio ejus. Sach.12:1.

---

13   33-36: 33,36 *DD*
30   Deus, Jehovah,: Jehovah Deus *DD*

A generation whose **spirit was not steadfast with God**. Ps.78:8.
A spirit of slumber was poured out over them. Isa.29:10.
Conceive chaff, bring forth stubble; **as to your spirit**, fire will devour you. Isa.33:11.

vi **Hellish life** 6

I will cause **the unclean spirit** to pass away from the land. Zech.13:2.
When **the unclean spirit** goes out of a person he goes through dry places, and after that links to himself seven other **spirits more evil** than himself, and they enter and dwell there. Matt.12:43-45.
Babylon has become a prison of every **unclean spirit**. Rev.18:2.

vii And then there are the hellish spirits themselves by whom people were tormented, Matt.8:16; 10:1; 12:43-45; Mark 1:23-27; 9:17-29; Luke 4:33-36; 6:17,18; 7:21; 8:2,29; 9:39,42,55; 11:24-26; 13:11; Rev.13:15; 16:13,14. 7

49 **Spirit is used to mean the life in one who is regenerate, which is called spiritual life.**

Jesus said, Unless people have been born of water and **the spirit**, they cannot enter the kingdom of God. John 3:5.
I will give you a new heart and **a new spirit**. I will put **My spirit** in the midst of you, and I will cause you to walk in My statutes. Ezek.36:26,27.
To give a new heart and **a new spirit**. Ezek.11:19.
Create in me a clean heart, O God, and renew **a steadfast spirit** within me. Bring back to me the joy of Your salvation, and let **a willing spirit** uphold me. Ps.51:10-12.
Make for yourselves a new heart and a new **spirit**. Why will you die, O house of Israel? Ezek.18:31.
You send forth Your **spirit**, they are created, and You renew the face of the ground. Ps.104:30.
The hour is coming, and now is, when the true worshippers will worship the Father in **spirit** and truth. John 4:23
God, Jehovah,[1] gives breath to the people, and **spirit** to those who walk on it. Isa.42:5.
Jehovah forms **people's spirit** within them. Zech.12:1.

---

1 The first and both later Latin editions of *DD* mean *Jehovah God*; but the original Hebrew, and the Latin version of Sebastian Schmidt, mean *God, Jehovah*.

Anima mea desideravi Te nocte, **spiritu meo** in medio mei exspectavi Te mane. Esai.26:9.
In die illo erit Jehovah in **spiritum judicii** sedenti in judicio. Esai.28:6.
Exultavit **spiritus meus** super Deo Salvatore meo. Luc.1:47.
5 Quiescere fecerunt **spiritum meum** in terra septentrionis. Sach.6:8.
In manum Tuam commendo **spiritum meum**, redemeras me. Ps.31:6.
Non fecit unus, et reliqui quibus **spiritus**. Mal.2:15.
Post tres dies et dimidium **spiritus vitae** a Deo intravit in binos testes occisos a bestia. Apoc.11:11.
10 Ecce, formator montium et creator **spiritus**. Amos 4:13.
Deus, **Deus spirituum** quoad omnem carnem. Num.16:22; 27:18.
Effundam super domum Davidis, et super habitatorem Hierosolymae, **spiritum gratiae et precum**. Sach.12:10.
Usque dum effuderit super nos **spiritum ex alto**. Esai.32:15.
15 Effundam aquas super sitientem, et rivulos super aridam. **Effundam spiritum Meum** super semen tuum. Esai.44:3.
Effundam **spiritum Meum** super omnem carnem, etiam super servos et ancillas; in diebus illis **effundam spiritum**. Joel 3:1,2.

Per effundere spiritum intelligitur regenerare; similiter per
20 dare cor novum et spiritum novum.
Quod per spiritum intelligatur vita spiritualis illis qui in humiliatione sunt,

Habito in contrito et **humili spiritu**, et ad vivificandum **spiritum humilium** et ad vivificandum cor contritorum. Esai.57:15.
25 Sacrificia Dei **spiritus infractus**, cor infractum et contritum Deus non spernit. Ps.51:19.
Dabit oleum gaudii loco luctus, et pallium laudis loco **spiritus contracti**. Esai.61:3.
Mulier deserta et **afflicta spiritu**. Esai.54:6.
30 Beati **pauperes spiritu**, quia illorum est regnum caelorum. Matt.5:3.

50 **Quod ubi dicitur Spiritus de Domino, intelligatur Divina Ipsius Vita, ita Ipse Dominus**, constat ex his –

---

1 desideravi: exspectavi *DD*
7 fecit: fuit *DD*
10 Ecce,: Ego Jehovah *DD*
10 Amos 4:13 *DD³*: Amos 4 *DD¹*, *DD²*
13 **gratiae et precum**: ex alto *DD*

With my soul I desired You in the night, with **my spirit** within me I waited for You in the morning. Isa.26:9.
On that day Jehovah will be **a spirit of judgment** to those who sit in judgment. Isa.28:6.
My spirit has rejoiced in God my Saviour. Luke 1:47.
They have caused **My spirit** to rest in the north land. Zech.6:8.
Into Your hand I commit **my spirit**; You have redeemed me. Ps.31:5.
Not one has done so, nor those remaining who had **spirit**. Mal.2:15.
After three and a half days **the spirit of life** from God entered the two witnesses slain by the beast. Rev.11:11.
Behold[1], He who forms the mountains and creates **the spirit**. Amos 4:13.
O God, **the God of the spirits** of all flesh. Num.16:22; 27:18.
I will pour out over the house of David, and over the inhabitant of Jerusalem, **a spirit of grace and supplications**. Zech.12:10.
Until **the spirit from on high** is poured out over us. Isa.32:15.
I will pour out waters upon the thirsty land, and streams upon the dry, **I will pour out My spirit** upon your seed. Isa.44:3.
I will pour out **My spirit** on all flesh, even on menservants and maidservants; in those days **I will pour out the spirit**. Joel 2:28,29.

Regenerating is meant by pouring out the spirit, and similarly by giving a new heart and new spirit.

Spirit is used to mean the spiritual life which they possess in whom there is humility. 2

I dwell in a contrite and **humble spirit**, and to enliven **the spirit of the humble** and to enliven the heart of the contrite. Isa.57:15.
The sacrifices of God are **a broken spirit**; a broken and contrite heart God does not despise. Ps.51:17.
He will give the oil of joy instead of mourning, the garment of praise instead of a feeble **spirit**. Isa.61:3.
A woman deserted and **grieved in spirit**. Isa.54:6.
Blessed are **the poor in spirit**, for theirs is the kingdom of heaven. Matt.5:3.

50   **Where Spirit is used in reference to the Lord, His Divine Life, and so the Lord Himself, is meant.** This is clear from the following places –

---

1 The text in the first and two later Latin editions means *I, Jehovah*, but the original Hebrew and Schmidt's Latin version mean *Behold*

Quem misit Pater, verba Dei loquitur; non ex mensura dedit Deus Ei **Spiritum**. Pater amat Filium, et omnia dedit in manum Ipsius. Joh.3:34,35.
Exibit virga de trunco Jischaji, quiescet super Ipso **Spiritus Jehovae**, **spiritus sapientiae** et intelligentiae, **spiritus consilii** et virtutis. Esai.11:1,2.
Dedi **Spiritum Meum** super Illum; judicium gentibus proferet. Esai.42:1.
Veniet sicut flumen angustum. **Spiritus Jehovae** signum inferet in Illo. Tunc veniet Zioni Redemptor. Esai.59:19,20.
Spiritus Domini Jehovih super Me, unxit Jehovah Me ad evangelizandum pauperibus. Esai.61:1; Luc.4:18.
Jesus, cognoscens **Spiritu Suo** quod sic cogitarent intra se. Marc.2:8.
Exultavit **Spiritu Jesus**, et dixit. Luc.10:21.
Jesus turbatus **Spiritu Suo**. Joh.13:21.
Jesus suspirans **Spiritu Suo**. Marc.8:12.

Spiritus pro Ipso Jehovah seu Domino,

Spiritus Deus est. Joh.4:24.
Quis direxit **Spiritum Jehovae** aut quis vir consilii Ipsius? Isa.40:13.
Spiritus Jehovae duxit illos per manum Mosis. Esai.63:14.
Quo abivero a **Spiritu Tuo**, et quo avolavero? Ps.139:7.
Dixit Jehovah, Non per robur sed per **Spiritum Meum** faciet. Sach.4:6.
Illi exacerbarunt **Spiritum Sanctitatis** Ipsius, unde conversus est illis in hostem. Esai.63:10; Ps.106:33.
Non arguet **Spiritus Meus** hominem in perpetuum, quia caro est. Gen.6:3.
Non in aeternum litigabo, quia **Spiritus** coram Me deficeret. Esai.57:16.
Blasphemia contra Spiritum Sanctum non remittetur; sed si quis dixerit verbum contra Filium Hominis remittetur.
Matt.12:31,32; Marc.3:28-30; Luc.12:10.

Blasphemia contra Spiritum Sanctum est blasphemia contra Divinum Domini: verbum contra Filium Hominis est aliquid contra Verbum, sensum ejus aliter interpretando, Filius Hominis enim est Dominus quoad Verbum, ut supra ostensum est.

    14   Spiritu Jesus *DD*[3]: spiritus Jesu *DD*[1], *DD*[2]
    19   Isa.40:13: Sach.4:6 *DD*[1], *DD*[2]; Isa.40:13; Sach.4:6 *DD*[3]
    24   Esai.63:10 *DD*[3]: om *DD*[1], *DD*[2]
    28   si quis: qui *DD*
    33   Verbum *DD*[3]: om *DD*[1], *DD*[2]

He whom the Father has sent speaks the words of God; God has not given Him **the Spirit** by measure. The Father loves the Son and has given all things into His hand. John 3:34,35.
There will come forth a shoot from the trunk of Jesse, and **the Spirit of Jehovah** will rest upon Him, **the spirit of wisdom** and understanding, **the spirit of counsel** and strength. Isa.11:1,2.
I have put **My Spirit** upon Him; He will bring forth judgment to the nations. Isa.42:1.
He will come like a narrow stream[1]; **the Spirit of Jehovah** will place a sign on Him. Then the Redeemer will come to Zion. Isa.59:19,20.
The Spirit of the Lord Jehovih is upon Me, Jehovah has anointed Me to bring good news to the poor. Isa.61:1; Luke 4:18.
Jesus, recognizing **in His Spirit** that this was what they were thinking among themselves. Mark 2:8.
Jesus rejoiced **in the Spirit** and said. Luke 10:21.
Jesus was troubled **in His Spirit**. John 13:21.
Jesus sighing **in His Spirit**. Mark 8:12.

Spirit stands for Jehovah or Lord Himself.

2

God is **a Spirit**. John 4:24.
Who has directed **the Spirit of Jehovah** or what man has been His advisor? Isa.40:13.
The Spirit of Jehovah led them by the hand of Moses. Isa.63:14.
Where shall I go from **Your Spirit**, and where shall I flee away? Ps.139:7.
Jehovah said, Not by might but by **My Spirit** will he act. Zech.4:6.
They aggravated His **Holy Spirit**, therefore He turned to be their enemy. Isa.63:10; Ps.106:33.
My Spirit will not reprove people for ever, for they are flesh. Gen.6:3.
I will not contend for ever, for **the Spirit** before Me would fail. Isa.57:16.
Blasphemy against the Holy Spirit will not be forgiven; but if anyone speaks a word against the Son of Man it will be forgiven. Matt.12:31,32; Mark 3:28-30; Luke 12:10.

Blasphemy against the Holy Spirit is blasphemy against the Lord's Divinity, a word said against the Son of Man is something said against the Word by misinterpreting its meaning, for the Son of Man is the Lord in respect of the Word, as has been shown above.

---

1   ie *a rushing stream*

51   **Quod per Spiritum, ubi de Domino, in specie intelligatur Vita Sapientiae Ipsius, quae est Divina Veritas,**

Ego **veritatem** vobis dico; prodest vobis ut Ego abeam, si enim non abivero, **Paracletus** non veniet ad vos. Si vero abivero, mittam Illum ad vos. Joh.16:7.
Quando venerit Ille **Spiritus Veritatis**, ducet vos in omnem **veritatem**. Non loquetur a Seipso, sed quaecunque audiverit loquetur. Joh.16:13.
Ille Me glorificabit, quia **ex Meo** accipiet et annuntiabit vobis. Omnia quaecunque Pater habet, Mea sunt; propter hoc dixi quod **de Meo** accepturus sit et annuntiaturus vobis. Joh.16:14,15.
Ego rogabo Patrem ut alium **Paracletum** det vobis, **Spiritus Veritatis**, quem mundus non potest accipere, quoniam non videt Illum nec cognoscit Illum. Vos autem cognoscitis Illum, quia apud vos manet et in vobis erit. Non relinquam vos orphanos; venio ad vos. Vos videbitis Me. Joh.14:16-19.
Quando venerit **Paracletus**, quem Ego missurus sum vobis a Patre, **Spiritus Veritatis**, Ille testabitur de Me. Joh.15:26.
Jesus clamavit, dicens, Si quis sitiverit, venito ad Me et bibito. Quisquis credit in Me, sicut dixit Scriptura, flumina e ventre Ipsius fluent aquae viventis. Hoc dixit de **Spiritu**, quem accepturi erant credentes in Ipsum. **Nondum erat Spiritus Sanctus quia Jesus nondum glorificatus erat**. Joh.7:37-39.
Jesus inspiravit in discipulos, et dixit, Accipite **Spiritum Sanctum**. Joh.20:22.

Quod Dominus per Paracletum, Spiritum Veritatis, et Spiritum Sanctum intellexerit Se Ipsum, patet ab illis Domini verbis **quod mundus Illum adhuc non cognosceret**, non enim adhuc cognoscebant Dominum; et cum dixit quod missurus sit Illum, addit, **Non relinquam vos orphanos, venio ad vos, et videbitis Me**, Joh.14:16-19,26,28. Et alibi, **Ecce Ego vobiscum sum omnibus diebus usque ad consummationem saeculi**, Matt.28:20. Et, cum Thomas dixit, Non scimus quo abis, dicit Jesus, **Ego sum via et veritas**, Joh.14:6.

4   abivero, **Paracletus**: abirem, **Paracletus** *DD*
16   16-19: 26,27 *DD*¹, *DD*²; 16-18 *DD*³

51 **In particular, where Spirit is used with reference to the Lord, the Life of His Wisdom, which is Divine Truth, is meant.**

I tell you **the truth**; it is to your advantage that I go away, for if I do not go away **the Paraclete**[1] will not come to you. But if I go away I will send Him to you. John 16:7.
When He **the Spirit of Truth** comes He will guide you into all **truth**. He will not speak from Himself, but whatever He hears He will speak. John 16:13.
He will glorify Me, for He will receive from **what is Mine** and declare it to you. All things whatever that the Father has are Mine; therefore I said that He will receive from **what is Mine** and declare it to you. John 16:14,15.
I will ask the Father to give you another **Paraclete, the Spirit of Truth**, whom the world cannot receive, because it neither sees Him nor knows Him. But you know Him, because He remains with you and will be in you. I will not leave you orphans; I will come to you. You will see Me. John 14:16-19.
When **the Paraclete** comes, whom I shall send to you from the Father, **the Spirit of Truth**, He will bear witness about Me. John 15:26.
Jesus cried out, saying, If anyone thirsts let them come to Me and drink. Whoever believes in Me, as the Scripture has said, Out of His belly will flow rivers of living water. This He said about **the Spirit** which those believing in Him were to receive. **The Holy Spirit was not yet because Jesus was not yet glorified.** John 7:37-39.
Jesus breathed on the disciples and said, Receive **the Holy Spirit**. John 20:22.

2 By Paraclete, Spirit of Truth and Holy Spirit, the Lord meant Himself. This is evident from the Lord's words, **that the world up to then did not know Him**, for up to then people did not know the Lord. It is also evident from the Lord's adding, when He said He would be sending Him, **I will not leave you orphans, I will come to you**, and **You will see Me**, John 14:16-19,26,28. And in another place, **I am with you at all times, even to the close of the age**, Matt.28:20. And, when Thomas said, We do not know where you are going, Jesus says, **I am the way and the truth**, John 14.6.

---

1 The Latin name or term, almost identical to the original Greek, is rendered variously in English versions of the Scriptures – *Comforter, Helper, Advocate*, etc., as well as *Paraclete*

Quia Spiritus Veritatis seu Spiritus Sanctus est idem cum Domino, qui est ipsa Veritas, ideo etiam dicitur, **Nondum erat Spiritus Sanctus, quia Jesus nondum glorificatus erat**, Joh.7:39. Nam post glorificationem seu plenariam unitionem cum Patre, quae facta est per passionem crucis, tunc erat Dominus ipsa Divina Sapientia ac Divina Veritas, ita Spiritus Sanctus. Quod Dominus inspiraverit in discipulos et dixerit, Accipite Spiritum Sanctum, erat quia omnis respiratio caeli est a Domino, angelis enim aeque ac hominibus est respiratio et micatio cordis. Illis respiratio est secundum receptionem Divinae Sapientiae a Domino, et illis micatio cordis seu pulsus est secundum receptionem Divini Amoris a Domino. Quod ita sit, videbitur in suo loco.

Quod Spiritus Sanctus sit Divina Veritas a Domino, patet adhuc ex his locis –

Quando tradiderint vos synagogis, ne solliciti estote quid dicturi. **Spiritus Sanctus** docebit vos in eadem hora quae oporteat dicere. Luc.12:11,12; Matt.10:19,20; Marc.13:11.
Dixit Jehovah, **Spiritus Meus**, qui super te, et verba Mea quae posui in ore tuo, non recedent ex ore tuo. Esai.59:21.
Exibit virga de trunco Jischaji. Percutiet terram virga oris Sui, et **spiritu labiorum Suorum** occidet impium. Erit **veritas** cingulum feminum Ejus. Esai.11:1,4,5.
Nam ore Ille praecepit et **Spiritus Ipsius** collegit illa. Esai.34:16.
Qui adorant Deum, in **spiritu et veritate** oportet adorare. Joh.4:24.
Spiritus est qui vivificat, caro non prodest quicquam. Verba quae Ego loquor vobis, **spiritus et vita sunt**. Joh.6:63.
Johannes dixit, Ego vos baptizo aqua in paenitentiam. Qui vero post me venturus est, baptizabit **Spiritu Sancto et igne**.
Matt.3:11; Marc.1:8; Luc.3:16.

Baptizare Spiritu Sancto et igne est regenerare per Divinum Verum quod est fidei, et per Divinum Bonum quod est amoris. Cum Jesus baptizabatur aperti sunt caeli, et vidit **Spiritum Sanctum** descendentem sicut columbam, Matt.3:16; Marc.1:10; Luc.3:21; Joh.1:32,33. Columba est repraesentativum purificationis et regenerationis per Divinum Verum.

18 Luc.12:11,12; Matt.10:19,20: Luc.12:12; 10:20 *DD*[1], *DD*[2]; Luc.12:12; 21:14 *DD*[3]
24 Nam: Nunc *DD*

Because the Spirit of Truth or Holy Spirit is the same as the Lord, who is Truth itself, it therefore also says, **The Holy Spirit was not yet because Jesus was not yet glorified**, John 7:39. For after His glorification, or complete union with the Father accomplished by His passion on the cross, the Lord was then Divine Wisdom and Divine Truth itself, thus the Holy Spirit. The reason why the Lord breathed on the disciples and said, Receive the Holy Spirit, was that in heaven all ability to breathe comes from the Lord, for angels, just the same as people, draw breath and have a heart that beats. Their actual ability to breathe depends on their acceptance of Divine Wisdom from the Lord, while their heartbeat or pulse depends on their acceptance of Divine Love from the Lord. This will be seen to be so in a place on its own.

From the following places it is more evident still that the Holy Spirit is Divine Truth coming from the Lord,

When they hand you over to synagogues do not be anxious about what you are going to say. **The Holy Spirit** will teach you in the same hour what you ought to say. Luke 12:11,12; Matt.10:19,20: Mark 13:11.

Jehovah said, **My Spirit** which is upon you, and My words which I have put in your mouth, will not depart out of your mouth. Isa.59:21.

There will come forth a shoot from the trunk of Jesse. He will smite the earth with the rod of His mouth, and with **the spirit[1] of His lips** He will slay the wicked. **Truth** will be the girdle of His loins. Isa.11:1,4,5.

For He has commanded with His mouth, and **His Spirit** has gathered them. Isa.34:16.

Those who worship God must worship in **spirit and truth**. John 4:24.

It is **the Spirit** which bestows life, the flesh profits nothing. The words which I speak to you, **they are spirit and life**. John 6:63.

John said, I baptize you with water for repentance. But He who comes after me will baptize you with **the Holy Spirit and with fire**. Matt.3:11; Mark 1:8; Luke 3:16.

To baptize with the Holy Spirit and with fire is to regenerate by means of the Divine Truth of faith and by means of the Divine Goodness of love. While Jesus was being baptized the heavens opened and He saw **the Holy Spirit** coming down like a dove, Matt.3:16; Mark 1:10; Luke 3:21; John 1:32,33. The dove is a symbol of purification and regeneration by means of Divine Truth.

---

1 ie *breath*

Quoniam per Spiritum Sanctum, ubi de Domino, intelligitur Divina Ipsius Vita, ita Ipse – et in specie Vita Sapientiae Ipsius, quae vocatur Divina Veritas – ideo per spiritum Prophetarum, qui etiam vocatur Spiritus Sanctus, intelligitur Divinum Verum a Domino. Ita in sequentibus his locis –

Spiritus dixit ecclesiis. Apoc.2:7,11,29; 3:1,3,6,13,22.
Septem lampades ignis ardentes coram throno sunt **septem spiritus Dei**. Apoc.4:5.
In medio seniorum Agnus stans, habens oculos septem, qui sunt **septem spiritus Dei** emissi in omnem terram. Apoc.5:6.

Lampades ignis et oculi Domini significant Divina Vera, ac septem significant sanctum.

Dixit **Spiritus**, ut requiescant a laboribus suis. Apoc.14:13.
Spiritus et sponsa dicunt, Veni. Apoc.22:17.
Cor suum posuerunt adamantem, ut non audirent legem aut verba quae misit **Jehovah in Spiritu Suo** per manum Prophetarum. Sach.7:12.
Spiritus Eliae venit super Elisaeum. 2 Reg.2:15.
Johannes praeivit **in spiritu** et virtute Eliae. Luc.1:17.
Spiritu Sancto impleta est Elisabetha, et prophetavit. Luc.1:41.
Zacharias impletus **Spiritu Sancto** prophetavit. Luc.1:67.
David dixit in **Spiritu Sancto**, Dixit Dominus Domino meo, Sede a dextris Meis. Marc.12:36.
Testimonium Jesu est Spiritus prophetiae. Apoc.19:10.

Quia nunc per Spiritum Sanctum in specie intelligitur Dominus quoad Divinam Sapientiam, et inde quoad Divinam Veritatem, patet unde est quod de Spiritu Sancto dicatur quod **illustret, doceat, inspiret**.

52   **Quod Ipse Jehovah, hoc est, Dominus, loquutus sit Verbum per Prophetas.**
De Prophetis legitur quod fuerint in **visione**, et quod **Jehovah loquutus sit cum illis**. Cum fuerunt in visione, non erant in suo corpore sed in suo spiritu, in quo statu viderunt talia quae in caelo sunt. Cum autem Jehovah loquutus est cum illis, tunc in corpore suo fuerunt, et audiverunt Jehovam loquentem. Hi bini status Prophetarum probe distinguendi sunt. In statu **visionis** aperti sunt oculi spiritus illorum et clausi oculi corporis illorum, ac tunc etiam sibi visi sunt auferri

       Since Holy Spirit, where this has reference to the Lord, is 5
used to mean His Divine Life, and so He Himself – and in particular
to mean the Life of His Wisdom, which is called Divine Truth – the
spirit of prophets, which too is called the Holy Spirit, means Divine
Truth from the Lord. This is so in the following places –

The spirit said to the churches. Rev.2:7,11,29; 3:1,3,6,13,22.
The seven lamps of fire that are burning before the throne are **the seven spirits of God**. Rev.4:5.
In the midst of the elders there was a Lamb standing, having seven eyes, which are **the seven spirits of God** sent out into all the earth. Rev.5:6.

Lamps of fire and the eyes of the Lord are signs of Divine Truth, and seven is a sign of what is holy.

Said **the spirit**, that they may rest from their labours. Rev.14:13.
The spirit and the bride say, Come. Rev.22:17.
They set their heart adamant, so that they might not hear the law or the words which **Jehovah** sent **in His Spirit** by the hand of the Prophets. Zech.7:12.
The spirit of Elijah came onto Elisha. 2 Kings 2:15.
John went before **in the spirit** and power of Elijah. Luke 1:17.
Elisabeth was filled with **the Holy Spirit**, and she prophesied. Luke 1:41.
Zechariah was filled with **the Holy Spirit** and prophesied. Luke 1:67.
David, in **the Holy Spirit**, said, The Lord said to my Lord, Sit at My right hand. Mark 12:36.
The testimony of Jesus is the spirit of prophecy. Rev.19:10.

Now since the Lord's Divine Wisdom and consequently Divine Truth are meant in particular by the Holy Spirit it is plain to see why the Holy Spirit is said **to enlighten, teach,** and **inspire.**

52   **Jehovah Himself, that is, the Lord, spoke the Word through the Prophets.**
We read of the Prophets that they were in **vision**, also that **Jehovah spoke to them**. When in vision they were not in their body but their spirit, and in that state they saw things such as exist in heaven. But when Jehovah spoke to them they were in their body and heard Jehovah speaking. A clear distinction must be drawn between these two states of the Prophets. In the state of **vision** the eyes of their spirit were open and those of their body closed, at which time it also seemed to them that they were taken from one place to another, while

e loco in locum, corpore manente in suo. In hoc statu fuerunt quandoque Ezechiel, Sacharias, Daniel, et Johannes cum scripsit Apocalypsin; et tunc dicitur quod essent in **visione**, aut in **spiritu**.

Dicit enim Ezechiel, Spiritus sustulit me et reduxit me in Chaldaeam ad captivitatem in **visione Dei**, in **spiritu Dei**; ita ascendit super me **visio** quam vidi. 11:1,24. Dicit quod sustulerit illum spiritus et audiverit post se terrae motum, et alia, 3:12,14, tum quod sustulerit illum spiritus inter terram et caelum, et abduxerit in Hierosolymam in **visionibus Dei**, et viderit abominationes, 8:3,seq. Quare similiter in visione Dei, seu in spiritu, vidit quatuor animalia, quae erant cherubi, cap.1 et cap.10, tum novam terram et novum templum, et angelum metientem illa, de quibus in cap.40-48. Quod tunc fuerit in visionibus Dei, dicit cap.40:2, et quod tunc sustulerit illum spiritus, 43:5.

Simile factum est cum Sacharia, in quo tunc angelus fuit, cum vidit virum equitantem inter myrtos, Sach.1:8, seq.; cum vidit quatuor cornua, et dein virum in cujus manu funiculus mensurae, 2:1,5,seq.; cum vidit Joschuam sacerdotem magnum, 3:1, seq.; cum vidit candelabrum et duas oleas, 4:1,seq.; cum vidit volumen volans et epham, 5:1,6; et cum vidit quatuor currus exeuntes inter duos montes, et equos. 6:1,seq.

In simili statu fuit Daniel cum vidit quatuor bestias ascendentes e mari, Dan.7:3, et cum vidit pugnas arietis et hirci, 8:1,seq. Quod viderit illa in visionibus, legitur 7:1,2,7,13; 8:2; 10:1,7,8. Quod angelus Gabriel ei visus sit in visione et loquutus cum illo, 9:21,22.

Simile factum est cum Johanne, cum scripsit Apocalypsin, qui dixit se fuisse **in spiritu** die Dominica, Apoc.1:10; quod delatus in desertum **in spiritu**, 17:3; in montem altum **in spiritu**, 21:10; quod viderit equos in **visione**, 9:17; et alibi quod **viderit** illa quae descripsit, ita in spiritu aut in visione, 1:12; 4:1; 5:1; 6:1; et in singulis sequentibus.

53   Quod autem ipsum Verbum attinet, non dicitur apud Prophetas quod loquuti sint illud ex Spiritu Sancto sed quod loquuti sint illud ex Jehovah, Jehovah Zebaoth, et Domino Jehovih. Nam legitur quod **Verbum factum sit a Jehovah ad me**, quod **Jehovah loquutus sit ad me**, tum saepissime, **Jehovah dixit**, et **Dictum Jehovae**. Et quia Dominus est

32   om 10 DD
37   et: ex DD

the body remained where it was. Ezekiel, Zechariah Daniel, and John when he wrote the Book of Revelation, at times experienced this state, and when they did it says that they were in **vision**, or else in **the spirit**.

Ezekiel says, The Spirit lifted me up and brought me back to Chaldea to the captives, in **a vision of God**, in **the spirit of God**. So the vision I saw went up above me, 11:1,24. He says that the spirit lifted him up and he heard an earthquake behind him, and other things, 3:12,14, also that the spirit lifted him up between earth and heaven and brought him in **the visions of God** to Jerusalem, and he saw abominations, 8:3 and following verses. Therefore he was in a like manner in a vision of God or in the spirit when he saw four living creatures, who were cherubs, in chapters 1 and 10, also a new earth and new temple, and an angel measuring these, in chapters 40-48. He says in 40:2 that these experiences were in the visions of God, and in 43:5 that they took place when the spirit had lifted him up.

Zechariah, who in that state had an angel present with him, had similar experiences – when he saw a man riding a horse among myrtle trees, 1:8 and following verses; when he saw four horns, and after that a man with a measuring line in his hand, 1:18-2:1 and following verses; when he saw Joshua the high priest, 3:1 and following verses; when he saw a lampstand and two olive trees, 4:1 and following verses; when he saw a flying scroll and an ephah, 5:1,6; and when he saw four chariots coming out between two mountains, and their horses, 6:1 and following verses.

Daniel was in that same state when he saw four beasts coming up out of the sea, 7:3, and when he saw the fight between the ram and the he-goat, 8:1 and following verses. We read in 7:1,2,7,13; 8:2; 10:1,7,8 that he saw those things in visions, in 9:21,22 that the angel Gabriel appeared to him in a vision and spoke to him.

John had similar experiences when he wrote the Book of Revelation – he said he was **in the spirit** on the Lord's day, 1:10, was carried away **in the spirit** into a wilderness, 17:3, onto a high mountain **in the spirit**, 21:10, saw horses **in a vision**, 9:17, and in other places said he **saw** the things he described, that is, when he was in the spirit or else in vision, 1:12; 4:1; 5:1; 6:1, and each succeeding chapter.

53   As for the Word itself however, the Prophets do not say that they spoke it from the Holy Spirit, but that they did so from Jehovah, Jehovah Zebaoth, and the Lord Jehovih. For we read that **the Word came from Jehovah to me**, that **Jehovah spoke to me**, as well as most often **Jehovah said**, and **the word of Jehovah**. And since the

Jehovah. ut supra ostensum est, ideo omne Verbum dictum est ab Ipso. Ut nemo dubitet quin ita sit, velim modo ex Jeremia afferre, ubi dicitur **Verbum ad me factum a Jehovah, Loquutus est Jehovah ad me, Dixit Jehovah,** et **Dictum Jehovae,** ut in his apud Jeremiam –

1:4,7,11-14,19; 2:1-5,9,19,22,29,31; 3:1,6,10,12,14,16; 4:1,3,9,17,27; 5:11,14,18,22,29; 6:6,9,12,15,16,21,22; 7:1,3,11,13,19-21; 8:1,3,12,13; 9:2,6,8,12,14,16,21,23,24; 10:1,2,18; 11:1,6,9,11,17,18,21,22; 12:14,17; 13:1,6,9,11-15,25; 14:1,10,14,15; 15:1-3,6,11,19,20; 16:1,3,5,9,14,16; 17:5,19-21,24; 18:1,5,6,11,13; 19:1,3,6,12,15; 20:4; 21:1,4,7,8,11,12; 22:2,5,6,11,16,18,24,29,30; 23:2,5,7,12,15,24,29,31,38; 24:3,5,8; 25:1,3,7-9,15,27-29,32; 26:1,2,18; 27:1,2,4,8,11,16,19,21,22; 28:2,12,14,16; 29:4,8,9,16,19-21,25,30-32; 30:1-5,8,10-12,17,18; 31:1,2,7,10,15-17,23,27,28,31-38; 32:1,6,14,15,25,26,28,30,36,42; 33:1,2,4,10-13,17,19,20,23,25; 34:1,2,4,8,12,13,17,22; 35:1,13,17-19; 36:1,6,27,29,30; 37:6,7,9; 38:2,3,17; 39:15-18; 40:1; 42:7,9,15,18,19; 43:8,10; 44:1,2,7,11,24-26,30; 45:1,2,5; 46:1,23,25,28; 47:1; 48:1,8,12,30,35,38,40,43,44,47; 49:2,5-7,12,13,16,18,26,28,30,32,35,37-39; 50:1,4,10,18,20,21,30,31,33,35,40; 51:25,33,36,39,52,58.

Haec solum apud Jeremiam. Simile dicitur apud omnes reliquos Prophetas, et non quod loquutus sit Spiritus Sanctus, nec quod Jehovah loquutus sit ad illos per Spiritum Sanctum.
54   Ex his nunc patet quod **Jehovah,** qui est **Dominus ab aeterno,** loquutus sit per Prophetas, et quod, ubi dicitur **Spiritus Sanctus,** sit Ipse. Consequenter, **Quod Deus sit unus et Persona et Essentia, et quod Ille sit Dominus.**

Lord is Jehovah, as was shown above, the whole Word was therefore declared by Him. To ensure that no one doubts this to be so I would like to draw on Jeremiah alone, where the expressions **the Word came to me from Jehovah, Jehovah spoke to me, Jehovah said**, and **the word of Jehovah** occur, as in the following places in Jeremiah –

1:4,7,11-14,19; 2:1-5,9,19,22,29,31; 3:1,6,10,12,14,16; 4:1,3,9,17,27; 5:11,14,18,22,29; 6:6,9,12,15,16,21,22; 7:1,3,11,13,19-21; 8:1,3,12,13; 9:2,6,8,12,14,16,21,23,24; 10:1,2,18; 11:1,6,9,11,17,18,21,22; 12:14,17; 13:1,6,9,11-15,25; 14:1,10,14,15; 15:1-3,6,11,19,20; 16:1,3,5,9,14,16; 17:5,19-21,24; 18:1,5,6,11,13; 19:1,3,6,12,15; 20:4; 21:1,4,7,8,11,12; 22:2,5,6,11,16,18,24,29,30; 23:2,5,7,12,15,24,29,31,38; 24:3,5,8; 25:1,3,7-9,15,27-29,32; 26:1,2,18; 27:1,2,4,8,11,16,19,21,22; 28:2,12,14,16; 29:4,8,9,16,19-21,25,30-32; 30:1-5,8,10-12,17,18; 31:1,2,7,10,15-17,23,27,28,31-38; 32:1,6,14,15,25,26,28,30,36,42; 33:1,2,4,10-13,17,19,20,23,25; 34:1,2,4,8,12,13,17,22; 35:1,13,17-19; 36:1,6,27,29,30; 37:6,7,9; 38:2,3,17; 39:15-18; 40:1; 42:7,9,15,18,19; 43:8,10; 44:1,2,7,11,24-26,30; 45:1,2,5; 46:1,23,25,28; 47:1; 48:1,8,12,30,35,38,40,43,44,47; 49:2,5-7,12,13,16,18,26,28,30,32,35,37-39; 50:1,4,10,18,20,21,30,31,33,35,40; 51:25,33,36,39,52,58.

These are places solely in Jeremiah. All the other Prophets use similar expressions, and they too do not ever say that the Holy Spirit spoke, or that Jehovah spoke to them by means of the Holy Spirit.

54 From all this it is now evident that **Jehovah**, who is **the Lord from eternity**, spoke by means of the Prophets, and that where the expression **Holy Spirit** occurs, He Himself is meant. Consequently, **God is one in both Person and Essence, and He is the Lord.**

Quod Doctrina Fidei Athanasianae concordet cum veritate, dum modo per Trinitatem Personarum intelligatur Trinitas Personae quae est in Domino

55 Quod Christiani tres Personas Divinas, ac ita sicut tres Deos, agnoverint, erat quia trinum in Domino est, ac unum vocatur Pater, alterum Filius, et tertium Spiritus Sanctus, et hoc trinum distincte nominatur in Verbo, sicut etiam distincte nominatur anima et corpus et quod ex illis procedit, quae tamen unum sunt. Verbum in sensu literae etiam tale est ut quae unum sunt distinguat sicut non forent unum. Inde est quod Jehovam, qui est Dominus ab aeterno, nominet nunc Jehovam, nunc Jehovam Zebaoth, nunc Deum, nunc Dominum, et simul Creatorem, Salvatorem, Redemptorem, et Formatorem, imo Schaddai; ac Humanum Ipsius quod assumsit in mundo, Jesum, Christum, Messiam, Filium Dei, Filium Hominis, et in Verbo Veteris Testamenti, Deum, Sanctum Israelis, Unctum Jehovae, Regem, Principem, Consiliarium, Angelum, Davidem.

Nunc quia Verbum tale est in sensu literae ut plures nominet qui tamen unum sunt, ideo Christiani, qui in initio simplices fuerunt et omnia secundum verba sensus literae intellexerunt, distinxerunt Divinitatem in tres Personas, quod etiam propter simplicitatem eorum permissum est. Sed tamen ita ut de **Filio** etiam crederent quod infinitus, increatus, omnipotens, Deus et Dominus esset, prorsus aequalis Patri, et insuper ut crederent quod non duo aut tres sint sed unus essentia, majestate, et gloria, ita Divinitate.

Qui illa secundum doctrinam simpliciter credunt, et non confirmant se in tribus Diis sed ex tribus unum faciunt, illi post obitum informantur a Domino per angelos quod Ipse sit ille unus ac illud trinum, quod etiam recipitur ab omnibus

The Teaching in the Athanasian Statement of Belief is in agreement with the truth, provided that Trinity of Persons is taken to mean the Trinity of Person which resides in the Lord

55   Christians have come to recognize three Divine Persons, thus three Gods, so to speak. One reason for this is the existence of the three essentials[1] in the Lord, one of which is called the Father, another the Son, and the third the Holy Spirit. And an added reason is that in the Word the Three are referred to by name as though they were distinct and separate – just as soul, body, and emanation from these are – when in fact they are a single whole. Furthermore in the literal sense of the Word the things which form a single entity are differentiated, as though they were not one such entity. So it is that Jehovah – that is, the Lord from eternity – is sometimes called Jehovah, sometimes Jehovah Zebaoth, sometimes God, sometimes Lord, and at the same time Creator, Saviour, Redeemer, and He who forms, or else Shaddai; while His Human which He took upon Himself in the world is called Jesus, Christ, Messiah, Son of God, Son of Man, and, in the Old Testament Word, God, Holy One of Israel, Jehovah's Anointed, King, Prince, Counsellor, Angel, David.

2   Now because the Word in its literal sense uses many different names for nevertheless a single entity, Christians – who in the beginning were simple people, understanding all things according to the literal meaning of the words there – consequently separated the Godhead into three Persons; and they were allowed to do so because of their simplicity. But this was to the end they would also believe that **the Son** was infinite, uncreated, almighty God and Lord, entirely equal to the Father, and above all would believe that they are not two or three but one in essence, majesty, and glory, and so in the Godhead.

3   After death those who in simplicity believe these things according to the teaching of the creed, yet do not come to believe firmly in three Gods but take the three to be one, are taught by the Lord through angels that He is that one God and those three

---

1 For the use of the expression *Three Essentials* here and in the rest of the present section, see note 1 on page 159

qui in caelum veniunt; nam nemo potest admitti in caelum qui tres Deos cogitat, utcunque ore dicit unum. Totius enim caeli vita, ac omnium angelorum sapientia, fundatur super agnitione et inde confessione Unius Dei et super fide quod ille Unus Deus sit etiam Homo, et quod Ipse sit Dominus, qui simul Deus et Homo.

Ex his patet quod ex Divina permissione factum sit quod Christiani in principio reciperent doctrinam de tribus Personis, modo reciperent simul quod etiam Dominus sit Deus infinitus, omnipotens, et Jehovah. Nam nisi id quoque recepissent, prorsus actum fuisset de ecclesia, quoniam ecclesia est ecclesia a Domino, et omnium vita aeterna est a Domino et non ab alio.

Quod ecclesia sit ecclesia a Domino, ex eo solo constare potest quod totum Verbum a principio ad finem de solo Domino agat, ut supra ostensum est, et quod in Ipsum credendum sit; et quod illis qui non credunt in Ipsum, non vita aeterna sit, imo quod ira Dei maneat super illis, Joh.3:36.

Nunc quia unusquisque in se videt quod si Deus unus est, sit **unus et Persona et Essentia** – nemo enim aliter cogitat, nec cogitare potest, dum cogitat quod Deus unus sit – velim nunc integram doctrinam quae ab Athanasio nomen habet, adducere, et postea demonstrare quod omnia quae ibi dicta sunt vera sint, modo loco Trinitatis Personarum intelligatur Trinitas Personae.

56   Doctrina haec est –

Qui vult salvari, illi necessarium est servare fidem hanc Catholicam (alii, Christianam); nisi quis illam fidem servaverit totam et integram absque dubio, in aeternum peribit.

Fides haec Catholica (alii, Christiana) est: quod colamus unum Deum in Trinitate, et Trinitatem in Unitate, neque commiscendo Personas, neque separando substantiam (alii, essentiam), quoniam est una Persona Patris, alia Filii, et alia Spiritus Sancti.

Sed Divinitas Patris, Filii, et Spiritus Sancti est una eadem, Gloria aequalis, et Majestas coaeterna.

Qualis est Pater, talis est Filius, et talis est Spiritus Sanctus.

Pater est Increatus, Filius est Increatus, et Spiritus Sanctus est Increatus.

essentials, which is also accepted by all who enter heaven. For none can be allowed into heaven who have three Gods in mind, however much they say One with their lips. The life of the whole of heaven and the wisdom of all angels rests on the acceptance and consequent profession of One God, and on the belief that the One God is also Man, and that He is the Lord, who is simultaneously God and Man.

From all this it is evident that in the beginning Christians were allowed by God to accept the teaching regarding three Persons, so long as they accepted at the same time also that the Lord is God – infinite, almighty, and Jehovah. For if they had not accepted this as well, the church would have come totally to an end, because the church derives its existence as a church from the Lord, and all obtain eternal life from the Lord and no one else.

That the church derives its existence as a church from the Lord is made clear by the single consideration that the whole of the Word from beginning to end has to do with the Lord alone, as was shown above, and that people should believe in Him. Those who do not believe in Him do not have eternal life; rather, the wrath of God remains on them, John 3:36.

Now because everyone can see in their own mind that if God is one He is **one in both Person and Essence** – for none think, nor are they able to think, anything other when they think that God is one – I would now like to quote the entire teaching that takes its name from Athanasius, and after this to show that everything stated there is true, provided that Trinity of Person is understood in place of Trinity of Persons.

56   The teaching is this –

Whosoever will be saved: before all things it is necessary that he hold the Catholick (*others* Christian) Faith.
Which Faith, except every one do keep whole and undefiled: without doubt he shall perish everlastingly.
And the Catholick (*others* Christian) Faith is this: that we worship one God in Trinity, and Trinity in Unity;
Neither confounding the persons: nor dividing the substance (*others* essence).
For there is one person of the Father, another of the Son: and another of the holy Ghost.
But the Godhead of the Father, of the Son, and of the holy Ghost is all one: the Glory equal, the Majesty co-eternal.
Such as the Father is, such is the Son: and such is the holy Ghost.
The Father uncreate, the Son uncreate: and the holy Ghost uncreate.

Pater est Infinitus, Filius est Infinitus, et Spiritus Sanctus est Infinitus; Pater Aeternus, Filius Aeternus, et Spiritus Sanctus Aeternus; et tamen non sunt tres Aeterni, sed unus Aeternus, et non sunt tres Infiniti, neque tres Increati, sed unus Increatus, et unus Infinitus.

Similiter ut Pater est Omnipotens, ita Filius est Omnipotens, et Spiritus Sanctus est Omnipotens, et tamen non sunt tres Omnipotentes sed unus Omnipotens.

Sicut Pater est Deus, ita Filius est Deus, et Spiritus Sanctus est Deus, et tamen non sunt tres Dii, sed unus Deus.

Quamvis Pater est Dominus, Filius est Dominus, et Spiritus Sanctus est Dominus, usque tamen non sunt tres Domini, sed unus Dominus. Quoniam sicut ex Christiana veritate obligati sumus agnoscere unamquamque Personam per se esse Deum et Dominum, usque tamen per Catholicam Religionem prohibiti sumus dicere esse tres Deos, aut tres Dominos (alii, usque tamen non possumus ex Christiana fide nominare tres Deos aut tres Dominos).

Pater a nullo factus est, neque creatus, neque natus; Filius est a solo Patre, non factus, nec creatus, sed natus; Spiritus Sanctus est ex Patre et ex Filio, neque factus, neque creatus, neque natus, sed procedens.

Ita est unus Pater, non tres Patres, unus Filius, non tres Filii, unus Spiritus Sanctus, non tres Spiritus Sancti; et in hac Trinitate nullus est primus et postremus, et nullus est maximus et minimus, sed omnes tres Personae sunt simul aeternae, et sunt prorsus aequales.

Ita ut prorsus sit, quemadmodum supra dictum est, quod Unitas in Trinitate, et Trinitas in Unitate, colenda sit (alii, quod tres Personae in una Divinitate, ac unus Deus in tribus Personis, colendus sit); quapropter qui vult salvari, illum oportet ita cogitare de Trinitate.

Porro etiam ad salutem necessarium est, ut quis rite credat Incarnationem nostri Domini Jesu Christi (alii, ut quis constanter credat quod noster Dominus sit verus Homo); quoniam vera Fides est, ut credamus et confiteamur quod noster Dominus Jesus Christus, Filius Dei, sit Deus et Homo; Deus, ex substantia (seu essentia, alii, natura) Patris, natus ante mundum, et Homo, ex substantia (alii, natura) matris, natus in mundo; perfectus Deus et perfectus Homo, ex rationali anima et humano corpore consistens, aequalis Patri

The Father incomprehensible, the Son incomprehensible: and the holy Ghost incomprehensible.
The Father eternal, the Son eternal: and the holy Ghost eternal.
And yet they are not three eternals: but one eternal.
As also there are not three incomprehensibles, nor three uncreated: but one uncreated, and one incomprehensible.
So likewise the Father is Almighty, the Son Almighty: and the holy Ghost Almighty.
And yet they are not three Almighties: but one Almighty.
So the Father is God, the Son is God: and the holy Ghost is God;
And yet they are not three Gods: but one God.
So likewise the Father is Lord, the Son Lord: and the holy Ghost Lord;
And yet not three Lords: but one Lord.
For like as we are compelled by the Christian verity: to acknowledge every person by himself to be God and Lord;
So are we forbidden by the Catholick Religion: to say, There be three Gods, or three Lords (*others* So are we not able by Christian belief to speak of three Gods, or three Lords).
The Father is made of none: neither created, nor begotten.
The Son is of the Father alone: not made, nor created, but begotten.
The holy Ghost is of the Father, and of the Son: neither made, nor created, nor begotten, but proceeding.
So there is one Father, not three Fathers; one Son, not three Sons: one holy Ghost, not three holy Ghosts.
And in this Trinity none is afore, or after other: none is greater, or less than another;
But the whole three persons are co-eternal together: and co-equal.
So that in all things, as is aforesaid: the Unity in Trinity, and the Trinity in Unity is to be worshipped (*others* that three Persons in one Godhead, and one God in three Persons is to be worshipped).
He therefore, that will be saved: must thus think of the Trinity.
Furthermore, it is necessary to everlasting salvation: that he also believe rightly the Incarnation of our Lord Jesus Christ (*others* that he believe unfailingly that our Lord is true Man).
For the right Faith is, that we believe and confess: that our Lord Jesus Christ, the Son of God, is God, and Man;
God of the substance (*or* essence; *others* nature) of the Father, begotten before the worlds: and Man of the substance (*others* nature) of his Mother, born in the world;
Perfect God, and perfect Man: of a reasonable soul, and humane flesh subsisting;

quoad Divinum, ac inferior (alii minor) Patre quoad Humanum.
Qui tametsi est Deus et Homo, non tamen sunt duo, sed unus Christus, unus non per conversionem Essentiae Divinae in Corpus sed per assumtionem Humani in Deum (alii, unus est Ille, non tamen ita quod Divinum transmutatum sit in Humanum, sed Divinum suscepit ad se Humanum), unus prorsus, non per confusionem (alii, commixtionem) substantiae, sed per Unitatem Personae (alii, Ille est prorsus Unus, non tamen ita quod binae naturae sint commixtae, sed Ille est Una Persona).
Quoniam sicut rationalis anima et corpus est unus homo, ita Deus et Homo est unus Christus.
Qui passus est propter salvationem nostri, descendit in infernum, et resurrexit tertio die ex morte, et ascendit in caelum, et sedet ad dextram Patris omnipotentis, unde venturus est ad judicandum vivos et mortuos, in cujus Adventu omnes homines resurgent cum suis corporibus et reddituri sunt de factis propriis rationem; et illi qui bona fecerunt, intrabunt in vitam aeternam, et qui mala fecerunt, in ignem aeternum.

57   Quod omnia hujus doctrinae quoad singula ejus verba sint vera, modo pro Trinitate Personarum intelligatur Trinitas Personae, videri potest ab eadem denuo exscripta, ubi haec Trinitas substituta est. Trinitas Personae est haec,
Quod **Divinum Domini sit Pater, Divinum Humanum Filius, et Divinum Procedens Spiritus Sanctus.**
Cum haec Trinitas intelligitur, tunc homo potest cogitare unum Deum, et quoque potest dicere unum Deum. Quod alioquin non possit nisi quam cogitare tres Deos, quis non videt? Et quoque vidit Athanasius, quare ejus doctrinae etiam haec verba inserta sunt –

Sicut ex Christiana veritate obligati sumus agnoscere unamquamque Personam per se esse Deum et Dominum,
usque tamen non possumus ex Catholica religione (aut, ex Christiana fide) dicere (seu, nominare) tres Deos, aut tres Dominos,

quod quasi est,

---

16   et reddituri sunt de factis propriis rationem *DD³*: *om DD¹, DD²*

Equal to the Father, as touching his Godhead: and inferior to (*others* less than) the Father, as touching his Manhood.
Who although he be God, and Man: yet he is not two, but one Christ;
One; not by conversion of the God-head into flesh: but by taking of the Manhood into God (*others* one is he, yet not such that Godhead was transformed into manhood, but Godhead took manhood upon himself);
One altogether; not by confusion (*others* intermingling) of substance: but by unity of person (*others* He is altogether one, yet not such that two natures are intermingled, but is one Person).
For as the reasonable soul and flesh is one man: so God and Man is one Christ.
Who suffered for our salvation: descended into hell, rose again the third day from the dead.
He ascended into heaven, he sitteth on the right hand of the Father, God Almighty: from whence he shall come to judge the quick and the dead.
At whose coming all men shall rise again with their bodies: and shall give account for their own works.
And they that have done good shall go into life everlasting: and they that have done evil into everlasting fire.[1]

57   All of this teaching, every word of it, is true – provided that in place of a Trinity of Persons a Trinity of Person is understood. This can be seen to be so when the same teaching has been written out again, with the former Trinity replacing the latter. The Trinity of Person is this –
The Lord's Divine is the Father, Divine Human the Son, and Divine Proceeding the Holy Spirit
When this is what people understand by the Trinity they are able to have one God in mind as well as to say one God. Who can fail to see that they would otherwise have three Gods in mind? Indeed Athanasius saw they would, which is why he also included in his teaching the following words –

For like as we are compelled by the Christian verity: to acknowledge every person by himself to be God and Lord;
So are we forbidden by the Catholick Religion (or Christian belief): to say (or speak of), There be three Gods, or three Lords

which is as if to say,

---

1   The text of the creed in §56 is transcribed from **BCP** of 1662. See pages x-xi above

Quamvis ex Christiana veritate licet agnoscere seu cogitare tres Deos et Dominos,
usque tamen non licet ex Christiana fide dicere seu nominare nisi quam unum Deum et unum Dominum,

cum tamen agnitio et cogitatio conjungit hominem cum Domino et cum caelo, non autem sola loquela. Praeterea, nemo comprehendit quomodo Divinum, quod unum est, potest dividi in tres Personas, quarum unaquaevis est Deus. Divinum enim non dividuum est, ac tres unum facere per essentiam aut substantiam non tollit ideam trium Deorum, sed modo dat ideam unanimitatis eorum.

58   Quod omnia illius doctrinae quoad singula ejus verba sint vera, modo pro Trinitate Personarum intelligatur Trinitas Personae, constare potest ex eadem denuo exscripta, quae nunc sequitur,

Qui vult salvari, illi necessarium est servare fidem hanc Christianam. Fides haec Christiana est: quod colamus unum Deum in Trinitate, et Trinitatem in Unitate,
non commiscendo Trinum Personae, neque separando Essentiam.
Trinum unius Personae est quod Pater, Filius, et Spiritus Sanctus vocatur.
Divinitas Patris, Filii, et Spiritus Sancti est una eadem, Gloria et Majestas aequalis.
Qualis est Pater, talis est Filius, et talis est Spiritus Sanctus.
Pater est Increatus, Filius est Increatus, et Spiritus Sanctus est Increatus;
Pater est Infinitus, Filius est Infinitus, et Spiritus Sanctus est Infinitus;
et tamen non sunt tres Infiniti, neque tres Increati, sed unus Increatus, et unus Infinitus.
Similiter ut Pater est Omnipotens, ita Filius est Omnipotens, et Spiritus Sanctus est Omnipotens,
et tamen non sunt tres Omnipotentes sed unus Omnipotens.
Sicut Pater est Deus, ita Filius est Deus, et Spiritus Sanctus est Deus, et tamen non sunt tres Dii, sed unus Deus.
Quamvis Pater est Dominus, Filius est Dominus, et Spiritus Sanctus est Dominus,
usque tamen non sunt tres Domini, sed unus Dominus.
Nunc sicut ex Christiana veritate agnoscimus Trinum in una Persona, quae Deus et Dominus,
ita ex Christiana fide possumus dicere unum Deum et unum Dominum.

Although the Christian verity allows people to acknowledge or have three Gods and Lords in mind,
Christian belief does not allow them to say or speak of anything other than one God and one Lord.

But what people accept and think is what links them to the Lord and to heaven, not just the words they utter. And what is more, no one understands how the Divine, who is one, can be divided into three Persons, each of whom is God. For the Divine is indivisible; and to make three one by virtue of their essence or substance does not take away the idea of three Gods, only conveys the idea of their unanimity.
58   The fact that all of that teaching, every word of it, is true – provided that Trinity of Person is understood instead of Trinity of Persons – becomes clear from the same teaching when written out again as follows –

Whosoever will be saved: before all things it is necessary that he hold the Christian Faith.
The Christian Faith is this: That we worship one God in Trinity, and Trinity in Unity;
Not confounding the Three Essentials of the Person: nor dividing the essence.
The Three Essentials of the one Person is what is called the Father, the Son, and the Holy Ghost.
The Godhead of the Father, of the Son, and of the Holy Ghost is all one: the glory and majesty equal.
Such as the Father is, such is the Son: and such is the Holy Ghost.
The Father uncreate, the Son uncreate: and the Holy Ghost uncreate.
The Father incomprehensible, the Son incomprehensible: and the Holy Ghost incomprehensible.
And yet there are not three incomprehensibles, nor three uncreated: but one uncreated, and one incomprehensible.
So likewise the Father is almighty, the Son almighty: and the Holy Ghost almighty.
And yet there are not three almighties: but one almighty.
So the Father is God, the Son is God: and the Holy Ghost is God.
And yet there are not three Gods: but one God.
So likewise the Father is Lord, the Son Lord: and the Holy Ghost Lord.
And yet not three Lords: but one Lord.
Now as by the Christian verity we acknowledge the Three Essentials in one Person, who is God and Lord,
So we are able by Christian belief to speak of one God and one Lord.

Pater a nullo factus est, neque creatus, neque natus;
Filius est ex solo Patre, non factus, nec creatus, sed natus.
Spiritus Sanctus est ex Patre et ex Filio, neque factus, neque creatus, neque natus, sed procedens.
Ita est unus Pater, non tres Patres, unus Filius, non tres Filii, unus Spiritus Sanctus, non tres Spiritus Sancti;
et in hac Trinitate nullus est maximus et minimus, sed sunt prorsus aequales.
Ita ut prorsus sit, quemadmodum supra dictum est, quod Unitas in Trinitate, et Trinitas in Unitate colenda sit.

59 Haec in doctrina de Trinitate et Unitate Dei. Postea sequitur ibi de assumtione Humani a Domino in mundo, quae vocatur Incarnatio. Illa quoque in doctrina, quoad omnia et singula ejus, vera sunt, modo distincte intelligatur humanum ex matre – in quo Dominus fuit, cum in statu humiliationis seu exinanitionis, et passus est tentationes et crucem – et Humanum ex Patre, in quo fuit in statu glorificationis seu unitionis. Nam Dominus Humanum in mundo conceptum a Jehovah, qui est Dominus ab aeterno, et natum a Maria Virgine, assumsit. Inde Ipsi fuit Divinum et humanum, Divinum a Divino Suo ab aeterno et humanum ex Maria matre in tempore; sed hoc humanum exuit et Humanum Divinum induit. Hoc Humanum est quod vocatur Divinum Humanum, et quod intelligitur in Verbo per Filium Dei. Cum itaque illa quae praecedunt in doctrina de Incarnatione, intelliguntur de humano materno, in quo fuit cum in statu humiliationis, et illa quae sequuntur ibi de Divino Humano, in quo fuit cum in statu glorificationis, tunc etiam omnia ibi coincidunt.

Cum humano materno, in quo fuit cum in statu humiliationis, coincidunt haec quae praecedunt in doctrina,

Quod Jesus Christus fuerit Deus et Homo,
Deus, ex substantia Patris, et Homo, ex substantia matris, natus in mundo;
perfectus Deus et perfectus Homo, ex rationali anima et humano corpore consistens,
aequalis Patri quoad Divinum, minor Patre quoad Humanum.

The Father is made of none: neither created, nor begotten.
The Son is of the Father alone: not made, neither created, but begotten.
The Holy Ghost is of the Father and of the Son: neither made, nor created, nor begotten, but proceeding.
So there is one Father, not three Fathers; one Son, not three Sons: one Holy Ghost, not three Holy Ghosts.
And in this Trinity none is greater or less: but entirely equal.
So that in all things, as is aforesaid: the Unity in Trinity, and the Trinity in Unity is to be worshipped.

59   These statements in the teaching have to do with the Trinity and Unity of God. They are followed in it by others which have to do with the Lord's taking on the Human in the world, which is called the Incarnation. These statements as well in the teaching, every single one, are true, provided that a clear distinction is made between the human derived from the mother – in which the Lord was when He was in a state of humiliation or exinanition, and endured temptations and the cross – and the Human derived from the Father, in which He was when in a state of glorification or union. For the Lord took on in the world a Human that was conceived from Jehovah, that is, the Lord from eternity, and born from Mary the virgin. Consequently the Lord had a Divine and He had a human; the Divine came from the Divine which was His from eternity, and the human from Mary His mother in time. But this human He cast off and put on a Human that was Divine. This Human is what is called the Divine Human and is what is meant in the Word by the Son of God. So when those statements regarding the Incarnation which come first in the teaching are taken to mean the maternal human in which He was when in a state of humiliation, and those that follow in it to mean the Divine Human in which He was in a state of glorification, everything there then stands in agreement with the truth.

The statements in agreement with it which come first in the teaching and refer to the maternal human, in which He was when in a state of humiliation, are these –

Jesus Christ was God and man;
God of the substance of the Father, and Man of the substance of the mother, born in the world;
Perfect God, and perfect man: of a reasonable soul and humane flesh subsisting;
Equal to the Father, as touching his Godhead: and less than the Father, as touching his Manhood.

Tum haec,

Quod Humanum illud non conversum sit in Divinum, nec ei commixtum, sed exutum, et pro eo assumtum Humanum Divinum.

Cum Humano Divino, in quo fuit in statu glorificationis, et nunc est in aeternum, coincidunt haec quae sequuntur in doctrina,

Tametsi noster Dominus Jesus Christus, Filius Dei, est Deus et Homo, usque non sunt duo, sed est unus Christus; imo est prorsus unus, est enim una Persona.

Quoniam sicut anima et corpus faciunt unum hominem, ita Deus et Homo est unus Christus.

60 Quod Deus et Homo in Domino, secundum doctrinam, non sint duo sed una Persona, et prorsus una, sicut anima et corpus sunt unum, patet clare a multis quae Ipse dixerat, ut, Quod Pater et Ipse unum sint; quod omnia Patris sua sint et omnia sua Patris; quod Ipse in Patre et Pater in Ipso sit; quod omnia data sint in manum Ipsius; quod Ipsi omnis potestas sit; quod Deus caeli et terrae sit; quod qui credit in Ipsum, vitam aeternam habeat; et quod qui non credit in Ipsum ira Dei maneat super illo; et porro, quod et Divinum et Humanum sublatum sit in caelum, et quod quoad utrumque sedeat ad dextram Dei, hoc est, quod omnipotens sit; et plura quae supra ex Verbo de Divino Humano Ipsius in multa copia allata sunt, quae omnia testantur quod
Deus sit unus tam Persona quam Essentia, in quo Trinitas, et quod ille Deus sit Dominus.

61 Quod haec de Domino nunc primum evulgata sint, est quia praedictum est in Apocalypsi, cap. 21 et 22, quod nova ecclesia in fine prioris a Domino instituenda sit, in qua hoc primarium erit. Haec ecclesia est quae per Novam Hierosolymam ibi intelligitur, in quam nemo intrare potest nisi qui solum Dominum pro Deo caeli et terrae agnoscit. Et hoc possum annuntiare, quod universum caelum Dominum solum agnoscat, et quod qui non agnoscit, non in caelum admittatur; caelum enim est caelum ex Domino. Ipsa illa

19-20 et quod qui non credit in Ipsum ira Dei maneat super illo *DP*: *om DD*
29 *om* a Domino *DP*
32 agnoscit. Et *DD*: agnoscit, quare illa Ecclesia ibi vocatur **Uxor Agni**. Et *DP*

And also this,

That manhood was not converted into or intermingled with the Godhead, but was cast off and the Divine Human taken on instead.

The statements in agreement with the truth which come after in the teaching and refer to the Divine Human, in which He was in a state of glorification and is now for ever, are these –

Although our Lord Jesus Christ, the Son of God, be God and man: yet he is not two, but one Christ;
Rather, He is one altogether, for He is one Person.
For as soul and body make one man: so God and Man is one Christ.

60 The idea, according to this teaching, that God and Man in the Lord are not two but one Person, altogether one, in the way soul and body are one, is shown very plainly to be true by many things He Himself stated, such as these: That the Father and He are one; all that is the Father's is His, and all that is His is the Father's; He is in the Father, and the Father in Him; all things have been given into His hand; He has all power; He is God of heaven and earth; whoever believe in Him have eternal life; and whoever do not believe in Him the wrath of God remains on them. In addition to these things He Himself said there are the references to both the Divine and the Human being carried up to heaven, to His sitting in respect of both at the right hand of God, meaning that He is almighty; and there are many more places in the Word concerning His Divine Human that have been quoted extensively above, all of which bear witness to this –
That God is one in both Person and Essence, in whom is the Trinity, and that the Lord is that God.
61 The reason why it is only now that these things concerning the Lord have been published is that it has been foretold, in chapters 21 and 22 of the Book of Revelation, that a new church, in which this will be the first and foremost item of belief, is to be established by the Lord when the previous one comes to an end. This church is what is meant in those chapters by the New Jerusalem, which no one can enter except those who take the Lord alone to be the God of heaven and earth. And I am able to say that this is what the whole of heaven takes Him to be, and that those who do not are not allowed into heaven; for heaven derives its existence as heaven from

agnitio ex amore et fide facit ut sint ibi in Domino et Dominus in illis, ut Ipse Dominus docet apud Johannem,

In die illo cognoscetis quod Ego in Patre Meo, et vos in Me et Ego in vobis. 14:20.

Tum apud eundem,

Manete in Me, etiam Ego in vobis. Ego sum vitis, vos palmites. Qui manet in Me et Ego in illo, hic fert fructum multum, nam sine Me non potestis facere quicquam. Nisi quis manserit in Me, ejectus est foras. 15:4-6; tum 17:22,23.

Quod hoc non prius e Verbo visum sit, est quia si prius visum fuisset, usque non receptum fuisset. Nondum enim Ultimum Judicium fuit peractum, et ante illud potentia inferni valuit supra potentiam caeli; et homo est in medio inter caelum et infernum, quare si prius visum fuisset, diabolus – hoc est, infernum – eripuisset illud e cordibus illorum, et insuper prophanavisset illud. Hic status potentiae inferni prorsus fractus est per Ultimum Judicium, quod nunc peractum est. Post illud, ita nunc, omnis homo qui vult illustrari et sapere, is potest, de qua re videantur quae in opere **De Caelo et Inferno**, n.589-596, et n.597-603, tum in opusculo **De Ultimo Judicio**, n.65-72, et n.73,74, scripta sunt.

6   sum *DP*: om *DD*

the Lord. The very acceptance of Him as such in love and faith by those there causes them to be in the Lord and the Lord in them, as the Lord Himself declares in John,

On that day you will know that I am in My Father, and you in Me and I in you. 14:20.

Also in the same gospel,

Abide in Me, and I in you. I am the vine, you are the branches. Those who abide in Me and I in them, they it is who bear much fruit, for apart from Me you cannot do anything. If people do not abide in Me they are cast out. 15:4-6; also 17:22,23.

2. The reason why this has not been seen before from the Word is that if it had been seen it would not have been accepted. For the Last Judgment, before which the power of hell was stronger than that of heaven, had not yet taken place, and people in the world exist midway between heaven and hell; therefore if it had been seen before then, the devil, that is, hell, would have snatched it away from their hearts and, more than that, defiled it. But that state of the power of hell has been completely broken by the Last Judgment that has now taken place. After that judgment, and so now, all who wish to be enlightened and be wise are able to be; regarding this, see what has been written in the work concerning **Heaven and Hell**, §§589-596 and §§597-603, as well as the small work concerning **The Last Judgment**, §§65-72 and §§73,74.

Quod Nova Ecclesia intelligatur per
Novam Hierosolymam in Apocalypsi

62 Postquam in Apocalypsi descriptus est status Ecclesiae Christianae, qualis erit in suo fine, et nunc est, et postquam in infernum conjecti sunt illi ab ea ecclesia qui per pseudoprophetam, draconem, meretricem magnam, et per bestias significantur, ita postquam Ultimum Judicium factum est, dicitur ibi,

Vidi caelum novum et terram novam, prius enim caelum et prior terra transivit. Tunc ego Johannes vidi **civitatem sanctam Hierosolymam** descendentem a Deo e caelo. Et audivi vocem magnam e caelo dicentem, Ecce tabernaculum Dei cum hominibus, qui habitabit cum illis, et illi populi Ejus erunt, et Ipse erit cum illis, Deus illorum. Dixit sedens super throno, Ecce nova omnia facio. Et dixit mihi, Scribe, quia haec verba vera et fidelia sunt. Apoc.21:1-3,5.

Per caelum novum, et per terram novam, quae vidit postquam prius caelum et prior terra transivit, non intelligitur novum caelum astriferum et atmosphaericum quod coram oculis humanis apparet, nec nova terra super qua habitant homines, sed intelligitur novum ecclesiae in mundo spirituali et novum ecclesiae in mundo naturali.

Quoniam novum ecclesiae in utroque mundo, tam spirituali quam naturali, factum est a Domino cum in mundo fuit, ideo simile apud Prophetas praedicitur, nempe quod novum caelum et nova terra tunc exstitura sint, ut Esai.65:17; 66:22, et alibi, per quae itaque non potest intelligi caelum aspectabile coram oculis et terra habitabilis ab hominibus. Per mundum spiritualem intelligitur mundus ubi habitant angeli et spiritus, et per mundum naturalem intelligitur mundus ubi habitant homines. Quod novum ecclesiae in mundo spirituali nuper factum sit, et quod novum ecclesiae in mundo naturali

6 *om* magnam DD

By the New Jerusalem in the Book of Revelation a New Church is meant

62 In the Book of Revelation, after its description of the state of the Christian Church as it would be, and now is, at the end of it, and then its description of the casting into hell of those belonging to that church who are meant by the false prophet, dragon, great prostitute, and by the beasts, that is, after the Last Judgment has been accomplished, it goes on to say –

I saw a new heaven and a new earth, for the former heaven and the former earth passed away. Then I John saw **the holy city**, **Jerusalem**, coming down from God out of heaven. And I heard a loud voice from heaven, saying, Behold, the tabernacle of God is with men, and He will dwell with them, and they will be His people, and He Himself their God will be with them. The one sitting on the throne said, Behold, I am making all things new. And He said to me, Write, for these words are true and faithful. Rev.21:1-3,5.

The new heaven and new earth that John saw after the former ones passed away does not mean a new starry sky and air visible to human eyes, or a new earth on which people are dwelling, but a new formation of the church in the spiritual world and a new formation of the church in the natural world.

[2] Because a new formation of the church in both worlds, spiritual as well as natural, was effected by the Lord while He was in the world, the Prophets contain similar predictions, that is to say, that a new heaven and new earth are going to be created, for example Isa.65:17; 66:22, and elsewhere, and therefore the visible sky in front of people's eyes and the earth on which they dwell cannot be what is meant. By spiritual world is meant the one where angels and spirits dwell, by natural world the one where people dwell. The fact that a new formation of the church has recently taken place in the spiritual world and a new formation of the church will do so in the natural world has been demonstrated

fiet, aliquibus ostensum est in opusculo **De Ultimo Judicio**, et plenius ostendetur in **Continuatione ejus**.

63   Per civitatem sanctam Hierosolymam intelligitur nova illa ecclesia quoad doctrinam; quare illa visa a Deo e caelo descendens, nam doctrina genuini veri non aliunde venit quam per caelum a Domino. Quia ecclesia quoad doctrinam per civitatem novam Hierosolymam intelligitur, ideo dicitur, Parata sicut sponsa ornata marito suo, vers.2, et postea,

Venit ad me unus de septem angelis, et loquutus mecum, dicens, Veni, ostendam tibi sponsam Agni uxorem. Et abstulit me in spiritu super montem altum et ostendit mihi civitatem magnam, sanctam Hierosolymam, descendentem e caelo a Deo. Vers.9,10.

Quod per sponsam et uxorem intelligatur ecclesia, cum per sponsum et maritum Dominus, notum est. Ecclesia sponsa est quando vult Dominum recipere, at uxor quando recepit. Quod Dominus per maritum ibi intelligatur, patet, nam dicitur, **Sponsa Agni Uxor**.

64   Quod per Hierosolymam in Verbo intelligatur ecclesia quoad doctrinam, est causa quia ibi in terra Canaane, et non alibi, templum erat, altare erat, sacrificia fiebant, ita ipse cultus Divinus, quare etiam tria festa quotannis ibi celebrabantur et ad illa omnis masculus totius terrae mandatus est ire. Ex eo est quod per Hierosolymam significetur ecclesia quoad cultum, et inde quoque ecclesia quoad doctrinam, nam cultus praescribitur in doctrina et fit secundum illam; tum quia Dominus in Hierosolyma fuit, et docuit in Suo templo, et postea ibi glorificavit Humanum Suum. Praeterea per urbem in Verbo in sensu ejus spirituali significatur doctrina; inde per civitatem sanctam, doctrina Divini Veri a Domino.*

---

* [Author's footnote] Quod per urbem in Verbo significetur doctrina ecclesiae et religionis, videatur in **Arcanis Caelestibus**, n.402,2449,2943,3216,4492,4493. Quod per portam urbis significetur doctrina, per quam fit introitus in ecclesiam, n.2943,4477. Quod ideo seniores sederint in porta urbis et judicaverint, ibid; egredi porta, quod sit recedere a doctrina, n. 4492,4493. Quod urbes et palatia in caelo repraesententur, quando angelis est sermo de doctrinalibus, n.3216, ibi.

13-14   per sponsum et maritum Dominus: per Dominum sponsus et maritus *DD*
32   2449 *DD³*: 2450 *DD¹*, *DD²*
33   4477: 4447,4478 *DD¹*; 4477,4478 *DD²*, *DD³*

to some extent in the small work concerning **The Last Judgment** and will be demonstrated more fully in the **Continuation**[1] of this.

63   This new church in respect of its teaching is what is meant by the holy city, Jerusalem; and this is why it was seen to be coming down from God out of heaven, for teaching containing real truth comes from no other source than the Lord by way of heaven. And because the church in respect of its teaching is meant by the city, new Jerusalem, it therefore says, in verse 2, Prepared as a bride adorned for her husband, and further on, in verses 9,10,

There came to me one of the seven angels, and spoke to me, saying, Come, I will show you the bride, the wife of the Lamb. And he carried me away in the spirit onto a high mountain and showed me the great city, the holy Jerusalem, coming down out of heaven from God.

It is a well-known idea that the church is meant by bride and wife when the Lord is meant by bridegroom and husband. The church is a bride when it is willing to accept the Lord, but a wife when it has accepted Him. The Lord is plainly meant here by husband, for it says, **The bride, the wife of the Lamb.**

64   The church in respect of its teaching is meant in the Word by Jerusalem because it was there and not anywhere else in the land of Canaan that the temple was situated, the altar stood, sacrifices were offered, and so Divine worship took place. Furthermore it was where the three annual feasts were held, which every male throughout the land was commanded to go to. This is the reason why Jerusalem means the church in respect of its worship, and therefore also in respect of its teaching, for worship is laid down in and conducted in accordance with its teaching. And another reason is that the Lord was present in Jerusalem, taught in His temple, and subsequently glorified His Human there. In addition teaching is meant in the Word, in its spiritual sense, by city; therefore teaching consisting of Divine Truth received from the Lord is meant by the holy city.*[2]

---

*   [Author's footnote] In the Word, teaching that is an aspect of the church and religion is meant by a city, see **Arcana Coelestia**, §§402,2449,2943,3216,4492,4493. Teaching, the means by which the entrance into the church is provided, is meant by the gate of a city, §§2943,4477. This is why the elders sat in the gate of their city and passed judgments there, ibid.; going away from the gate means departing from its teaching, §§4492,4493. Cities and palaces are represented in heaven when angels are discussing aspects of that teaching, §3216.

1   ie the work published in 1763
2   In the works published in 1758 Swedenborg frequently refers his reader back to **Arcana Coelestia**, either in a footnote, as here, or in some other way

Quod per Hierosolymam intelligatur ecclesia quoad doctrinam, etiam ex aliis in Verbo patet, ut ex his – Apud Esaiam,

Propter Zionem non tacebo et propter Hierosolymam non quiescam, usque dum exeat sicut splendor justitia ejus, et salus ejus sicut lampas ardeat. Tunc videbunt gentes justitiam tuam, et omnes reges gloriam tuam. Et vocabitur tibi nomen novum quod os Jehovae enuntiabit. Et eris corona decoris in manu Jehovae, et cidaris regni in manu Dei tui. Beneplacebit Jehovae in te, et terra tua maritabitur. Ecce salus tua veniet; ecce merces Ipsius cum Ipso. Et vocabunt illos, Populus sanctitatis, Redempti Jehovae; et tu vocaberis, Quaesita Urbs, Non Deserta. 62:1-4,11,12.

Agitur in toto illo capite de adventu Domini et de nova ab Ipso instauranda ecclesia. Nova haec ecclesia est quae intelligitur per Hierosolymam, cui vocabitur nomen novum quod os Jehovae enuntiabit, quaeque erit corona decoris in manu Jehovae, et cidaris regni in manu Dei, in qua Jehovae beneplacebit, et quae vocabitur Urbs Quaesita, Non Deserta. Per haec non potest intelligi Hierosolyma in qua, cum Dominus in mundum venit, fuerunt Judaei, nam illa erat in omni contrario, quae potius vocanda erat Sodoma, ut quoque vocatur, Apoc.11:8; Esai.3:9; Jer.23:14; Ezech.16:46,48. Alibi apud Esaiam,

Ecce Ego creans caelum novum et terram novam; non commemorabuntur priora. Laetamini et exultate in aeternitates quae Ego creans. Ecce Ego creaturus Hierosolymam exultationem, et populum ejus laetitiam, ut exultem super Hierosolyma et laeter super populo Meo. Tunc lupus et agnus pascent simul. Non malum facient in toto monte sanctitatis Meae. 65:17-19,25.

Etiam in hoc capite agitur de adventu Domini et de ecclesia ab Ipso instauranda, quae non instaurata est apud illos qui in Hierosolyma sed apud illos qui extra illam erant, quare haec ecclesia intelligitur per Hierosolymam quae erit Domino exultatio, et cujus populus erit Ipsi laetitia; tum ubi lupus et agnus pascent simul, et ubi non malum facient. Hic quoque

9   Jehovae: Jehovah *DD*
17 qua Jehovae: qua Jehovah *DD*

That the church in respect of its teaching is meant by 2
Jerusalem is also evident from other places in the Word – for instance,
in Isaiah,

For Zion's sake I will not keep silent and for Jerusalem's sake I will not
rest, until her righteousness goes forth as brightness and her salvation as
a lamp that is burning. At that time the nations will see your righteousness, and all the kings your glory. And you will be called by a new name
which the mouth of Jehovah will declare. And you will be a crown of
beauty in the hand of Jehovah, and a royal turban in the hand of your
God. Jehovah will take pleasure in you, and your land will be married.
Behold, your salvation will come; behold, His reward will be with Him.
And they will call them, The Holy People, the Redeemed of Jehovah; and
you will be called, A City Sought Out, Not Forsaken. 62:1-4,11,12.

The subject in the whole of this chapter is the coming of the Lord
and a new church to be established by Him. This new church is what
is meant by a Jerusalem that will be called by a new name which
the mouth of Jehovah will declare, and which will be a crown of
beauty in the hand of Jehovah and royal turban in the hand of God,
in which Jehovah will take pleasure and which will be called A City
Sought Out, Not Forsaken. These descriptions of it cannot be taken
to mean the Jerusalem inhabited by Jews when the Lord came into
the world, for this Jerusalem was the complete opposite of them and
ought instead to have been called Sodom, as it is in fact called in
Rev.11:8; Isa.3:9; Jer.23:14; Ezek.16:46,48. In another place in Isaiah, 3

Behold, I am creating a new heaven and a new earth; the former things
will not be remembered. Be glad and rejoice for ever in the things I am
creating. Behold, I will create Jerusalem to be a joy, and her people to be
a gladness, that I may rejoice in Jerusalem and be glad in My people. At
that time the wolf and the lamb will feed together. They will do no evil
on all My holy mountain. Isa.65:17-19,25.

In this chapter too the subject is the coming of the Lord and a new
church to be established by Him, which was established not among
the inhabitants of Jerusalem but of places away from there. This
church therefore is the one that is meant by the Jerusalem which
will be a joy to the Lord and its people a gladness for Him, also a
place where wolf and lamb will feed together, and a place where

dicitur quemadmodum in Apocalypsi, quod Dominus creaturus caelum novum et terram novam, per quae etiam similia intelliguntur, et quoque dicitur quod creaturus Hierosolymam. Alibi apud Esaiam,

5 Excitare, excitare, indue robur tuum, Zion, indue vestes decoris tui, Hierosolyma urbs sanctitatis; quia non addet ut veniat in te amplius praeputiatus et immundus. Excute te e pulvere, surge, sede, Hierosolyma. Cognoscet populus nomen Meum in die illo, nam Ego ille qui loquens, Ecce Me. Consolatus est Jehovah populum Suum,
10 redemit Hierosolymam. 52:1,2,6,9.

Etiam in eo capite agitur de adventu Domini et de ecclesia ab Ipso instauranda, quare per Hierosolymam, in quam non amplius veniet praeputiatus et immundus, et quam Dominus redimet, intelligitur ecclesia; et per Hierosolymam
15 urbem sanctitatis, ecclesia quoad doctrinam a Domino. Apud Zephaniam,

Jubila, filia Zionis; laetare ex omni corde, filia Hierosolymae. Rex Israelis in medio tui; ne time malum amplius. Laetabitur super te cum gaudio, acquiescet in amore Suo, exultabit super te cum jubilo.
20 Dabo vos in nomen et in laudem omnibus populis terrae. 3:14-17,20.

Similiter hic de Domino et de ecclesia ab Ipso, super qua Rex Israelis, qui est Dominus, laetabitur cum gaudio, exultabit cum jubilo, et in cujus amore requiescet, et quos dabit in nomen et in laudem omnibus populis terrae. Apud Esaiam,

25 Sic dixit Jehovah Redemptor tuus et Formator tuus; dicens Hierosolymae, Habitaberis, et urbibus Jehudae, Aedificabimini. 44:24,26.

Et apud Danielem,

Scito et percipito, ab exitu Verbi usque ad restituendum et ad
30 aedificandum Hierosolymam, usque ad Messiam Principem, septimanae septem. 9:25.

19 Suo: tuo *DD*

those people will do no evil. Similar things are meant in this chapter where it is stated, as in the Book of Revelation, that the Lord is going to create a new heaven and a new earth as well as a Jerusalem. In another place in Isaiah,

Awake, awake, put on your strength, O Zion, put on your beautiful garments, O Jerusalem, the holy city; no more may there come into you the uncircumcised and the unclean. Shake yourself from the dust, arise, sit, O Jerusalem. The people will know My name on that day, for I am He who is saying, Behold Me. Jehovah has comforted His people, He has redeemed Jerusalem. 52:1,2,6,9.

In this chapter as well the subject is the coming of the Lord and the church to be established by Him, and therefore Jerusalem, which the uncircumcised and the unclean will no more come into and which the Lord will redeem, means the church, and Jerusalem, the holy city, the church in respect of that teaching which comes from the Lord. In Zephaniah,

Sing aloud, O daughter of Zion; rejoice with all your heart, O daughter of Jerusalem. The King of Israel is in your midst, fear not evil any more. He will rejoice over you with gladness, He will quiet you by His love, He will exult over you with loud song. I will give you fame and praise among all the peoples of the earth. 3:14-17,20.

Here in like manner the subject is the Lord and the church to be established by Him, over which the King of Israel – that is, the Lord – will rejoice with gladness, exult with loud song, quiet them by His love, and give them fame and praise among all the peoples of the earth. In Isaiah,

Thus said Jehovah your Redeemer, He who formed you, He who says to Jerusalem, You will be inhabited, and to the cities of Judah, You will be built. 44:24,26.

And in Daniel,

Know and perceive that from the going forth of the Word to restore and to build Jerusalem until the Messiah, the Prince, there will be seven weeks. 9:25.

Quod per Hierosolymam etiam hic intelligatur ecclesia, patet, quoniam haec a Domino restituebatur et aedificabatur, non autem Hierosolyma sedes Judaeorum.

Per Hierosolymam intelligitur ecclesia a Domino etiam in sequentibus locis – Apud Sachariam,

Sic dixit Jehovah, Revertar ad Zionem et habitabo in medio Hierosolymae, unde vocabitur Hierosolyma, Urbs Veritatis; et mons Jehovae Zebaoth, Mons Sanctitatis. 8:3,20-23.

Apud Joelem,

Tunc cognoscetis quod Ego Jehovah Deus vester, habitans in Zione, monte sanctitatis; et erit Hierosolyma sanctitas. Et fiet in die illo, stillabunt montes mustum, et colles fluent lacte; et Hierosolyma sedebit in generationem et generationem. 4:17-21.

Apud Esaiam,

In die illo erit germen Jehovae in decus et in gloriam. Et fiet, relictus in Zione, et residuus in Hierosolyma, sanctus dicetur, omnis scriptus ad vitam in Hierosolyma. 4:2,3.

Apud Micham,

In extremitate dierum erit mons domus Jehovae constitutus in caput montium. Nam e Zione exibit doctrina, et verbum Jehovae ex Hierosolyma. Ad te veniet regnum prius, regnum filiae Hierosolymae. 4:1,2,8.

Apud Jeremiam,

In tempore illo vocabunt Hierosolymam thronum Jehovae; et congregabuntur omnes gentes ob nomen Jehovae Hierosolymam; neque ibunt amplius post confirmationem cordis sui mali. 3:17.

Apud Esaiam,

Specta Zionem urbem festi stati nostri. Oculi tui videant Hierosolymam, habitaculum tranquillum, tabernaculum quod non

It is self-evident that in these places as well Jerusalem means the church, because the church was what the Lord restored and built, not Jerusalem where the Jews were settled.

The church to be established by the Lord is meant by Jerusalem in the following places also – In Zechariah,

Thus said Jehovah, I will return to Zion and dwell in the midst of Jerusalem, therefore Jerusalem will be called the City of Truth, and the mountain of Jehovah Zebaoth the Holy Mountain. 8:3,20-23.

In Joel,

Then you will know that I am Jehovah your God, dwelling on Zion, My holy mountain; and Jerusalem will be holy. And it will happen on that day, that the mountains will drip new wine, and the hills will flow with milk, and Jerusalem will abide from generation to generation. 3:17-21.

In Isaiah,

On that day the branch of Jehovah will be beautiful and glorious. And it will happen, that whoever remains in Zion, and whoever is left in Jerusalem, will be called holy, everyone who has been written for life in Jerusalem. 4:2,3.

In Micah,

In the latter days the mountain of the house of Jehovah will be established as the head of the mountains. For out of Zion will go forth teaching, and the word of Jehovah from Jerusalem. The former kingdom will come to you, the kingdom of the daughter of Jerusalem. 4:1,2,8.

In Jeremiah,

At that time they will call Jerusalem the throne of Jehovah, and all the nations will be gathered together, because of Jehovah's name, to Jerusalem; nor will they go any more after the stubbornness of their own evil heart. 3:17.

In Isaiah,

Look upon Zion, the city of our appointed feast. May your eyes see Jerusalem, a quiet dwelling place, a tent which will not be overthrown.

dissipabitur; non removebuntur clavi ejus in perpetuum, et omnes funes ejus non avellentur. 33:20.

Praeter etiam alibi, ut apud Esaiam 24:23; 37:32; 66:10-14; apud Sachariam 12:3,6,8-10; 14:8,11,12,21; apud Malachiam 3:4; apud Davidem Pss.122:1-7; 137:5-7.

Quod per Hierosolymam in illis locis intelligatur ecclesia quae a Domino instauranda erat et quae etiam instaurata est, et non Hierosolyma in terra Canaane a Judaeis habitata, constare etiam potest a locis in Verbo, ubi de hac dicitur quod prorsus deperdita sit et quod destruenda, ut Jer.5:1; 6:6,7; 7:17,18,seq.; 8:6-8,seq.; 9:10,11,13,seq.; 13:9,10,14; 14:16; Thren.1:8,9,17; Ezech.4:1-fin.; 5:9-fin.; 12:18,19; 15:6-8; 16:1-63; 23:1-49; Matt.23:37,38; Luc.19:41-44; 21:20-22; 23:28-30; et multis aliis in locis.

65 Dicitur in Apocalypsi, **Novum caelum et nova terra**, et postea, **Ecce nova omnia facio**, per quae non aliud intelligitur quam quod in ecclesia nunc a Domino instauranda, **nova doctrina erit**, quae in priore ecclesia non fuit. Quod non fuerit, est causa quia si fuisset, non recepta fuisset, nondum enim Ultimum Judicium peractum fuit, et ante illud potentia inferni praevaluit potentiae caeli, quare si prius ex ore Domini data fuisset, apud hominem non mansisset. Nec hodie manet nisi quam apud illos qui Dominum solum adeunt et Ipsum Deum caeli et terrae agnoscunt, videatur supra, n.61. Eadem haec doctrina prius quidem data est in Verbo, sed quia ecclesia non ita diu post instaurationem ejus versa est in Babyloniam et apud alios postea in Philisthaeam, ideo illa non potuit ex Verbo videri; nam ecclesia non aliter videt Verbum quam ex principio religionis suae et ejus doctrina.

Nova, quae in hoc opusculo sunt, in genere haec sunt –

i Quod Deus sit unus Persona et Essentia, et quod Ille sit Dominus
ii Quod tota Scriptura Sacra de Ipso solo agat
iii Quod in mundum venerit ut subjugaret inferna ac ut glorificaret Humanum Suum, et quod utrumque fecerit per tentationes in Se admissas, et plene per ultimam illarum, quae

---

4   3:4: 3:2,4 *AR, DD*
5   5-7 *AR*²: 4-6 *AR*¹, *DD*
13 37,38 *AR*: 37,39 *DD*¹, *DD*²; 33,38,39 *DD*³

Its pegs will never be removed, and none of its ropes will be pulled away. 33:20.

And in other places in addition to these, such as Isaiah 24:23; 37:32; 66:10-14; Zechariah 12:3,6,8-10; 14:8,11,12,21; Malachi 3:4; Psalms of David 122:1-7; 137:5-7.

The fact that Jerusalem in these places means the church that was to be established by the Lord, and also was established, not the Jerusalem in the land of Canaan where Jews lived, becomes even more clear from places in the Word where it says that this Jerusalem was completely ruined and was to be destroyed, as in Jer.5:1; 6:6,7; 7:17,18, and following verses; 8:6-8, and following verses; 9:10,11,13, and following verses; 13:9,10,14; 14:16; Lam.1:8,9,17; Ezek.4:1-end; 5:9-end; 12:18,19; 15:6-8; 16:1-63; 23:1-49; Matt.23:37,38; Luke 19:41-44; 21:20-22; 23:28-30; and in many other places.

65 The Book of Revelation speaks about **a new heaven and new earth**, after which comes the statement, **Behold, I am making all things new**. By this nothing else is meant than that in the church to be established now by the Lord **there will be a new teaching**, which did not exist in the previous church. It did not exist there because if it had it would not have been accepted, for the Last Judgment had not been accomplished yet, before when the power of hell was stronger than that of heaven, and therefore even if it had been delivered to people from the mouth of the Lord it would not have stayed put with them. Nor at the present day does it do so except with those who go to the Lord alone and take Him to be God Himself of heaven and earth, see §61 above. This same teaching, it is true, had been delivered previously within the Word, but because the church not so long after its establishment was turned into Babylon, and afterwards among some into Philistia, it could not be seen from within the Word; for a church does not look at the Word from any other position than its fundamental religious principles and teaching consisting of these.

In general terms the new things contained in this small work are these –

i   God is one in Person and Essence, and the Lord is that God
ii   The whole of Sacred Scripture has to do with Him alone
iii   He came into the world to subdue the hells and to glorify His Human; He accomplished both of these things by means of the temptations He underwent, and completely so by means of the final

fuit passio crucis; et quod per id Redemptor et Salvator factus sit, et quod per id Ipsi soli meritum et justitia

iv   Quod impleverit omnia Legis, sit quod impleverit omnia Verbi

v   Quod per passionem crucis non abstulerit peccata, sed quod illa portaverit sicut Propheta, quod est quod passus sit ut in Se repraesentaretur ecclesia, quomodo illa malefecerat Verbo

vi   Quod imputatio meriti non sit aliquid nisi per illam intelligatur remissio peccatorum post paenitentiam Haec in hoc opusculo. In sequentibus, quae erunt **De Scriptura Sacra**, **De Doctrina Vitae**, **De Fide**, et **De Divino Amore et Divina Sapientia**, nova adhuc videbuntur.

---

12   De **Doctrina Vitae** *DD²*, *DD³*: in Doctrina vitae *DD¹*

one, which was His passion on the cross; and by accomplishing all this He became the Redeemer and Saviour, to whom alone merit and righteousness belong

iv   By His fulfilling all things of the Law is meant His fulfilling all things of the Word

v   By His passion on the cross He did not take away sins but as *the* Prophet carried them, that is, He suffered on it in order that in Him the way in which the church mistreated the Word might be represented

vi   Nothing else is meant by the imputation of His merit than the forgiveness of sins following repentance These things are covered in this small work. Still more new things will be seen in those that follow, which will deal with **Sacred Scripture**, **Life**, **Faith**, and **Divine Love and Wisdom**.

TABLE OF PARALLEL PASSAGES

DD 60,61   DP 263
   64   AR 880